XML Programming with VB & ASP

XML Programming with VB & ASP

MARK WILSON
TRACEY WILSON

MANNING

Greenwich
(74° w. long.)

For electronic browsing and ordering of this book, visit http://www.manning.com
The publisher offers discounts on this book when ordered in quantity.
For more information, please contact:

Special Sales Department
Manning Publications Co.
32 Lafayette Place   Fax: (203) 661-9018
Greenwich, CT 06830   email: orders@manning.com

Library of Congress Cataloging-in-Publication Data
Wilson, Mark, 1969-
        XML programming with VB and ASP /Mark Wilson, Tracey Wilson.
            p.   cm.
        Includes bibliographical references and index.
        ISBN 1-884777-87-2
        1. XML (Document markup language).   2. Microsoft Visual BASIC.
        3. ASP (Computer network protocol) I. Wilson, Tracey. II. Title.
        QA76.76.H94 W596   1999
        005.7'2--dc21
                        99-055358

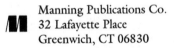

Manning Publications Co.   Production Services: *TIPS* Technical Publishing
32 Lafayette Place   Copyeditor: Jeannine Kolbush
Greenwich, CT 06830   Typesetter: Lynanne S. Fowle
                                   Cover designer: Leslie Haimes

Printed in the United States of America
   2 3 4 5 6 7 8 9 19 – CM – 02 01 00

Dedicated to our loved ones, especially Tracey's Dad

contents

list of figures   xv
list of tables   xvii
introduction   xix
acknowledgments   xxiii
about the cover illustration   xxv

1 Why XML? 1

1.1   Overview   2

1.2   XML enables data sharing   3

    Building your own markup language   5

    What else can we do with XML?   6

    Who is the W3C? (Worldwide Web Consortium)   7

2 XML boot camp 9

2.1   Overview   10

2.2   XML and its derivatives is a huge topic   10

    Learning more about the XML syntax   11

    The X(ML) files   11

    Step 1: Discovering the structure   12

    Step 2: Building an XML file   17

    Step 3: Using style in your design   25

    RDF (Resource Description Framework)   26

3 Why would a business use XML?   29

3.1 Overview   30

3.2 The business problem   30

3.3 User scenarios   30

    Scenario 1—Bandwidths and customization   30

    Scenario 2—Immediately usable data that is reliable   31

    Scenario 3—New layouts   31

    Scenario 4—New requirements   32

3.4 Solving the problem with XML and XSL   33

4 Programming with XML   35

4.1 Overview   36

4.2 The W3C Document Object Model   36

    Understanding Nodes and child Nodes   39

4.3 Navigating the Microsoft XML DOM   39

4.4 Data Islands—getting started with XML   40

    How do Data Islands work?   42

    How do you take your HTML: DIV(ed) or SPAN(ed)?   45

    Binding other HTML elements to a Data Island

    recordset   46,   Output of source code   48,

    Full source code   48

    Accessing a standalone Data Island   48

    Full source code   49

    Saving your Data Island changes   49

    Limiting the number and moving through the records   49

    Output of source code   51,   Full source code   51,

    Adding new records to a Data Island   52

    Output of source code   53,   Full source code   54,

    Getting an ADO recordset from XML Data Islands   54

4.5 Getting the Microsoft XML objects onto your PC   55

4.6 Creating the objects   55

4.7   Loading a file synchronously   *55*

4.8   Loading a file asynchronously   *56*
            Using WithEvents in VB   56

4.9   A roundtrip on using the DOM object with a
            TreeView   *57*
            Preparing to run the example   58
            Module variables   59
            Populating the TreeView from the DOMDocument   59

4.10   Saving an XML document to a file in ASP   *70*

4.11   Handling errors and debugging   *71*

4.12   Accessing the XML with ASP   *71*

4.13   Sending data back to the user   *71*
            *Creating XML on the server from your relational
            database   72*
            Returning an ADO 2.1 recordset as XML   75

4.14   Communicating with the server from VB
            using XMLHTTPRequest   *77*
            Receiving an XML DOMDocument object in VB   78

5 *XSL—adding style to XML*   *81*

5.1   Overview   *82*

5.2   What can XSL do?   *82*
            What can the Microsoft XSL implementation do?   83
            Where can I see a demo of XSL?   83

5.3   Debugging your XML and XSL with IE5   *84*
            Connecting up your XML and XSL files   85
            XML + XSL = HTML in a browser   86

5.4   Building the HTML output   *87*
            xsl:for-each   90,   xsl:value-of   90,
            Processing all the children   90,   Full source code   91,
            Using XSL as a Data Island   92
            Switching styles with TransformNode   94

5.5   Patterns   *99*

    Sorting   99,   Context   99,

    Pattern operators   100

    Filtering and logical operators   101

    Using patterns   102

5.6   How to make a hyperlink   *105*

5.7   Summary   *106*

6   **Building XML solutions   107**

6.1   Overview   *108*

6.2   What do we want to achieve in these examples?   *109*

    Data brokering   109

    Communications between objects   110

    Beyond the network, into the Internet   110

    Simplifying frameworks   111

    Disconnected programs and data   111

6.3   A quick overview of the examples   *112*

6.4   Implements   *115*

6.5   Techniques for reusing business objects   *117*

6.6   Creating the projects   *118*

6.7   SimpleUI—just the basics   *118*

    frmAdos and the objects   120

    frmBO and the objects   120

    How the ADO-only approach works   121

    How the business object approach works   125

    How the ASP approach works   139

6.8   XMLDemo—a more complete example   *146*

    The code for getRecs   149

    *The DOMtoBO class code—populating the client-side
business object   158*

    The People and Person class   162

6.9   Summary   *164*

7 The Microsoft DOM objects in detail 167

7.1 Overview 168

7.2 DOM objects 168

DOMDocument 170

XMLDOMElement 170

XMLDOMNode 171

XMLDOMNodeList 172

XMLDOMNamedNodeMap 172

XMLDOMCDATASection 173

XMLDOMAttribute 173

XMLDOMDocumentType 173

XMLDOMEntity 174

XMLDOMProcessingInstruction 175

XMLDOMParseError 175

XMLHTTPRequest 176

7.3 DOM object properties 176

async 180, Attributes 181,
childNodes 183, docType 188,
documentElement 190
firstChild, lastChild, nextSibling, and
previousSibling 191
length 192, namespaceURI 193,
nodeName 194, nodeType 197,
nodeTypedValue 208, nodeTypeString 209,
nodeValue 210, ondataavailable 212,
ownerDocument 213, parentNode 214,
parsed 214, parseError 215,
prefix 216, preserveWhiteSpace 217,
resolveExternals 218, tagName 219,
text 219, url 220,
validateOnParse 221, value 221,

7.4 DOM object methods 222

abort() 224, appendChild() 225,
cloneNode() 228
createAttribute(), createCDATASection(),
createComment(), createElement(),
createEntityReference(), createProcessingInstruction(),
createTextNode() 228
createNode() 233, getAttribute() 235,
getAttributeNode() 236
getElementsByTagName() 236
getNamedItem() 238, hasChildNodes() 240,
insertBefore() 241, load() 241,
loadXML() 242, nextNode() 24,2
nodeFromID() 244, removeAttribute() 245,
removeAttributeNode() 246, removeChild() 247,
removeNamedItem() 248
replaceChild() 249, reset() 250,
save() 250, selectNodes() 252,
selectSingleNode() 253, send() 254
setAttribute() 254, setAttributeNode() 255,
setNamedItem() 256, transformNode() 257,
transformNodeToObject() 259

8 *Schemas, BizTalk, and eCommerce* 261

8.1 An introduction to eCommerce 262

8.2 Why do our systems need a Schema? 263
Development of flexible web applications 263
So, how does it work then? 263

8.3 Using the data types that are available 266
Full list of Microsoft data types supported 267
Primitive Types 268
Supported data type conversions 269

8.4   BizTalk, where it's all happening!   *270*
       A BizTalk XML example   *270*
       Get your schemas here!   *272*
       Cool tools and websites   *272*
       How different are all the Schemas?   *273*
8.5   Summary   *277*

Where to go from here   279

9.1   The End   *280*
9.2   Check out the online glossary   *280*
9.3   Investigate future technologies   *280*
9.4   Join the http://www.vbxml.com VB, ASP, and XML discussions   *280*
9.5   Author Online at http://www.manning.com   *280*
9.6   Newsgroups   *281*
9.7   W3C discussion groups   *281*
9.8   Links, links, and more links   *281*

index   *285*

list of figures

Figure 1.1   XML is suitable for exchanging information   4

Figure 1.2   XML provides structure for your data   5

Figure 2.1   Three basic files   11

Figure 2.2   DTDs provide standards   13

Figure 2.3   Typical development pattern   17

Figure 2.4   Namespaces ensure uniqueness   23

Figure 3.1   The XML possibilities are endless   32

Figure 4.1   The DOM for an HTML table   37

Figure 4.2   An XML file and its DOM equivalent   38

Figure 4.3   Nodes and NodeLists in the DOM object   40

Figure 4.4   Data Island within an HTML page   41

Figure 4.5   Data Island—displaying the records   44

Figure 4.6   Data Island—binding a text box   48

Figure 4.7   Data Island—moving through records   51

Figure 4.8   Data Island—adding a new record   53

Figure 4.9   DOM sample screen-shot   58

Figure 4.10   Retrieving an XML pick list of people from a
              database   72

Figure 4.11   Saving ADO as XML application   76

Figure 5.1   IE5 debugging an XML error   84

Figure 5.2   XSL adds style to XML   85

Figure 5.3   XSL as a Data Island   93

Figure 5.4   A plain text style   96

Figure 5.5   Choosing the table stylesheet   97

Figure 6.1   Sample UML sequence diagram   112

Figure 6.2   Sample UML three tier services model   113

Figure 6.3   Three-tier diagram for Example A   115

Figure 6.4   The SimpleUI project   118

Figure 6.5   The SimpleUI application   119

Figure 6.6   Sequence diagrams for frmAdo   120

Figure 6.7   The business object sequence diagram   121

Figure 6.8   The ASP or Webclass sequence diagram   122

Figure 6.9   The ADO example   122

Figure 6.10   The basic SimpleUI project functionality   123

Figure 6.11   The business object example   126

Figure 6.12   Business object sequence diagram   127

Figure 6.13   The DBToXml VB project   128

Figure 6.14   The ASP example   139

Figure 6.15   Example B user interface   147

Figure 6.16   Example B XML Demo   148

Figure 6.17   Collection builder in the Class Builder Utility   163

Figure 6.18   Class Builder Utility   164

Figure 7.1   Nodes and NodeLists in the DOM Object   168

Figure 7.2   Returned childNodes from the DOMDocument root   185

Figure 7.3   Returned childNodes from the DOMDocument root element   186

Figure 7.4   Returned childNodes from an element   186

Figure 7.5   Local View in VB of XMLDOMDocumentType   190

Figure 7.6   ChildNodes property of the docType in the VB Local Views window   204

Figure 7.7   NodeList returned from the documentElement property   237

Figure 7.8   NodeList returned from the getElementsByTag-Name() method   238

list of tables

Table 2.1	The XML document content model	22
Table 4.1	XML document with descriptions	39
Table 4.2	HTML elements that can be bound to Data Islands	46
Table 5.1	XSL	90
Table 5.2	XSL query operators	100
Table 5.3	Code examples of XSL operator	100
Table 5.4	XSL Logical operators	101
Table 5.5	XSL examples of logical operators	101
Table 5.6	XSL commonly used examples of logical operators	102
Table 6.1	Source code listing for projects	148
Table 7.1	XML DOM Objects	169
Table 7.2	XML object naming conventions	169
Table 7.3	Built-in entities that the DOMDocument automatically parses	174
Table 7.4	DOMDocument properties	177
Table 7.5	Return values for the different XMLDOM interfaces	195
Table 7.6	Return values for XMLDOM interfaces with no nodeNames	196

Table 7.7   The 12 Node types   198

Table 7.8   nodeTypeString return values   210

Table 7.9   nodeValue returned for nodeTypes   211

Table 7.10   DOMDocument methods   222

Table 7.11   Signature of the createNode method   233

Table 7.12   Specifications of values to insert in createNode signature   234

Table 7.13   save() method return values   251

Table 8.1   The growth of DNS hosts on the Internet   262

Table 8.2   Datatypes that are supported   267

Table 8.3   Supported W3C primitive types   269

Table 8.4   Datatype conversions supported by Microsoft XML processors   269

introduction

XML (eXtensible Markup Language) is the best thing since sliced bread. What HTML (Hypertext Transport Protocol) did for the World Wide Web and for distributing data around the globe is what XML is doing for eCommerce and data exchange.

We are in the midst of a growing and unprecedented amount of business-to-consumer (known as *B2C*) and business-to-business (known as *B2B*) information exchange. Selling your wares via the web, intelligent agents haggling for the best price, transparent data exchange between businesses—XML makes all of this possible and affordable!

Where will it be used? The short answer is *everywhere*! XML will be used on the Internet in web pages. It will be used in the Microsoft BackOffice to structure your knowledge. It will be used across platforms, across applications, and across languages. It will be the centerpiece in all distributed solutions built in the future.

Not only software developers will use XML; it will be in almost all of the products we use in the future. Wherever there is data exchange or persistence, XML will be there. You may not even know when you are using it. For example, in Microsoft Word (in Office 2000) when you choose the *Save as web page* menu choice, you save your document in an HTML format with XML embedded in it.

Note XML is everywhere: In Microsoft Word 2000, when you choose the *Save as web page* menu choice, you save your document as an XML-HTML hybrid.

XML is an infinitely extensible language with which you can create your own markup languages. This is why XML is also referred to as a metalanguage, or a language in which you can specify other languages. This book does not go into detail on how to create your own markup languages or into the syntax details of XML. (There are thousands of books and websites for that.) What we discuss is how to apply it to your development projects. We show you code examples of how you can use the power of XML in your development projects.

The focus of this book

As more developers become familiar with the promise of XML, the Internet requirements of businesses will move beyond the simple interactive HTML pages. Businesses will want to create more wealth from their information. It has been said many times that *information wants to be free*, and XML will achieve this.

In this book, *XML Programming with VB and ASP*, we will walk you through using XML in your Microsoft IE5 (Internet Explorer 5), Microsoft Visual Interdev, and Microsoft Visual Basic 6.0 applications.

Development projects will enable direct data exchange between objects, between servers, and between remote companies across the Internet. The promise of EDI (Electronic Data Interchange) will become real, and it will be inexpensive to apply. The shift to transparent communication of almost all information will be sudden and widespread.

That is why we think this book is your key to a whole new future as a developer or IT worker. With XML and this book as your roadmap, you will discover how to build truly flexible and powerful solutions.

What will the readers of this book learn?

When you are finished reading *XML Programming with VB and ASP*, you will understand the basic concepts of XML and how best to use it in ASP and VB code.

The following table lists the major topics that we will discuss.

Topic	Major topics presented
Consulting	How your clients can benefit from XML
	Why your company should be using XML in your projects
	How XML will influence the future of the Internet and software development
XML	Understanding and using the XML, DTD, and XSL files
	Understanding and using the Document Object Model document (DOM)
	Understanding Schemas, entities, elements, validation, parsing, and many more XML topics
IE5	Automating the Microsoft IE5 web browser in your code

	Using IE5 object models to expose objects such as tables and DSO 9Data Source Objects9
	Data Islands: how, where, when and why
VB	DOM—using the Document Object Model
	Designing and using webclasses
	Using XML in a multitier solution with business objects
	Communicating between objects using XML
ASP	Various ASP code examples of manipulating an XML file
	Using ASP pages as a central distribution point for your XML data
	Passing parameters to your ASP file and receiving the reply

After reading this book, you are welcome to come to our home website at http://www.vbxml.com or http://www.thespot4.com to find more training links, articles, and information on discussion groups that you can join.

If you would like to meet the authors, please visit the Manning Publications website. The url http://www.manning.com/wilson has a link to the Author Online forum for this book, where you can make comments, ask technical questions, and receive help from the authors and from other users.

Target PC configuration for readers

Often a book with extensive examples of code and solutions (such as this one) can make your life as a reader quite tough by using obscure software components or having different versions of components. Many times a book will use expensive components that readers cannot afford to purchase.

We have intentionally developed these solutions on a PC that has standard, bundled, or free software components. For example, the Microsoft PWS (Personal Web Server) is easy to get a hold of and is free! Ditto for IE5 and the MDAC 2.1 (Microsoft Data Access Components), which has Y2K updates and contains ADO 2.1 (ActiveX Data Object), which the code in this book uses.

For ADO 2.1 there is an upgrade if you have the older versions of ADO 1.5 or ADO 2.0. Windows 2000 provides ADO 2.5; however, this book does not cover 2.5 features (although some useful pointers to changes in how the technologies are used are provided).

This code was developed and tested on a PC with the configuration listed here. To execute the examples provided in this book, you must have the same or newer components.

- IE5 web browser
- ADO 2.1 data access components
- Microsoft PWS 1.0a
- PWS has the ASP.EXE extensions installed
- PWS has the Microsoft FrontPage extensions installed

Source code downloads

All source code for the examples posted in *XML Programming with VB and ASP* is available to purchasers of the book from the Manning website. The url http://www.manning.com/wilson includes a link to the source code files and to the Author Online forum. The code is also available at www.vbxml.com.

Conventions used in this book

The following typographical conventions are used throughout the book:

Code examples and fragments are set in a fixed-width font. `Courier` is used for VB code. `Letter Gothic` is used for XML code.

Comments in code are set off with an apostrophe at the beginning of each comment line. The comment line or lines precede the line or lines of code being referenced.

Code annotations accompany certain segments of code. Footnotes are tagged with ❶ .

Code line continuations are indented.

acknowledgments

I had often heard that writing a book was hard and stressful, but I never believed it. With a somewhat naive and casual enthusiasm, I took on this project of writing a book on XML programming with VB and ASP. Now, I know the truth.

To Trace, my gorgeous wife, thank you for your patience and for your incredible contribution to this book. To our family, extended family, and friends all around the world, this is for you!

I would like to thank all of the proofreaders and the members of the VBXML discussion group. Your contributions have been crucial to the success of this book.

We express our appreciation to the following reviewers, who provided invaluable insight into what the readers want and for the time and effort they took to read our manuscript in the various stages of development: Armand Datema, Bill Eddins, Brian Breneman, Carlos Palmisciano, Charles Hoffman, Chris Million, Earl Cox, Govind Kanshi, Howard Bolling, Jian Wang, Nikita Ogievetsky, Robert Green, Simon North, and Steve Ball.

I would also like to thank God for giving me this opportunity.

— Mark Wilson

Writing this book has been a wonderful experience—especially knowing that this work will help so many people with this wonderful, growing technology.

My most endearing acknowledgment is to Mark.

To all our family, you give us so much love; thank you for always being so caring. Even though we are all spread out across the world, our hearts are not far. To our friends, old and new, thank you for meaning so much to Mark and me.

Special thanks also go to the patient crew from Manning Publications (Marjan Bace, Ted Kennedy, Mary Piergies, Ed Toupin, Leslie Haimes, Chris Hillman, Lee Fitzpatrick, Peter Schoenberg, Bob Kern, Jeannine Kolbush, Lynanne Fowle, and the rest of the TIPS crew, and many more people), who have assisted us through this gestation period.

I want to thank my kind Father.

— Trace Wilson

about the cover illustration

The cover illustration of this book is from the 1805 edition of Sylvain Maréchal's four-volume compendium of regional dress customs. This book was first published in Paris in 1788, one year before the French Revolution. Its title alone requires no fewer than 30 words.

> *Costumes Civils actuels de tous les peuples connus dessinés d'après nature gravés et coloriés, accompagnés d'une notice historique sur leurs coutumes, moeurs, religions, etc., etc., redigés par M. Sylvain Maréchal*

The four volumes include an annotation on the illustrations: "gravé à manière noire par Mixelle d'après Desrais et colorié." Clearly, the engraver and illustrator deserved no more than to be listed by their last names—after all they were mere technicians. The workers who colored each illustration by hand remain nameless.

The colorful variety of this collection reminds us vividly of how culturally apart the world's towns and regions were just 200 years ago. Dress codes have changed everywhere and the diversity by region, so rich at the time, has faded away. It is now hard to tell the inhabitant of one continent from another. Perhaps we have traded cultural diversity for a more varied personal life—certainly a more varied and exciting technological environment. At a time when it is hard to tell one computer book from another, Manning celebrates the inventiveness and initiative of the computer business with book covers based on the rich diversity of regional life of two centuries ago, brought back to life by Maréchal's pictures. Just think, Maréchal's was a world so different from ours people would take the time to read a book title 30 words long.

Why XML?

1

1.1 Overview

XML will become the *lingua franca* for communication between devices, web browsers, computers, servers, and applications. In time, any two applications (regardless of who built them or when) will be able to exchange information (such as prices, availability, and so on) without ever having been designed to talk to each other.

Imagine a world where computer programs can talk to each other, discover new sources of information, and use them almost immediately.

There will be companies that are data brokers, because all they do is provide repackaged data from websites and databases all over the world. Your programs will be able to understand, categorize, and use this data correctly and quickly. What would the future look like if all software programs simply displayed the same data in different ways? A word processor could extract only the information it needs to show, but an email system could display the same information in a different way. In a sense, this is what OLEDB is intended to deliver: one pipe through which to suck different information types and use them in a common way.

XML can be considered a simplified dialect of SGML (Standard Generalized Markup Language).

With XML, the data storage format itself will change. Data will become far more useful. Currently we know of several companies that are designing what could be called an xGUI, or an eXtensible Graphical User Interface. This is where the boundaries of XML and applications will begin to blur, and true document centricity will become the norm. Without ever leaving your current document, you may be able to edit it in several different programs—because underneath it all is XML with different stylesheets being applied.

With this increasingly common information and knowledge structure, eCommerce and transparent data communication between businesses will transform our world of business. Entirely new categories of software will pop up to manage this data flow, to take a *toll charge* as the data flows about. New types of components will emerge that are simply *data broker* objects.

Have you used a search engine and found exactly what you want the first time you asked?

XML and its derivatives will eventually be capable of describing metadata in a way that is machine-readable.

Have you used a search engine and found exactly what you want the first time you asked? If you used a search engine to search for the resumés of all Visual Basic programmers, for example, you could get over a million hits. And of those, only a few would actually be resumés, the rest being a statement such as *email me for my resume*.

We are sure search engine developers would like to see websites structure their data and categorize themselves sufficiently for the engines to provide accurate answers to queries. HTML doesn't allow this, but XML does. In the broader XML scheme of things, this is the promise being made—that XML and its derivatives will be capable of describing *metadata* (complex information and relationships) in a way that is consistent and machine-readable.

These are only some of the promises of XML, and this book can show you how to get started on building this future. XML is being designed through a discussion between the major interested groups and individuals at the W3C (World Wide Web Consortium).

1.2 *XML enables data sharing*

To illustrate the need for the same data to be available in different formats to different companies, let's imagine a company called News R Us that gathers news information around the world, compiles it, and provides it electronically to other companies. News R Us typically receives news snippets and announcements in many different formats, massages the information into one central database, and exports various relevant topics in an acceptable output for the various News R Us customers.

All these customers have different information needs, in different formats, at different times. However, many will also have binary or platform issues to deal with as well! Some of the customers could be using PCs, mainframes, or UNIX boxes. Many could have a combination of these needs.

XML is ideal for this type of situation. You see, XML is not vendor-specific, and because it is only a text file, it doesn't require you to have a particular operating system or hardware. It is a metalanguage and can handle a staggering array of data structures and relationships. You can also apply stylesheets to XML in order to manipulate the data into any format you require. Even better, these stylesheets can be reused.

XML is an ideal data format for this type of complex situation. XML is not vendor-specific and doesn't require you to have a particular operating system or hardware, since it is only a text file.

If we compare the flexibility of XML to programs that most developers currently write, we will be able to see some of the benefits of XML more clearly. With many existing applications distributed across the world via the Internet, intricate data-exchange mechanisms are developed to ensure timely data delivery and use. However, these systems are notoriously expensive. With the Internet, web servers, and XML, you will see more and more distributed solutions communicating and exchanging data using the HTTP protocol. That means we can build solutions that exchange data inexpensively, anywhere and anytime. However, XML goes one step further than simply holding data, as you can see in figure 1.1.

News R Us also exchanges their information with other news organizations that add information to it and then send the enriched information back. This can happen several times, perhaps in one day. You imagine that building a solution that is flexible enough to cope with data that changes so frequently is a nightmare, right? The problem is that radically changing data may not comply with your database design and could cause errors in your applications.

In most systems, the trouble comes when the data file changes over time. The new data is lost, or the old data is seen as incompatible by the database or applications.

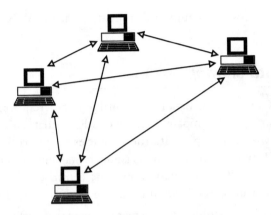

Figure 1.1   XML is suitable for exchanging information

If you take a moment to think back, as a developer you may remember when a program crashed or displayed error messages. When you looked for the reason, you found that the data source or text file your customer/colleague/etc. had given you had changed in a minute (or major!) way—a few spaces here, another column there, or perhaps a whole new category of information. With XML that is not a problem. XML has a document to *explain* your data structure.

For more information on a news exchange format, see http://www.xml-news.org/

Now, each of the participating systems can exchange news clippings, or even billing information, as long as they provide a document that explains the structure of the XML data they are sending. That way, when the document grows, changes, or evolves, nothing will go awry as long as the format structure of the document is updated. If your data storage device is aware of the structure of the data being presented, it can map the data to the structure, and then be able to correctly store or update the correct tables or fields.

Now the relationship between the companies (in terms of document exchange) is as shown in figure 1.2.

Here you can see computer programs exchanging data and accessing the structure information. If the structure of the data and the structure listed in the document are both changed simultaneously, then no errors should occur.

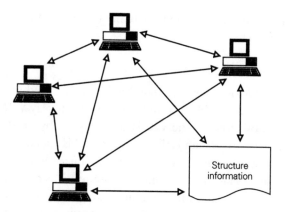

Figure 1.2 XML provides structure for your data

1.2.1 *Building your own markup language*

As we mentioned, XML is a metalanguage. It has and can cope with a wide variety or rich information. How does it do this? It is a markup language with which you can create other markup languages. You use it to define a vocabulary of words and the relationships between those words that represent your data.

XML is a markup language with which you can create or use other markup languages.

For example, if your industry is book publishing, then you could use or define a book markup language. If you are in the sports industry, then you could use a sports markup language. Already the chemical industry has defined a markup language called CML (Chemical Markup Language). There is a markup language for music called MusicML, and a mathematics markup language called MathML. Many other markup languages already exist in different vertical industries.

That's why XML is the next biggest thing since sliced bread, or at least since HTML. It is an eXtensible Markup Language in which you can create your own tags.

XML provides structure for your document by using tags. The names of these tags are defined in your structure document. Doesn't HTML provide tags? Yes, HTML provides tags such as <B> for bold or <I> for italics, but you cannot simply create your own tags such as <AUTHOR> or <CAR_PART>, because web browsers will simply ignore the tags they don't know how to display. HTML is therefore very difficult to extend.

That's where the extensible part of *eXtensible Markup Language* comes in. XML enables you to build a markup language that suits your needs. A whole new world opens up that can encompass our imagination. XML is hardly out the door, and already RDF (Resource Description Framework) is being used on the Internet. RDF is based on XML and is designed for representing and manipulating metadata. Now that sounds serious, right? If we take a closer look, RDF is used to create machine-readable descriptions of objects. In other words, an XML-aware or

RDF-aware application should be able to actually understand that a `<CAR:MIRROR>` tag refers to a part of a vehicle.

1.2.2   *What else can we do with XML?*

VRML (Virtual Reality Modeling Language) is being changed so that it is based on XML. That will mean that XML-aware browsers can display VRML. Hopefully we can kiss that extra download of the VRML viewer goodbye as the browser renders the virtual reality worlds dynamically, using the XML data.

What about all the ways you can use XML in the burgeoning eCommerce and EDI industry? What about all the companies whose job it is to sit in between you (the consumer) and the supplier company that makes the product you are looking for, such as a suit or DVD player? If the supplier company makes the details of their products available on the web, then you can conceivably imagine that the middle-persons (otherwise known as intermediaries or infomediaries) could find themselves being bypassed by you and your trusty Internet browser!

How about all those documents that don't work because they were made in one program and no other program can read them? Not a problem if the format is XML and the display and structure documents are available. How about data stored on one operating system, and your own operating system won't read it? That's no problem if the file is written in XML and the structure is publicly available.

Unknown graphics files and future formats? Not a problem if the graphics format is XML-based, because your XML-aware browser will be able to read it and understand it. VML (Vector Markup Language) is currently under development. Rather than describing an image in a vector or mathematical format, VML uses XML. Now the image can be dynamically categorized and manipulated in many different ways.

Microsoft's *push* or *channel* technology is implemented in XML. Push delivers your website to the viewer via *channels* rather than having the viewers come to you all the time. The technology that implements Microsoft's push technology is called CDF (Channel Definition Framework), and CDF is written in XML. So when you create a push channel for your website, you create an XML file that tells another program details about your push channel.

Any program can access the CDF file because it is written in a text file and uses XML as its open format. Therefore, CDF is suitable as a standard that can be applied throughout the industry.

Textual markup makes your website more useful

Another immediately useful application of XML would be to mark up data that is on your homepage or corporate web page. You know that one of the limitations with HTML is that you are confined to the tags that HTML provides. In HTML if you need a tag such as a `<PRICE>` tag to explicitly identify your item prices, you cannot use one. All the browsers out there will simply ignore your wonderful new tag. However, with XML you can use that new tag and any other tags you want!

Let's look at the following paragraph:

> You can have a discussion with Mark Wilson on the book *XML Programming With VB and ASP* at the Manning website. Look for the author online section. To meet other Visual Basic developers focusing on XML, go to http://www.vbxml.com.

SGML and HTML are both based on 8-bit ASCII, which is a long way from being able to deal with Asiatic and Oriental languages. XML is based on unicode *from the ground up. This makes it far more capable of dealing with international commerce.*

This could be marked up as follows to make its content more explicit to search engines:

```
<review subject-type="book"/>You can have a discussion with
<AUTHOR>Mark Wilson<AUTHOR> on the book <BOOK_NAME>XML Programming
With VB And ASP</BOOK_NAME> at the <PUBLISHER>Mannings</PUBLISHER>
website. Look for the <LINK_AREA> author online section</LINK_AREA>.
To meet other <USER_TOPIC>Visual Basic developers</USER_TOPIC>
focusing on <BOOK_TOPIC>XML</BOOK_TOPIC>, go to <URL>http://
www.vbxml.com</URL>.
```

As we discovered earlier, marking up text in this fashion enables an XML-aware program to accurately understand the information on your website.

If you try typing that snippet into IE5, it will not display properly. The code to the right is correct for IE5.

```
<?xml version="1.0" encoding="UTF-8"?><info><review subject-
type="book"/>You can have a discussion with <AUTHOR>Mark Wil-
son<AUTHOR> on the book <BOOK_NAME>XML Programming With VB And ASP</
BOOK_NAME> at the <PUBLISHER>Mannings</PUBLISHER> website. Look for
the <LINK_AREA> author online section</LINK_AREA>. To meet other
<USER_TOPIC>Visual Basic developers</USER_TOPIC> focusing on
<BOOK_TOPIC>XML</BOOK_TOPIC>, go to <URL>http://www.vbxml.com</
URL>.</info>
```

The benefits of XML should be clear from these examples. Exactly how you can use XML in Visual Basic or ASP to solve the problems and to harness the opportunities is the topic of this book.

1.2.3 *Who is the W3C? (Worldwide Web Consortium)*

The W3C was founded in October 1994. Its goal is to develop common protocols by forming an international industry consortium to discuss technologies and technical issues and provide recommendations.

The W3C does not police or enforce their recommendations.

At the W3C you can find:

- a repository of information about the WWW for developers and users
- reference code implementations for the various recommendations
- various prototype and sample applications to demonstrate the use of new technology being fostered at the W3C

The W3C procedures

A group makes a submission on a technology (or technical issue) to the W3C. After discussion and consulting, a draft proposal is created. After more discussion, a recommendation may be issued —where the design, model, or technology is considered ready for widespread industry use.

The W3C is a collection of interested parties that meet to thrash out various new Internet technologies. Their process is quite substantial and inclusive and results in a consensus decision (although there are stories on the web of strong-arming within the working groups). However, the end result does carry substantial momentum.

If industry-wide support of your technical specification is important to you, then the W3C is an environment where the industry can meet to discuss your proposals and eventually eke out a draft specification that finally becomes a recommendation. The basic steps that a submission to the W3C can go through are as follows:

Notes

A Note is an idea, comment, or document. It does not mean the W3C will do any work related to the items or topics listed in the Note.

Working drafts

A Working Draft represents work in progress, but it does not imply consensus on the issues by the group involved or W3C.

Proposed recommendations

A Proposed Recommendation is work that (1) represents consensus within the group that produced it and (2) has been proposed by the Director to the Advisory Committee for review.

Recommendations

To see some of the activities and projects within the W3C, go to http:// www.w3.org/ Consortium/ Activities

A Recommendation is work that represents consensus within W3C and has the Director's stamp of approval. W3C considers whether the ideas or technology specified by a Recommendation are appropriate for widespread deployment and promote W3C's mission.

The W3C is not a *policeperson*. They do not enforce the agreements made or the technologies designed. Each of the parties involved can (and sometimes does) *extend* or *improve* upon the designs.

XML boot camp 2

2.1   Overview

Let's look at the goals set out for XML by the W3C as stated on their website:

- XML shall be straightforwardly usable over the Internet
- XML shall support a wide variety of applications
- XML shall be compatible with SGML
- It shall be easy to write programs that process XML documents
- The number of optional features in XML is to be kept to the absolute minimum, ideally zero
- XML documents should be human-legible and reasonably clear
- The XML design should be prepared quickly
- The design of XML shall be formal and concise
- XML documents shall be easy to create
- Terseness in XML markup is of minimal importance

To be honest, we don't think this needs explaining. What this says to us is that XML should be easy to use, legible to humans, Internet-friendly, and basically all things to all people.

2.2   *XML and its derivatives is a huge topic*

As you may have already seen, XML (being so extensible) is already an incredibly diverse and complex topic. You can be a guru on an issue or area and be completely ignorant of another up-and-coming area. New XML application servers, solutions, markup languages, and W3C recommendations appear almost every day. In the middle of this information overdose, *XML Programming With VB And ASP* will keep your ship on a steady course in this sea of knowledge.

We will focus on the basics of XML and assume that you can discover the more complex details for yourself. We will restrict our scope of interest to focus on XML from the perspective of a Visual Basic or ASP developer. Also, we'll try to keep the XML syntax at a minimum and keep the solutions and example code at a maximum.

XML was born from SGML and should be compatible. You may be wondering where XML came from. XML was born from SGML, which is a complex, flexible, and just plain hard-to-work-with markup language. Needless to say, XML has taken off like a rocket because it has some of the best ingredients of SGML without many of the downsides. (We can almost hear all those SGML aficionados reading this as they open their email programs to send us emails on why SGML rules.)

As you have seen, XML was designed from the ground up to be extensible and to be simple to implement. As a result, it seems that attempt to be simple and flexible has resulted in the massive adoption of XML in the computing industry. Unfortunately anything that is so flexible and extensible will be used for a bewildering array of uses, and eventually the number of choices and solutions begin to overlap and perhaps compete with each other.

2.2.1 Learning more about the XML syntax

To learn more about XML syntax, we recommend reading John E. Simpson's book Just XML *by Prentice Hall.*

Although we will cover a substantial amount of technical detail in this book that will definitely get you more than started, we recommend you source some kind of XML syntax reference book.

If you would like to learn about the details of the syntax of XML, we recommend reading John E. Simpson's book *Just XML*.

2.2.2 The X(ML) files

XML has three basic files: XML, DTD, and XSL.

Most XML solutions have three files, as shown in figure 2.1:

1 XML file that contains the data

2 DTD (or Schema) file that provides structure for the XML file (optional)

3 XSL that provides the *look* or user interface of the XML file (optional)

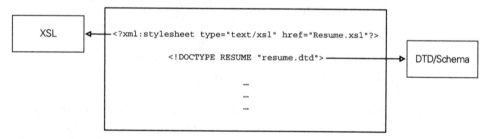

Figure 2.1   Three basic files

We have not yet explained DTDs, Schemas, or XSL, but we will soon. Figure 2.1 is only an overview to get you started. Bear in mind that XML files do not need to have DTD or XSL files, as they are optional and serve different purposes to the core XML file. However, in our examples in this book, we will build all three files.Bear in mind that XML files do not need to have DTD or XSL files, as they are optional.

Let's look at the three steps involved in building a simple XML data file that you can use for your current data. There are many ways to approach this, but we have boiled it down to three simple steps:

1 Discover (or establish) the structure of your data

2 Build the XML file that holds the data

3 Apply (or create) the XSL formatting

2.2.3 *Step 1: Discovering the structure*

This is the first step in creating an XML document. We need to look at our data and extract the important concepts. To do this, ask yourself what each section or sentence is about conceptually. In essence you are building up a vocabulary that can be reused across similar documents. To demonstrate this, let's build a sample resumé or CV. Now this is something we are all intimately familiar with, we imagine!

First we will define the words we need and then we will set them out in a hierarchical order. We will not put actual information inside this vocabulary; rather we will only define the data structure. Of course, there are many things we can put in this vocabulary, but let's only create a basic structure. A possible vocabulary for an XML document that contains a resumé could be:

```
Name
Telephone number
Company (which is made up of)
Company name
Contact person
Contact telephone number
Contact email
Position
Description
```

Now that you know the XML file will hold all of its data in between a beginning and end tag (this is correctly referred to as an element), we can also understand the benefit of separating the structure from the data. As we mentioned before, that means that many different XML files can reuse the same structure file. This structure file is formally known as a DTD (Document Type Declaration).

DTDs: Reusing the structure in your data and industry

As XML becomes widespread, your industry association or company is likely to have one or more published DTDs that you can use and link to. These DTDs define tags for elements that are commonly used in your applications. You don't need to recreate these DTDs—you just point to them in your XML file and follow their structure when you create your XML document.

Note   Schemas are a better structure document than DTDs for industry-wide data exchange. Schemas provide better datatypes, and they are already being used in document repositories such as http://www.biztalk.org

---

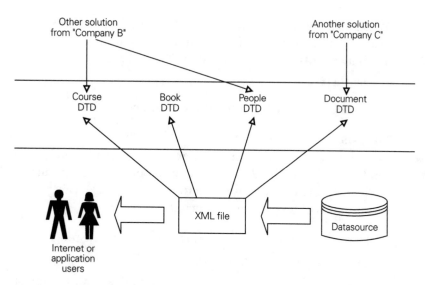

Figure 2.2   DTDs provide standards

We have already seen how we can use XML and a DTD to simplify the exchange of information between different sources. In addition, the increasingly widespread use of vertical industry DTDs means that systems can use these common DTDs to exchange information with each other, regardless of each business's internal format or storage architecture. In this way, industries will begin to reuse common formats as shown in figure 2.2.

Elements

An element consists of a start tag, an end tag, and what's between them.

As you already know, similar to HTML, XML also uses tags to define the beginning and end of each piece of data or concept. Actually, the correct word for this is an element. Each element can hold many other elements. In this way, we saw the company element holding other elements, including CONTACT NAME, CONTACT PERSON, and CONTACT TELEPHONE NUMBER.

Let's have a closer look. What consists of a start tag, an end tag, and what's between them is an element:

```
<BOOK>...<TITLE>XML Programming With VB And ASP</TITLE>...</BOOK>
```

<BOOK> and <TITLE> are both elements, even though <TITLE> is within the <BOOK> element.

Attributes

When elements contain properties, they are called attributes. In the following example, the element is BOOK and the attribute is TITLE. The value of the attribute is XML Programming With VB And ASP.

```
<BOOK TITLE="XML Programming With VB And ASP">...</BOOK>
```

Attributes are parts or properties of elements.

Entities

To put it simply, any file or web resource that can be *included* into an XML file can be called an entity. Any file or web resource that can be included into an XML file is an entity. Entity is also used to refer to special character representations and substitutions of text strings and includes.

Here's an example of substituting entities for text strings:

```
<!ENTITY BookName "XML Programming With VB And ASP">
```

Now you can use the entity &BookName; in a document, and wherever you refer to it, the entire string of XML Programming With VB And ASP will be substituted. In VB, this is similar to using a constant. Also, by defining this in a DTD and keeping the DTD external, you can ensure that the same definitions are reused accurately across all your XML files.

Say we placed this in our DTD:

```
<!ENTITY Introduction SYSTEM "http://mark/xmlcode/intro.xml">
```

Then wherever we used the keyword &Introduction; the XML text in intro.xml at our website would be included.

Just as useful is being able to include graphics. Say we used:

```
<!NOTATION gif SYSTEM "http://mark/xmlcode/gifviewer.exe">
<!ENTITY mypic SYSTEM "http://mark/xmlcode/mypic.gif" NDATA gif >
```

The mypic.gif would be placed wherever we use the &mypic; keyword.

Of course you may have been wondering about the <!NOTATION piece. Well, that is the location of a helper program that can view the gif. The parser knows to look for this notation because at the end of the !ENTITY line, NDATA gif was inserted, indicating that a notation for the gif is included.

To attribute or to element, that is the question!

An interesting similarity between attributes and elements is that this BOOK element contains an attribute of PUBLISHER:

```
<Book Publisher="Manning">XML Programming With VB And ASP</Book>
```

But you could also change the attribute into its own element. Then you would use:

```
<Publication>
        <Book>XML Programming With VB And ASP</Book>
        <Publisher>Manning</Publisher>
</Publication>
```

The two alternatives shown above don't look the same, but they are in fact the same in many ways. Of course, there are some subtle differences between elements and attributes. When choosing how to structure your data, consider the following:

- The order of attributes cannot be controlled
- You cannot specify different types of elements, though you can specify (to a limited extent) the contents of elements through the use of a DTD or Schema
- You can specify an attribute as an "ID" type of attribute, which can then be used from various DOM methods
- Attributes cannot contain subelements; only elements can contain other elements

Inline or standalone?

Bearing in mind that the structure or vocabulary is held in a DTD document, let's look at various ways to use this vocabulary we have identified. We have at least three possibilities:

- We can create a DTD that is *standalone*, external to the XML document, and therefore reusable across several documents
- We can create a DTD that is held within our XML file and is therefore only available to this file
- We can avoid defining a DTD file completely (since it is an optional file) and simply get on with creating an XML data file itself

In the solution in this book, we will create and use standalone and reusable resume structures.

A simple DTD (Document Type Definition)

Because a DTD defines the structure of our XML document, our DTD file could look like this:

```
<!-- This is a comment within an example resume.dtd -->
<!ELEMENT MYNAME ANY>
<!ELEMENT MYTELEPHONENUMBER ANY>
<!ELEMENT COMPANY (COMPANYNAME , CONTACTPERSON , CONTACTTELEPHONENUMBER ,
  CONTACTEMAIL , POSITION , DESCRIPTION )>
<!ELEMENT COMPANYNAME (#PCDATA )>
<!ELEMENT CONTACTPERSON (#PCDATA )>
```

```
<!ELEMENT CONTACTTELEPHONENUMBER (#PCDATA )>
<!ELEMENT CONTACTEMAIL (#PCDATA )>
<!ELEMENT POSITION (#PCDATA )>
<!ELEMENT DESCRIPTION (#PCDATA )>
```

DTDs can be much more complex than this example—and they typically are—but this gives you a sense of what they can do. It's just a matter of structuring your data and figuring out the *parts* of your content.

An XML document only has one root element, and in this case, it is the `<RESUME></RESUME>` element. This is not listed within the DTD file, but within this root element, we define a dataset element called `<COMPANY>` that is made up of six different parts:

```
<!ELEMENT COMPANY (COMPANYNAME, CONTACTPERSON,
CONTACTTELEPHONENUMBER, CONTACTEMAIL, POSITION, DESCRIPTION)>
```

If you are interested, HTML is rumored to have 26 or more DTDs that you can use. You can read about one of them at: http://www.w3.org/TR/REC-html40/loose.dtd

We then identify each of the parts within the dataset. What we want to do is identify what type of information each one can and will hold.

So far in this book, we have occasionally mentioned Schemas. Let's take a closer look at them and how they compare to DTDs.

Schemas and DTDs—what's the difference?

DTDs have four major things going for them:

- They are easy to learn and are a standard
- They are mature and are used in several thousand applications
- They have an enormous number of trained developers already using them from the SGML heyday
- There are many tools out there for using DTDs

Schemas were born out of the limitations to DTDs. For example:

- DTDs are not written in XML, and therefore they are not available via the DOM
- DTDs do not have support for namespaces
- DTDs are good at describing structure, but not the data contents—their data typing is poor and limited. There is no support for currencies and so on

Schemas, on the other hand:

- Are built in XML and can therefore be used via the DOM in Visual Basic or VBScript in ASP
- Provide datatypes such as float, currencies, and so on
- Provide better relationships between elements
- Enable you to create your own user-defined data types

- Indicate some form of inheritance
- Support namespaces

Since Schemas are XML documents themselves, there is a DTD (or Schema) available for evaluating if your Schema itself is valid.

While Schemas will definitely figure into your future projects, a consensus view is that the final proposal of the working group on Schemas will not look like the current implementation of Schemas within Microsoft IE5. For example, in August 1998 the Schema syntax changed substantially. It is expected that will happen again once the working draft becomes a recommendation. Therefore this book will be focusing mainly on DTDs and giving pointers to Schemas. For more information, see chapter 8, "Schemas, BizTalk, and eCommerce."

2.2.4 Step 2: Building an XML file

Let's create our first XML file now. We have defined our DTD and now we can create an XML document that conforms to the structure of the DTD.

In a nutshell, most XML applications will extract data from a database, mark it up with XML, and send it to the user. There are many choices of what to do to the file during the markup stage. As a result, several different types of documents can end up at the client's browser.

Overall, the pattern shown in figure 2.3 is followed.

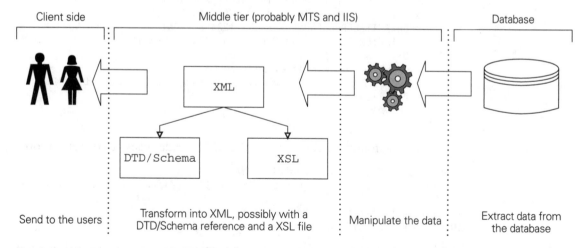

Figure 2.3   Typical development pattern

What you see below is an XML file with standard headings, followed by some (fictitious) personal details, and then followed by details on two companies we have (fictitiously) worked for. Note how there are no spaces within the tag names, as a sample company name becomes <COMPANYNAME>. Also note how the tag <COMPANY> holds six tags within itself (just as our DTD said it would).

Our resume.xml file looks like this:

```
<?xml version="1.0" encoding="UTF-8"?>
<!-- This is a sample file for the Resume XML application we are going to
build -->
<?xml:stylesheet type="text/xsl" href="resume.xsl"?>
<!DOCTYPE RESUME SYSTEM "resume.dtd">
<RESUME>
    <MYNAME>Mark Wilson</MYNAME>
    <MYTELEPHONENUMBER>001 123456</MYTELEPHONENUMBER>
        <COMPANY>
          <COMPANYNAME>Indigo web design</COMPANYNAME>
          <CONTACTPERSON>Sandy Robinson</CONTACTPERSON>
          <CONTACTTELEPHONENUMBER/>
          <CONTACTEMAIL>important@indigoweb.com</CONTACTEMAIL>
          <POSITION>
            <ROLE>Webmaster</ROLE>
            <DESCRIPTION>This was an exciting project where we worked on
              integrating...</DESCRIPTION>
          </POSITION>
        </COMPANY>
        <COMPANY>
          <COMPANYNAME>Purple people eaters web design</COMPANYNAME>
          <CONTACTPERSON>Robin Sandyson</CONTACTPERSON>
          <CONTACTTELEPHONENUMBER>(003) 123456</CONTACT-TELEPHONENUMBER>
          <CONTACTEMAIL>important@ppweb.com</CONTACTEMAIL>
          <POSITION>
            <ROLE>Senior web developer</ROLE>
            <DESCRIPTION>I developed their intranet solution...</DESCRIPTION>
          </POSITION>
        </COMPANY>
</RESUME>
```

We're sure the following four lines in the XML header caught your attention:

```
<?XML version="1.0" encoding="UTF-8"?>
<!-- This is a sample file for the resume XML application we are going to
  build -->
<?xml:stylesheet type="text/xsl" href="resume.xsl"?>
<!DOCTYPE RESUME SYSTEM "resume.dtd">
```

The following line tells the reader (for example, a web browser) which version of XML and which text encoding you are using (UTF-* is the default):

```
<?xml version="1.0" encoding="UTF-8"?>
```

<? and ?> are delimiters that tell the reader that there is a PI (processing instruction), which in this case is the version of XML that is being used.

Note in the following line that the characters `<!--` begin a comment and the characters `-->` end the comment:

```
<!-- This is a sample file for the resume XML application we are going to
build -->
```

This comment will go unprocessed and not be displayed. It can even hold characters such as < and >.

This line tells the reader that there is a document called a stylesheet, which will explain to the reader (for example, a Web browser) how to display our resume.xml file:

```
<?xml:stylesheet type="text/xsl" href="resume.xsl"?>
```

CSS (Cascading Stylesheet) provides a way to define a look (such as *use bold and italics on the heading in font size 10*) across several HTML pages. With an external XSL (eXtensible Stylesheet Language), you have an easy way to define a look (or presentation) for more than just one XML file.

This line tells the reader that there is a document against which the structure of this XML file should be checked:

```
<!DOCTYPE RESUME SYSTEM "resume.dtd">
```

This new document is called a DTD. A DTD for a document need not always be an external file. The DTD for our resume.xml can be held within itself. However, since one of the useful points of a DTD is that it provides a way to use a common structure across a company or across an industry, it makes sense to provide it in an external or separate file. Using the keyword `SYSTEM` means the DTD can be found outside of the current XML document.

Validation and parsing

Since our resume.xml contains a reference to a DTD, when our resume.xml document is parsed, its structure is compared with the resume.dtd to ensure that the structure is correct (assuming, of course, that the parser intends to validate the document). This comparison process is called validation and is performed by a tool called a parser.

Although the specification calls for programs to automatically validate XML files when displaying the XML file, IE5 does not. It is assumed that web surfers don't need to know if the file structure is incorrect. Logically, the onus is on the developer to get the implementation of the XML file right before releasing it to the public.

To have IE5 validate your XML file, you need to use code or scripting. This book covers this issue and many other code examples.

The difference between well-formed and valid documents

Valid means your XML file does not break any of the rules imposed on XML and correctly uses all external references—such as a DTD.

Before we go any further, let's clarify an important concept—the differences between *well-formed* and *valid*. You will find many explanations of these two terms, but for our needs, here is the simplest interpretation:

> XML files that follow the standard syntax for XML are *well-formed*. XML files that are well-formed and also correctly follow the structure of a DTD are considered *valid*.

A few things to remember about XML and DTDs

Valid is a superset of well-formed, and it is easier to be well-formed than it is to be valid.

- XML files do not need to have DTDs unless the developer is sure that a specific structure must always be followed
- DTDs can be held internally within the XML document. Alternatively, if you need to share a common structure across several XML files, you can make the DTD standalone. In thiscase, you use the SYSTEM keyword
- XML files that follow the standard syntax for XML are well-formed
- XML files that are well-formed and also correctly follow the structure of a DTD are considered valid
- XML is by design case-sensitive (though tool builders may not adhere to this)
- Every XML document can only have one root element

What does the syntax look like if the structure goes deeper than just one level, as we have above? In addition, how do we show no information between tags?

Our new resume1.xml file looks like the following. Note that the `<POSITION>` tag now contains the `<ROLE>` and `<DESCRIPTION>` tags.

```
<?xml version="1.0" encoding="UTF-8"?>
<!-- This is a sample file for the Resume XML application we are going to
    build -->
<?xml:stylesheet type="text/xsl" href="resume.xsl"?>
<!DOCTYPE RESUME SYSTEM "http://mark/xmlcode/resume.dtd">
<RESUME>
    <MYNAME>Mark Wilson</MYNAME>
    <MYTELEPHONENUMBER>001 123456</MYTELEPHONENUMBER>
        <COMPANY>
            <COMPANYNAME>Indigo web design</COMPANYNAME>
            <CONTACTPERSON>Sandy Robinson</CONTACTPERSON>
            <CONTACTTELEPHONENUMBER/>
            <CONTACTEMAIL>important@indigoweb.com</CONTACTEMAIL>
            <POSITION>
                <ROLE>Webmaster</ROLE>
                <DESCRIPTION>This was an exciting project where we
                    worked on integrating...</DESCRIPTION>
            </POSITION>
        </COMPANY>
```

```
<COMPANY>
   <COMPANYNAME>Purple people eaters web design</COMPANYNAME>
   <CONTACTPERSON>Robin Sandyson</CONTACTPERSON>
   <CONTACTTELEPHONENUMBER>(003) 123456</CONTACTTELEPHONENUMBER>
   <CONTACTEMAIL>important@ppweb.com</CONTACTEMAIL>
   <POSITION>
    <ROLE>Senior web developer</ROLE>
    <DESCRIPTION>I developed their intranet solution...</DESCRIPTION>
   </POSITION>
</COMPANY>
</RESUME>
```

We declared the DTD with:

```
<!DOCTYPE RESUME SYSTEM "http://mark/xmlcode/resume.dtd">
```

You can see we inserted the keyword SYSTEM and followed it with the name of an external (to the document) DTD file.

The format of a DTD declaration is:

```
<!DOCTYPE name externalDTDpointer [internalDTDsubset]>
```

To show an empty tag, you could use:

```
<CONTACTTELEPHONENUMBER> </CONTACTTELEPHONENUMBER>
```

This is the shortened version:

```
<CONTACTTELEPHONENUMBER/>
```

We also saw the following new line.

```
<?xml:stylesheet type="text/xsl" href="resume.xsl"?>
```

To SYSTEM or not to SYSTEM, that is the question! Making the DTD standalone means you can reuse the same DTD across several XML files.

Up to this point we have been dealing with two files: the XML file and the DTD file. We know that the data is held in the XML file and structures are held in the DTD file, but what we have not seen yet is how this data will be displayed. That is the role of a stylesheet. We will focus on stylesheets a bit later. For the moment, we will concentrate on understanding a more complex DTD for the resume1.xml file.

CDATA and #PCDATA

In some instances you may be working with restricted characters, or you may want to have script or HTML passed directly through without the parser accessing the data. There are several element declarations you can use; two of the most popular—CDATA and #PCDATA—are described below.

In a very elegant way, XML has managed to separate the data from structure and the display. All three will typically be in separate files and can be reused across an organization or an industry.

In the examples above, we handled the restricted character of < by changing it to >, and we then placed it into a CDATA section.

character data (CDATA):

By design this should receive no parsing, but this depends of course on the parser, which could look for the use of]]> and other XML-reserved sets of characters. The contents are treated as characters to be passed to the application.

parsed character data (#PCDATA):

For example, > will be parsed into < on output. (The # ensures that this tag is not seen as a tag that the designer has created.)

Namespaces provide uniqueness

We know that XML is a language for creating markup languages, and the whole point of XML is to enable users to be able to create unique tags that identify their information in more meaningful ways than simply applying the basic set of HTML tags to all documents. While this gives users great flexibility, it poses problems for interchange and software integration. What happens when two documents make use of the same tag names in different contexts?

Table 2.1 shows all your alternative element declarations.

Table 2.1   The XML document content model

Type	Element Declaration	Description
Parsed character data	#PCDATA	The contents should be ignored by the parser
Character data	CDATA	Certain parts of the contents shuld be converted to characters
Empty data	EMPTY	Declares that an element cannot contain any contents
Any data	ANY	This type of element can contain any contents allowed by the DTD
Mixed	#PCDATA|x|y|z	Provides a set alternative

The W3C definition of namespaces is at http:// www.w3.org/TR /REC-xml-names/

For example, within a single XML document, the tag <TITLE> may refer to the name of the employer whom you worked for:

```
<CONTACTPERSON>
<TITLE>Dr.</TITLE>
<SURNAME>Andrews</SURNAME>
</CONTACTPERSON>
```

It could also refer to the title of the document itself:

```
<TITLE>Mark Wilson's resume</TITLE>
```

In addition, if you have a section where you listed books or training courses, you may have:

```
<COURSESANDBOOKS>
<TITLE>Book1</TITLE>
<TITLE>Course1</TITLE>
<TITLE>Course2</TITLE>
<TITLE>Book2</TITLE>
</COURSESANDBOOKS>
```

What you need is to explain how each instance of the <TITLE> tag is different from the other ones. How can you help a software program know what each one is? That's the basic reason why current search engines are not perfect. They have to guess which context applies to which words.

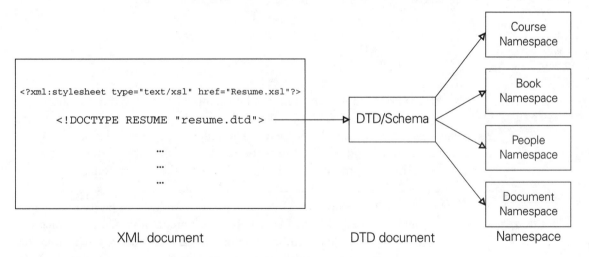

Figure 2.4   Namespaces ensure uniqueness

Enter XML namespaces. Namespaces allow tags like <TITLE> to have uniqueness and a specific context for each instance of <TITLE>. Then when you refer to a <TITLE> tag, you can include a reference to the context. The uniqueness is provided by pointing to a URI (Universal Resource Indicator), which is similar to but broader than a URL. And because each URI is unique, that makes each namespace unique.

> *Note* It is important to understand that there is no document at the URI indicated by the URI. The URI is only used to ensure uniqueness for each instance of a tag.

While the human reader can distinguish between the different interpretations of the `<TITLE>` element, a computer program does not have the context to tell them apart. Namespaces solve this problem by associating a namespace with a tag name. For example, the titles can be written as (see figure 2.4):

```
<BookInfo:TITLE>Eating Mr. Bigglesworth</BookInfo:TITLE>
<AuthorInfo:TITLE>Mini me</AuthorInfo:TITLE>
```

The name preceding the colon refers to the name of the namespace and ensures that identically named elements are not confused. Both humans and computers can tell which `<TITLE>` *is being referred to.*

Now, in the DTD for our own document, we can refer to these namespaces. The default declaration declares a namespace for all elements within scope. The scope below is from

```
<BOOK> to </BOOK>
```

All tags within this scope reference the stated namespace:

```
<?xml version="1.0" encoding="UTF-8"?>
<BOOK xmlns="urn:BookLovers.org:BookInfo">
<TITLE>Book1 </TITLE>
 <PRICE currency="US Dollar">34.95</PRICE>
</BOOK>
```

You can also declare a default namespace at the start of your XML document; any tags without prefixes are assumed to be in the default namespace.

But this is not complex enough. In the example above, we did not show two `<TITLE>` elements, right? What we need to do is to declare several namespaces and somehow use them within the elements. The following example declares BOOK and COURSE to be shorthand for the full names of their respective namespaces. Now, each element can have the same name but reference different namespaces!

> *Note* The W3C definition of XML namespaces is: An XML namespace is a collection of names, identified by a URI, which are used in XML documents as element types and attribute names. XML namespaces differ from the namespaces conventionally used in computing disciplines in that the XML version has internal structure and is not, mathematically speaking, a set.

Now we can use the following tags in our XML document because we have included those namespaces in the DTD:

```
<?xml version="1.0" encoding="UTF-8"?>
<BOOK xmlns:bk="urn:BookLovers.org:BookInfo"
      xmlns:COURSE="urn:Training.org:Courses">
```

```
<COURSE:TITLE>Learning XML</COURSE:TITLE>
<bk:TITLE>Book1</bk:TITLE>
<bk:TITLE>Dr.No</bk:TITLE>
<bk:TITLE>My resume</bk:TITLE>
</BOOK>
```

What you can see above is that we defined a namespace of bk and COURSES within the root tag of BOOK. We have then prefixed the <TITLE> element with the namespace <COURSE> and the other <TITLE> element with the bk namespace. Now humans and machines can easily differentiate between the two elements.

2.2.5 *Step 3: Using style in your design*

W3C XSL Working Draft is at http:// www.w3.org/ TR/WD-xsl

XSL is a language for expressing stylesheets. In the past CSS provided the *look and feel* for HTML documents on the web. However, now CSS2 adds support for *paged media*, which mainly relates to paper or transparencies. While CSS continues to evolve in this way, and many XML pundits still use CSS as their preferred stylesheet over XSL, we will be delving into XSL as our preferred stylesheet for this book.

You can find out more about the working draft of one of the modules of the new CSS3 at http:// www.w3.org/TR/ CSS3-selectors

However, before we get going on the Microsoft XSL implementation, be aware that the XSL specification has already expanded and changed since IE5 and its objects were shipped. Although you can use XSL in Microsoft IE5, it is undergoing major changes at the W3C. They call it "modularization." Let's describe the W3C changes that you will be encountering in the future before we discuss the XSL implementation, which you can find in the Microsoft XML Objects in IE5.

Here we describe some of the W3C changes that you will encounter in the future, not the current Microsoft IE5 XSL implementation.

XSL can be used in two ways. It can be used to transform (this is called XSL Transformations, or XSLT) and for rendering (by using the XSL Formatting Objects). Although there are an increasing number of tools available, there is at the time of writing no browser implementation for native XML/XSL. For example, in IE5, your XML documents must first be converted to HTML (using either CSS or XSL) before IE5 can display it. Netscape 5.0 (also named Mozilla) shows great promise of working with XML natively and being totally standards-compliant.

XSLT: a transforming stylesheet

XSLT is a modular part of XSL, as there is a separate XSL specification. Both are a part of the W3C *Style Sheets* activity, and XSLT is expected to become recommended before XSL does. It is not a general-purpose display language as XSL is; rather XSLT is designed primarily for the kinds of transformation that are needed when transforming one XML document into another XML or HTML document.

Note   If you are interested in having a look at Mozilla, then for a bit of fun go to http://www.mozillazine.org and check out their developers, the discussions, and all kinds of interesting uses they are putting XML to (such as extensible and custom user interfaces). You can download the latest development version of Mozilla at http://www.mozilla.org

---

The latest working draft of XSLT can be found at http:// www.w3.org/ TR/xslt

The intention of XSLT is neatly demonstrated in this way. As you may already know, XML DOM objects can be referred to as a *tree*. In this analogy, an XSLT describes rules for transforming a source tree into a result tree. A *pattern* is matched against the source tree, and this creates the result tree, with the result tree being separate from the source tree. That's the important thing! It is intended to be a separate tree that can have a completely different structure from the source tree. The pattern that is applied may filter, order, or add structure to the new result tree.

We can summarize by saying that XSLT is designed primarily for the kinds of transformation that are needed when transforming one XML document into another XML or HTML document. It is not a general-purpose language like XSL for specifying the display (or rendering) of XML documents.

Note   The W3C Style Sheets activity can be found at http://www.w3.org/Style/Activity

---

The Microsoft implementation of XSL

XSLT is not a part of the Microsoft IE5 objects, as this proposal appeared after the browser was shipped. However, the good news is that the Microsoft IE5 objects provide all of the functionality you are looking for.

More good news is that this book does not focus on the (evolving) W3C XSL standards, but on the Microsoft IE5 implementation of XSL as objects. This means you can read this book, learn from its examples, and get going immediately regardless of the changes to underlying specification. The Microsoft IE5 objects provide a rich set of methods to use on your next project, and we will show you how to use them.

2.2.6   RDF (Resource Description Framework)

RDF is good at providing a way to express complexity and complex data (metadata).

RDF has been described as an *application* of XML, an *API* to XML, and also as a way of associating metadata to anything that has a URI or a web address.

Either way, it inherits all the benefits of XML, and it goes one better by providing *machine-readable* descriptions of objects. Eventually all web resources will be described either in or through RDF, and thereafter even the relationships between objects will be explained as well. We can just see those search engines revving to go!

RDF is good at providing a way to express complexity and complex data (metadata) and it will be a good way to allow applications to exchange their metadata. RDF is targeted at application areas such as: the description of Internet resources, site-maps, content rating for websites, electronic commerce, EDI, collaborative applications, or services.

Note   W3C activity for RDF can be found at http://www.w3.org/Metadata/ Activity. Also, for the Dublin Core for A Simple Content Description Model for Electronic Resources, check http://purl.oclc.org/dc/for.

Why would a business use XML?

What this chapter covers:
- The benefits of XML to a business
- Design considerations
- Scenarios

3.1 Overview

Let's imagine the company Resumes R Us! is a one-person Internet startup. It intends to gather and distribute resumes from software developers and distribute the information across the Internet. Its competitive edge will be the customizable and immediate way it can provide its data.

3.2 The business problem

The clients require the resumé data to be available in different formats. Some clients dial up via modem and cannot take images; other clients require completely formatted information, which they can simply print off. Still other clients simply want the information to be sent in a recordset form that they can incorporate into their databases on a regular basis.

Some users cannot be limited to using only programs written in Java, Visual Basic, HTML, or other languages; they must be able to query and receive replies across mediums such as email, HTML, or perhaps even a telephone. Still more clients will not be making the requests for information themselves, but will reply upon automated programs to fetch the data at irregular intervals, requiring immediate delivery of the information in the requested format.

For Resumes R Us!, this wide variety of requirements poses substantial challenges, both in technology and in time to provide these services. Since this is currently a one-person startup, these services need to be automated and flexible. Ideally the solution provided will enable the client to design their own solutions and relieve the small company from the workload. Also, if Resumes R Us! adds more information as it becomes available, the computer programs that the customer uses must not be made unstable at all.

How can XML help us achieve these grand goals?

3.3 User scenarios

Here is a selection of scenarios where the customer's needs are met by our XML-oriented designs.

3.3.1 Scenario 1—Bandwidths and customization

The client requests that specific data be returned in a specific format. A selection is made in a Visual Basic application or on a web page, and the submit button is pressed. The reply must be received quickly and with the requested format.

The business problem for Resumes R Us! is that the format could be in a huge variety of colors, sizes, and bandwidths! The client may want summarized financials, tables, images, colors, or simple text for printing immediately. Clients may also want the data formatted for high-bandwidth online viewing with no database access (images included, maximum information) or low-bandwidth online viewing with no database access (no images, less information).

Behind the scenes, the standard XML is transformed using XSL *on the fly*. What this means is that one dataset can be returned in many different formats. Now Resumes R Us! can associate different bandwidths and customization requirements with each of their clients and apply the appropriate XSL stylesheet in order to fulfill each client's needs.

3.3.2   Scenario 2—Immediately usable data that is reliable

The client has set up a program on its server that will automatically request data at intervals. The data should be returned in a package that the receiving program can unpack and use immediately. Robustness is a vital issue for this scenario.

The Resumes R Us! business problem is that the contents of the database will change from time to time, and it is important that the solution that is eventually created can handle all the changes. Not only that, but the customer's software must also be able to extract the fields it is expecting without crashing when it comes across data it didn't expect.

Behind the scenes the data can be returned in the format of:

- XML text file with a DTD (either inline or referenced externally), and/or
- An ADO 2.1 persisted recordset file format.

The Microsoft ADOs are record-sets with function-ality similar to RDO and DAO recordset functionality.

When using an XML file, the receiving program can read the DTD and look in the XML file for the data it needs. This removes the issue of programs expecting certain data formats, exact placing of characters, or consistent columns in comma-delimited formats. The data is also immediately usable. If the solution uses the ADO 2.1 persisted-file approach, the file is reloaded from XML back into an ADO 2.1 recordset and is immediately available for use as a data-source object.

3.3.3   Scenario 3—New layouts

The customer regularly has a new layout for their data and must receive the infor-mation from Resumes R Us! in the new format promptly. Any delay in the turn-around would have a negative impact on the relationship with the client.

The business problem is that Resumes R Us! cannot afford the time to extend the existing Visual Basic programs and cannot afford to be seen as ignoring the custom needs of the client.

Behind the scenes, the client designs their own layout using XSL and uses a web page or small Visual Basic program (using FTP) to upload the new XSL file to the server. When Resumes R Us! receives the new XSL file, it is immediately available in a layout in which the client's data can be returned.

Note   The ability for the ADO objects to save the recordsets as XML is provided by version 2.1 of the ADO objects. As long as the file is not changed, another program using ADO 2.1 can unpack the recordset file back in the original XML text file.

3.3.4 *Scenario 4—New requirements*

Occasionally Resumes R Us! creates new ways to retrieve resumes from their database. One idea they are toying with is to email their customers a contact telephone number that can be used to listen to the latest resumes. This service also guarantees that the voice messages are up-to-date and not prerecorded.

The business problem for Resumes R Us! is the time and cost involved in setting up these new solutions. This solution in particular cannot be a prerecorded voice; it must be dynamically generated on the fly in order to be up-to-date.

Behind the scenes, using XSL, Resumes R Us! can return data to the clients in almost any format that an XML-aware text-reading program can read. A suitable application for reading the XML file would be an application that manages call centers.

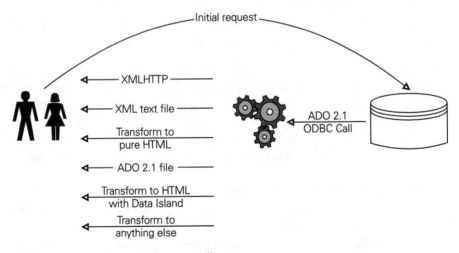

Figure 3.1   The XML possibilities are endless

3.4 *Solving the problem with XML and XSL*

One of the key patterns we see above is that XML combined with XSL can provide the same data in several different ways. This is a key benefit of XML; as a text file, it can be read, written, and passed across all platforms, as shown in figure 3.1.

It's beginning to sound like XML is the all-healing, world-peace-inducing snake oil for computing! Sadly, it is not, but it does bring some useful characteristics to the computing universe. Read on to find out how to use it in your applications and solutions.

Programming with XML

What this chapter covers:

- Getting started in ASP and in VB
- XML in Microsoft IE5
- Data Islands explained
- Sending and receiving XML over the web
- Using the DOM
- Different versions of ADO

4.1 Overview

In this chapter, we will expand on all the basic XML-related code you will need to create, open, read, close, and manipulate an XML DOM Document or XML file. Some of these examples are in ASP; others are provided in VB. Since the syntax of the two is so similar, you should be able to learn from either one and apply the techniques to the other.

4.2 The W3C Document Object Model

W3C Activity for DOM can be found at http:// www.w3.org/ DOM/Activity

By now you have seen the acronym DOM several times in this book, and it is time to take a closer look at the objects that provide methods to manipulate XML files. What's in a name? DOM stands for Document Object Model. It's the way we can treat a document as an object and extract information, make changes, and query the document from code. This is where we begin to come to the core of this book: how to programmatically manipulate all the above objects (and more)— that's where the action is, right? It's all fine and good knowing in detail about XML, DTDs, and Schemas and so on, but you want to know how to use all of this in your VB programs and ASP scripts!

The methods that are eventually proposed for all the W3C objects and for the current Microsoft objects may eventually be different.

The W3C DOM intends to provide programmers with an object model that will allow programs and scripts to access and update the content, structure, and style of documents in a standard way and in a platform- and language-neutral way. By creating a standard DOM interface, scripting and software development across many different software platforms becomes possible.

> **Note** The W3C DOM intends to provide programmers with an object model that will allow programs and scripts to access and update the content, structure, and style of documents in a standard way and in a platform- and language-neutral way.

To understand what a document object model is, first let's look at some HTML code for an HTML table. Then we will look at the HTML from a DOM perspective:

```
<TABLE>
<TBODY>
<TR>
<TD>XML Programming With VB And ASP</TD>
<TD>Mark Wilson</TD>
</TR>
<TR>
<TD>Another book </TD>
<TD>Someone Else</TD>
</TR>
```

```
</TBODY>
</TABLE>
```

This code would show up in an HTML page as a garden-variety table made in HTML. It has no borders, headers or anything else and looks like this:

XML Programming With VB And ASP	Mark Wilson
Another book	Someone Else

From the DOM perspective, you won't see the table as the user does. Instead, you'll see it as a series of objects linked to each other as shown in figure 4.1.

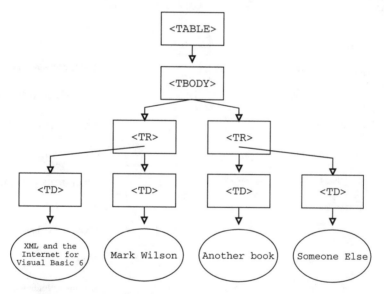

Figure 4.1   The DOM for an HTML table

If you used VBScript or VB code to loop through this table, you would find that the TABLE contains one TBODY, which contains two TR (table rows). Each TR contains a TD (table column), and each of the TDs has a value. Now that you have seen how an HTML table looks from a DOM perspective, let's look at an XML file and its DOM equivalent.

How does your XML look when viewed through a DOM? Like the HTML table, which had one <TABLE> object as its root, in XML there is only one root, called a "Node" In our case, the Node is named <RESUME>. OK, this may sound a bit confusing. We said that everything in an XML document DOM was an element, right? Well, they are also called Nodes, because they can hold information such as tag names, values, and children.

Note Think of an XML file as a tree or branches and leaves. The branches hold the leaves. On the other hand, think of them as parents and children. However there is always one root Node from which all the others can hang.

The DTD declaration and the XSL stylesheet link are Nodes from the root Node that appear before the root element.

Think of an XML file as a tree or branches and leaves. The branches hold the leaves. You already know that both the branches and leaves are elements in XML. Now in an XML DOM, they are both called Nodes. If a Node has sub Nodes under it, the sub Nodes are called *children*. Let's take a look in figure 4.2.

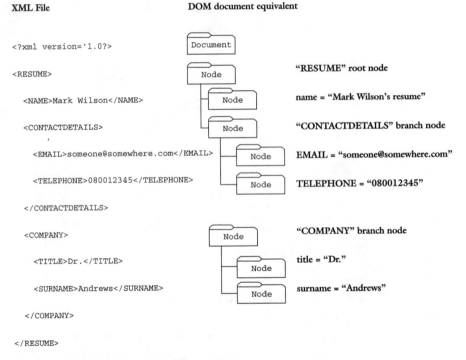

Figure 4.2   An XML file and its DOM equivalent

If you don't get it yet, bear with us for a minute; this should clear everything up.

4.2.1   *Understanding Nodes and child Nodes*

Let's dig a bit deeper and look at the XML document in table 4.1.

Table 4.1   XML document with descriptions

XML line	Description
`<?xml version='1.0'?>`	This is the opening statement of an XML document.
`<RESUME>`	This is the root Node.
`<NAME>Mark Wilson</NAME>`	This is a Node. The nodeType is "element."
`<CONTACTDETAILS>`	The CONTACTDETAILS Node has two children, EMAIL and TELEPHONE.
`<EMAIL>someone@somewhere.com</EMAIL>`	This EMAIL Node does not have any children.
`<TELEPHONE>080012345</TELEPHONE>`	The tag for this Node (or element) is TELEPHONE and the value is "080012345".
`</CONTACTDETAILS>`	This closes the CONTACTDETAILS tag or element.
`</RESUME>`	This closes the root Node.

In table 4.1, you can see that each line inside the XML document is an element. It is also a Node from the DOM perspective. Some Nodes have children and some do not. The properties for Nodes that you are likely to use are *tag* and *value*.

Microsoft has shipped some very useful objects with IE5 that can be used from any programming language that can make use of COM objects. In our case, we will focus on VBScript (in ASP text files) and VB.

4.3   *Navigating the Microsoft XML DOM*

Since XML is just a text file, you may have spent some time thinking about how you will programmatically create or manipulate all those text files. Luckily for us, most programming languages either have or are about to ship a set of objects that encapsulate the text file.

The Microsoft XML objects provide designers and developers with methods and properties to expose all the elements, Nodes, tags, values, and all the other XML syntax you need to work with XML. The XML document(s) that we have been discussing and working with have a programmatic equivalent called a DOM, and the W3C and its members have worked extensively on standardizing it.

In the source code of this book, we will focus exclusively on the Microsoft objects that expose the W3C DOM. We are sure you will be pleased to hear that the differences are relatively minor, and the Microsoft website gives several assurances that those differences will be removed in the future.

*To best under-
stand code or de-
scriptions about
the DOM, think
of an XML docu-
ment as a tree.
Another useful
analogy is to think
of parents and
their children.*

Figure 4.3 shows how the Microsoft DOM structures your XML documents.

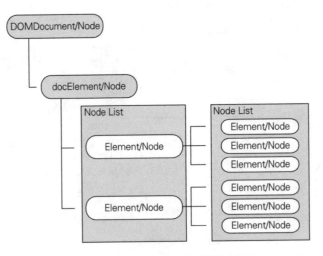

Figure 4.3   Nodes and NodeLists in the DOM object

*See chapter 7,
"The Microsoft
DOM objects
in detail,"
for a detailed
explanation of
objects, properties,
and methods.*

As you can see, there is one root Node within the object, called the DOMDocument. It is known as a Node. The actual elements are held within the `documentEle-ment`, which also is a Node. Within the `documentElement` are the actual elements and Nodes that contain your data. Just like a tree, a Node can hold further elements.

Perhaps it is time to explore how you can use XML in a practical way. We will not jump to detailed VB or ASP code just yet. First let's look at a very simple way to make use of XML in your IE5 HTML web pages. It's called a Data Island.

4.4   Data Islands—getting started with XML

Using a Data Island is an easy way to begin to see how to you can use XML in your web development projects. A Data Island is simply a way to hold XML code within an HTML page in Microsoft IE5 without using the `<OBJECT>` tag.

*Data Islands are
not standard
HTML; this is
a Microsoft
IE5-only feature.*

Data Islands are sometimes referred to as a DSO (Data Source Object) since they are a source of data. Almost anything that can be in a well-formed XML document can be inside a Data Island. A very useful feature of Data Islands is to hold the XML snippet *inline* on the HTML page itself and then bind textboxes, tables, and other IE5 DHTML objects to it. Figure 4.4 shows this.

Another very exciting aspect of Data Islands is the familiarity with VB that developers already have with the DHTML and XML object model. If you are familiar with HTML, it will come as a big surprise to think that you can bind HTML tables to data sources. Even more incredible is that the tables expose an

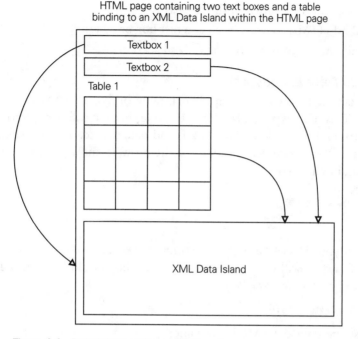

Figure 4.4   **Data Island within an HTML page**

object model that you can work with. The Data Islands expose recordsets, and they have all the familiar properties and methods you are used to in your VB applications, such as `movefirst()`, `movelast()`, and `addnew()`.

This is a fantastic solution if you need to distribute your code to the client side. Rather than hit the server for each data request, you can simply send your data to the client and display parts of it, manipulate it, and eventually send back the records for updates to your database. And best of all, it's easy to do! However, there is one big limitation. You cannot manipulate large XML files without a delay. Even if the customer has an extremely fast connection to the Internet or on your intranet, loading a 3.8-megabyte XML file on a P266 with 64Mb RAM will take 8–10 seconds.

However, given that you probably would not be using that amount of data in a solution such as this, you will find Data Islands a very useful feature of the Microsoft IE5 implementation of XML for smaller-sized data solutions. Settle in for a tour of various easy ways to use a Data Island in an HTML page. We will use examples to find out how to:

- Move through the records using buttons
- Display only a subset of the records
- Bind HTML controls (such as a text box or table)
- Add new records to the Data Island

4.4.1 *How do Data Islands work?*

The example below creates an HTML table of five columns across and five rows down. This table is a standard HTML table, but we will use Microsoft IE5 extensions to bind the table to the Data Island data source. The following lines are the normal HTML document headers (so the browser knows to display the contents as HTML, not as XML):

```
<HTML>
<HEAD> </HEAD>
<TITLE>List of people example</TITLE>
<BODY>
```

Start your Data Island with the snippet `<XML ID=xmlPeople>`. When you bind to this DSO, you will use the ID attribute, so this should be a meaningful label. In this case, we will use *xmlPeople*:

```
<XML ID=xmlPeople>
```

Use the standard XML header line:

```
<?xml version="1.0" ?>
```

Open the root Node and put in your XML elements:

```
<PEOPLE>
<PERSON>
 <NAME>Mark Wilson</NAME>
 <ADDRESS>911 Somewhere Circle, Canberra, Australia</ADDRESS>
 <TEL>(++612) 12345</TEL>
 <FAX>(++612) 12345</FAX>
 <EMAIL>Mark.Wilson@somewhere.com</EMAIL>
</PERSON>
<PERSON>
 <NAME>Tracey Wilson</NAME>
 <ADDRESS>121 Zootle Road, Cape Town, South Africa</ADDRESS>
 <TEL>(++2721) 531 9090</TEL>
 <FAX>(++2721) 531 9090</FAX>
 <EMAIL>Tracey.Wilson@somewhere.com</EMAIL>
</PERSON>
<PERSON>
 <NAME>Jodie Foster</NAME>
 <ADDRESS>30 Animal Road, New York, USA</ADDRESS>
 <TEL>(++1) 3000 12345</TEL>
 <FAX>(++1) 3000 12345</FAX>
```

```
 <EMAIL>Jodie.Foster@somewhere.com</EMAIL>
</PERSON>
<PERSON>
 <NAME>Lorrin Maughan</NAME>
 <ADDRESS>1143 Winners Lane, London, UK</ADDRESS>
 <TEL>(++94) 17 12345</TEL>
 <FAX>++94) 17 12345</FAX>
 <EMAIL>Lorrin.Maughan@somewhere.com</EMAIL>
</PERSON>
<PERSON>
 <NAME>Steve Rachel</NAME>
 <ADDRESS>90210 Beverly Hills, California, USA</ADDRESS>
 <TEL>(++1) 2000 12345</TEL>
 <FAX>(++1) 2000 12345</FAX>
 <EMAIL>Steve.Rachel@somewhere.com</EMAIL>
</PERSON>
```

Close the root Node in your XML:

```
</PEOPLE>
```

Close your XML Data Island:

```
</XML>
```

Create your HTML table, but insert the Microsoft IE5 extension that will bind the table to the xmlPeople data source using the snippet `DATASRC=#xmlPeople`:

```
<TABLE DATASRC=#xmlPeople>
```

Let's put in a table header line that tells us which column holds what information:

```
<THEAD>
  <TR>
<TH>NAME</TH>
<TH>ADDRESS ID</TH>
<TH>TEL</TH>
<TH>FAX</TH>
<TH>EMAIL</TH>
  </TR>
</THEAD>
```

Now insert your <TR> (which is literally a "table row"):

```
<TR>
<TD><DIV datafld="NAME"></DIV></TD>
<TD><DIV datafld="ADDRESS"></DIV></TD>
<TD><DIV datafld="TEL"></DIV></TD>
<TD><DIV datafld="FAX"></DIV></TD>
<TD><DIV datafld="EMAIL"></DIV></TD>
</TR>
</TABLE>
```

```
</BODY>
</HTML>
```

The key part is specifying the data source (DATASRC attribute) for the table. Of course, the data source is the XML Data Island called xmlPeople. The table is now populated by the contents of the Data Island, regardless of whether the Data Island is inline or external to the HTML file.

Output of code

Figure 4.5 shows the output of the source code.

NAME	ADDRESS ID	TEL	FAX	EMAIL
Mark Wilson	911 Somewhere Circle, Canberra, Australia	(++612) 12345	(++612) 12345	Mark.Wilson@somewhere.com
Tracey Wilson	121 Zootle Road, Cape Town, South Africa	(++2721) 531 9090	(++2721) 531 9090	Tracey.Wilson@somewhere.com
Jodie Foster	30 Animal Road, New York, USA	(++1) 3000 12345	(++1) 3000 12345	Jodie.Foster@somewhere.com
Lorrin Maughan	1143 Winners Lane, London, UK	(++94) 17 12345	++94) 17 12345	Lorrin.Maughan@somewhere.com
Steve Rachel	90210 Beverly Hills, California, USA	(++1) 2000 12345	(++1) 2000 12345	Steve.Rachel@somewhere.com

Figure 4.5   Data Island—displaying the records

Full source code

To successfully run this sample code, you need

- Internet Explorer 5 (IE5)
- A text editor to create an HTML file

To view this solution in action, type the full course code (below) into a text file, save it as myfile.htm, and then open it in IE5.

```
<HTML>
<HEAD> </HEAD>
<TITLE>List of people example</TITLE>
<BODY>
<XML ID=xmlPeople>
<?xml version="1.0" ?>
<PEOPLE>
<PERSON>
<NAME>Mark Wilson</NAME>
<ADDRESS>911 Somewhere Circle, Canberra, Australia</ADDRESS>
<TEL>(++612) 12345</TEL>
<FAX>(++612) 12345</FAX>
<EMAIL>Mark.Wilson@somewhere.com</EMAIL>
</PERSON>
<PERSON>
<NAME>Tracey Wilson</NAME>
<ADDRESS>121 Zootle Road, Cape Town, South Africa</ADDRESS>
<TEL>(++2721) 531 9090</TEL>
```

```
<FAX>(++2721) 531 9090</FAX>
<EMAIL>Tracey.Wilson@somewhere.com</EMAIL>
</PERSON>
<PERSON>
<NAME>Jodie Foster</NAME>
<ADDRESS>30 Animal Road, New York, USA</ADDRESS>
<TEL>(++1) 3000 12345</TEL>
<FAX>(++1) 3000 12345</FAX>
<EMAIL>Jodie.Foster@somewhere.com</EMAIL>
</PERSON>
<PERSON>
<NAME>Lorrin Maughan</NAME>
<ADDRESS>1143 Winners Lane, London, UK</ADDRESS>
<TEL>(++94) 17 12345</TEL>
<FAX>++94) 17 12345</FAX>
<EMAIL>Lorrin.Maughan@somewhere.com</EMAIL>
</PERSON>
<PERSON>
<NAME>Steve Rachel</NAME>
<ADDRESS>90210 Beverly Hills, California, USA</ADDRESS>
<TEL>(++1) 2000 12345</TEL>
<FAX>(++1) 2000 12345</FAX>
<EMAIL>Steve.Rachel@somewhere.com</EMAIL>
</PERSON>
</PEOPLE>
</XML>

<TABLE DATASRC=#xmlPeople>
<THEAD>
  <TR>
<TH>NAME</TH>
<TH>ADDRESS ID</TH>
<TH>TEL</TH>
<TH>FAX</TH>
<TH>EMAIL</TH>
  </TR>
</THEAD>
<TR>
<TD><DIV datafld="NAME"></DIV></TD>
<TD><DIV datafld="ADDRESS"></DIV></TD>
<TD><DIV datafld="TEL"></DIV></TD>
<TD><DIV datafld="FAX"></DIV></TD>
<TD><DIV datafld="EMAIL"></DIV></TD>
</TR>
</TABLE>

</BODY>
</HTML>
```

4.4.2 *How do you take your HTML: DIV(ed) or SPAN(ed)?*

Most of the HTML coding in the examples above is simple. You assign data to an element or you bind an element to a DSO. In many of these cases, the element was contained in a tag called DIV or SPAN. Just in case you were wondering, here is a brief outline of what these two are.

If you don't do much program-ming that is viewed through Internet Explorer 4 or 5 (and above), then you can skip this section.

This pair of tags is useless in normal HTML:

```
<SPAN>...</SPAN>
```

But in IE5 DHTML, it is invaluable! The `<SPAN>` tag is used as a container tag for text, images, or other media types. The unique characteristic of the `<SPAN>` tag is that it is an inline element. This means that there is no break before or after the tag (unlike the DIV tag).

You can use the SPAN tag to bind data directly into the text of the page, without breaking the text up. This pair of tags in HTML is also a very useful pair of tags in IE5 DHTML:

```
<DIV>...</DIV>
```

Like the `<SPAN>` tags, the `<DIV>` tags are also a container but behave more like the `<P>...</P>` tags—which means that there is a line break in the HTML before and after the `<DIV>` section.

Both DIV and SPAN can be bound (still using IE5 DHTML) to DSO recordsets.

4.4.3 *Binding other HTML elements to a Data Island recordset*

These HTML elements can be bound in IE5. As you can see in table 4.2, although they can all be bound, only some are updateable. You can retreive more information on these HTML elements from the Microsoft website.

Table 4.2   HTML elements that can be bound to Data Islands

Element	Updateable	Bound Property
A	False	href
APPLET	True	property value via PARAM
BUTTON	False	innerText, innerHTML
DIV	False	innerText, innerHTML
FRAME	False	src
IFRAME	False	src
IMG	False	src
INPUT TYPE=CHECKBOX	True	checked
INPUT TYPE=HIDDEN	True	value
INPUT TYPE=LABEL	True	value
INPUT TYPE=PASSWORD	True	value
INPUT TYPE=RADIO	True	checked
INPUT TYPE=TEXT	True	value
LABEL	False	innerText, innerHTML
MARQUEE	False	innerText, innerHTML
SELECT	True	obj.options(obj.selectedIndex).text

Table 4.2   HTML elements that can be bound to Data Islands (continued)

SPAN	False	innerText, innerHTML
TEXTAREA	True	value

Binding a textbox

To simplify things, we will only focus on the table and the textbox (or TEXT-AREA in HTML). Let's extend the code of our previous example to include a textbox in the last column called EMAIL.

Here is the code to bind a text box to the EMAIL field:

```
<TABLE DATASRC='#xmlPeople' BORDER CELLPADDING=3>
<THEAD>
  <TR>
<TH>NAME</TH>
<TH>ADDRESS ID</TH>
<TH>TEL</TH>
<TH>FAX</TH>
<TH>EMAIL</TH>
  </TR>
</THEAD>
  <TR>
    <TD><SPAN DATAFLD="NAME"></SPAN></TD>
    <TD><SPAN DATAFLD="ADDRESS"></SPAN></TD>
    <TD><SPAN DATAFLD="TEL"></SPAN></TD>
    <TD><SPAN DATAFLD="FAX"></SPAN></TD>
```

And here is what you were looking for! Into the normal HTML textbox (in HTML, it's created with the code INPUT TYPE=text) you simply insert DATAFLD="EMAIL", and the text box is bound to the EMAIL field!

```
<TD>EMAIL: <INPUT TYPE=TEXT DATAFLD="EMAIL"></TD>
  </TR>
</TABLE>
```

The important difference here is the snippet EMAIL: <INPUT TYPE=TEXT DATAFLD="EMAIL">, which binds the text box (INPUT TYPE=TEXT) to the EMAIL field (DATAFLD="EMAIL") in the Data Island that is connected to the table. However, what if you do not place the text box within a table that defines a DSO? Or, what if the table doesn't define one? Perhaps each HTML text box should have its own one! No problem. Just define your own within the HTML, like this:

```
<INPUT TYPE=TEXT DATASRC=#xmlPeople DATAFLD=EMAIL>
```

Well, that was painless!

4.4.4 Output of source code

Figure 4.6 shows the output of the source code.

NAME	ADDRESS ID	TEL	FAX	EMAIL
Mark Wilson	911 Somewhere Circle, Canberra, Australia	(++612) 12345	(++612) 12345	Mark.Wilson@somewhei
Tracey Wilson	121 Zootle Road, Cape Town, South Africa	(++2721) 531 9090	(++2721) 531 9090	Tracey.Wilson@somewh
Jodie Foster	30 Animal Road, New York, USA	(++1) 3000 12345	(++1) 3000 12345	Jodie.Foster@somewhe
Lorrin Maughan	1143 Winners Lane, London, UK	(++94) 17 12345	++94) 17 12345	Lorrin.Maughan@somew
Steve Rachel	90210 Beverly Hills, California, USA	(++1) 2000 12345	(++1) 2000 12345	Steve.Rachel@somewhe

Figure 4.6   Data Island—binding a text box

4.4.5 Full source code

```
<TABLE DATASRC='#xmlPeople' BORDER CELLPADDING=3>
<THEAD>
  <TR>
<TH>NAME</TH>
<TH>ADDRESS ID</TH>
<TH>TEL</TH>
<TH>FAX</TH>
<TH>EMAIL</TH>
  </TR>
</THEAD>
  <TR>
    <TD><SPAN DATAFLD="NAME"></SPAN></TD>
    <TD><SPAN DATAFLD="ADDRESS"></SPAN></TD>
    <TD><SPAN DATAFLD="TEL"></SPAN></TD>
    <TD><SPAN DATAFLD="FAX"></SPAN></TD>
    <TD>EMAIL: <INPUT TYPE=TEXT DATAFLD="EMAIL"></TD>
  </TR>
</TABLE>
```

4.4.6 Accessing a standalone Data Island

If the Data Island is external to the HTML page, you need to provide a reference through a SRC attribute on the XML tag in your HTML document.

If the data is on a network or the Internet, use:

```
<XML ID=xmlPeople SRC="http://mark/xmlcode/people.xml"></XML>
```

On the other hand, if the data is local, you can use:

```
<XML ID=xmlPeople SRC="people.xml"></XML>
```

Then your DATASRC for your table can point to the ID attribute that is preceded by the # sign (in this case, it's #xmlPeople), as shown in the full source code example below.

4.4.7 *Full source code*

```
<XML ID=xmlPeople SRC="people.xml">
</XML>

<TABLE DATASRC=#xmlPeople>
<TR>
<TD><DIV datafld="NAME"></DIV></TD>
<TD><DIV datafld="ADDRESS"></DIV></TD>
<TD><DIV datafld="TEL"></DIV></TD>
<TD><DIV datafld="FAX"></DIV></TD>
<TD><DIV datafld="EMAIL"></DIV></TD>
</TR>
</TABLE>
```

4.4.8 *Saving your Data Island changes*

If your user has changed the value of the EMAIL text box, the change has already been synchronized to the bound Data Island DSO. So now, to send the data back to the server to be saved, use the following line of code to place a clone of the document in the variable objDOMDocument:

```
set objDOMDocument = xmlPeople.cloneNode(true)
```

Now you can send the objDOMDocument object back to the server to be saved back to your database.

4.4.9 *Limiting the number and moving through the records*

Let's say the Data Island contains 100 lines and when it loads into your table, the table completely fills several screens. This is not very useful to you or your user, so what you really want to do is have some way of limiting the number of records shown and, of course, have some way of moving through the unseen records— something like a forward or back button.

Well, if this were pure HTML, you could not even begin *thinking* about trying to achieve this! However, in IE5 we have DHTML (which is different from Netscape's DHTML), and when you use DHTML (and its extensions for tables) and, of course, spice all that up with our Data Island, well... let's have a look!

To get access to the Microsoft IE5 extensions and make more use of the HTML table (not the Data Island, please note!), give it a name. In the following example, we add to the <TABLE... line:

```
"ID=tblPeople"
```

To limit the number of records it displays, we also insert

```
"DATAPAGESIZE=10"
```

If you are using the source code as is, don't forget to include the Data Island called xmlPeople here.

Now the table will display the first 10 records of the Data Island it is bound to! If you are using the source code *as is*, don't forget to include the Data Island called xmlPeople here, and then follow it with:

```
<TABLE ID=tblPeople DATASRC='#xmlPeople' BORDER =1 CELL-
   PADDING=3 DATAPAGESIZE=10>
   <THEAD>
   <TR>
   <TH>NAME</TH>
   <TH>ADDRESS ID</TH>
   <TH>TEL</TH>
   <TH>FAX</TH>
   <TH>EMAIL</TH></TR>
   </THEAD>
   <TR>
     <TD><SPAN DATAFLD="NAME"></SPAN></TD>
     <TD><SPAN DATAFLD="ADDRESS"></SPAN></TD>
     <TD><SPAN DATAFLD="TEL"></SPAN></TD>
     <TD><SPAN DATAFLD="FAX"></SPAN></TD>
     <TD><INPUT DATAFLD="EMAIL"
   id=text1 name=text1></TD>
     </TR></TR>
</TABLE>
```

Now we provide a textbox to allow the user to change the number of records viewed. Note the code onblur="tblPeople.dataPageSize = this.value that sets the datasize property of the tblPeople table to the value that the user enters into the text box. The tables are automatically updated as soon as the user clicks away from the text box.

```
<INPUT TYPE=TEXT VALUE=10 onblur="tblPeople.dataPageSize = this.value;">
```

Now, to enable the user to move forward, backward, to the first record, and to the last record, we provide a button called cmdfirstPage. When you click on it, the following code is run, and the table will move to the first record.

```
<BUTTON ID=cmdfirstPage onclick="tblPeople.firstPage()">&lt;&lt;</BUTTON>
```

To move to the previous datapage is very similar. This time we use the function tblPeople.previousPage(), which moves the table one page back. Note that DataPageSize will affect exactly how many records back we move:

```
<BUTTON ID=cmdpreviousPage onclick="tblPeople.previousPage()">&lt;</BUTTON>
```

To move to the next datapage is also very similar. This time we use the function `tblPeople.nextPage()`, which moves the table one page forward. Again, DataPageSize will affect exactly how many records back we move.

```
<BUTTON ID=cmdnextPage onclick="tblPeople.nextPage()">&gt;</BUTTON>
```

Ditto for moving to the last record. The function called is `tblPeople.lastPage()`:

```
<BUTTON ID=cmdlastPage onclick="tblPeople.lastPage()">&gt;&gt;</BUTTON>
```

4.4.10 Output of source code

In the example code we have, there are a total of five records. However, the table is permitted to show ten records. If you reduce the number viewed to two records, you will be able to navigate between the records (see figure 4.7).

NAME	ADDRESS ID	TEL	FAX	EMAIL
Mark Wilson	911 Somewhere Circle, Canberra, Australia	(++612) 12345	(++612) 12345	Mark.Wilson@somewher
Tracey Wilson	121 Zootle Road, Cape Town, South Africa	(++2721) 531 9090	(++2721) 531 9090	Tracey.Wilson@somewh
Jodie Foster	30 Animal Road, New York, USA	(++1) 3000 12345	(++1) 3000 12345	Jodie.Foster@somewhe
Lorrin Maughan	1143 Winners Lane, London, UK	(++94) 17 12345	++94) 17 12345	Lorrin.Maughan@somew
Steve Rachel	90210 Beverly Hills, California, USA	(++1) 2000 12345	(++1) 2000 12345	Steve.Rachel@somewhe

Change the number of records viewed here: |10

Move backwards `<< < > >>` and forwards.

Figure 4.7   Data Island—moving through records

Note   If you limit the number of records you can see in the table to less than the total number of records in the recordset, then you can create forward and backward buttons to navigate through the rest of the records.

4.4.11 Full source code

If you are using the source code *as is*, don't forget to include the Data Island called xmlPeople here, and then follow it with:

```
<TABLE ID=tblPeople DATASRC='#xmlPeople' BORDER =1 CELL-
PADDING=3 DATAPAGESIZE=10>
  <THEAD>
  <TR>
  <TH>NAME</TH>
```

```
<TH>ADDRESS ID</TH>
<TH>TEL</TH>
<TH>FAX</TH>
<TH>EMAIL</TH></TR>
</THEAD>
<TR>
  <TD><SPAN DATAFLD="NAME"></SPAN></TD>
  <TD><SPAN DATAFLD="ADDRESS"></SPAN></TD>
  <TD><SPAN DATAFLD="TEL"></SPAN></TD>
  <TD><SPAN DATAFLD="FAX"></SPAN></TD>
  <TD><INPUT DATAFLD="EMAIL"></TD>
  </TR></TR>
</TABLE>

<p>Change the number of records viewed here:
<INPUT TYPE=TEXT VALUE=10 STYLE="width:20"
onblur="tblPeople.dataPageSize = this.value;">
</p>
<p>
Move backwards 
<BUTTON ID=cmdfirstPage onclick="tblPeople.firstPage()">&lt;&lt;</BUTTON>
<BUTTON ID=cmdpreviousPage onclick="tblPeople.previousPage()">&lt;</BUT-
  TON>
<BUTTON ID=cmdnextPage onclick="tblPeople.nextPage()">&gt;</BUTTON>
<BUTTON ID=cmdlastPage onclick="tblPeople.lastPage()">&gt;&gt;</BUTTON>
 and forwards.
</p>
<p>Add another record here (move off the record to save it):
<INPUT ID="add" TYPE=BUTTON VALUE="Add Employee" onClick="xmlid.record-
  set.addNew()">
</p>
```

4.4.12 *Adding new records to a Data Island*

This time, we use text boxes to display the data and to insert a new record.

In the code you can see the HTML for a label and the corresponding textbox (textboxes are called input boxes in HTML):

```
<P>Name: <INPUT TYPE=TEXT DATASRC=#xmlPeople DATAFLD=NAME></P>
<P>ADDRESS: <INPUT class=regText DATASRC=#xmlPeople DATAFLD="ADDRESS"></P>
<P>TEL: <INPUT class=regText DATASRC=#xmlPeople DATAFLD="TEL"></P>
<P>FAX: <INPUT TYPE=TEXT class=regText DATASRC=#xmlPeople DATAFLD="FAX"></P>
<P>EMAIL: <INPUT TYPE=TEXT DATASRC=#xmlPeople DATAFLD=EMAIL><P>
```

We have seen the *move first* trick before, but this time something important has changed. If you look at the table <TABLE... code, you will see that the DATASRC for the entire table is defined. But now the input box is not contained within a table, so we must specify both the DATASRC and the DATAFLD in the input box details.

Also, since we will not be moving the DATASRC via the table object, in order to move all the text boxes back a record or forward a record, we manipulate the underlying recordset, which is exposed by the xmlPeople Data Island.

In the next piece of code, you see the first of the four buttons, called first. When it is clicked, the code onClick="xmlPeople.recordset.moveFirst() is run. Here you can see that the xmlPeople recordset is moved.

```
</P><INPUT ID="first" TYPE=button VALUE="<<" onClick="xmlPeople.record-
   set.moveFirst()"></P>
```

Ditto for manipulating the Data Island recordset with the method .movePrevious():

```
<INPUT ID="prev" TYPE=button VALUE="<" onClick="if (xmlPeople.record-
   set.absoluteposition > 1) xmlPeople.recordset.movePrevious()">
```

Ditto for manipulating the Data Island recordset with the method .moveNext():

```
<INPUT ID="next" TYPE=button VALUE=">" onClick="if (xmlPeople.record-
   set.absoluteposition < xmlPeople.recordset.recordcount) xmlPeo-
   ple.recordset.moveNext()">
```

Ditto for manipulating the Data Island recordset with the method .moveLast():

```
<INPUT ID="last" TYPE=button VALUE=">>" onClick="xmlPeople.record-
   set.moveLast()">
```

And to add a record to the recordset, we have another button called add, which displays the label Add Person and tells the recordset to addNew().

```
<INPUT ID="add" TYPE=BUTTON VALUE="Add Person" onClick="xml-
   People.recordset.addNew()">
```

4.4.13 *Output of source code*
Figure 4.8 shows the output of the source code.

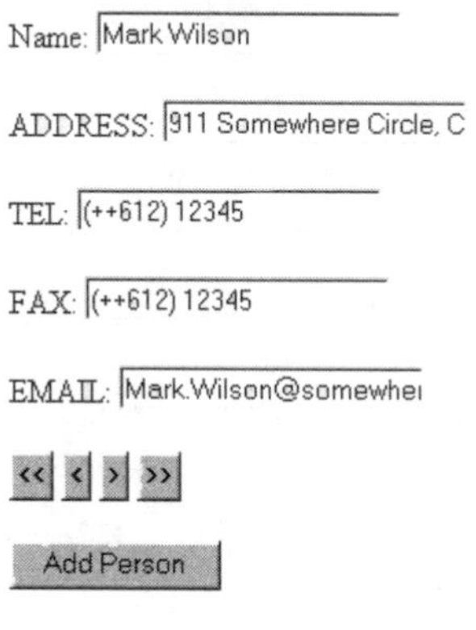

Figure 4.8   Data Island—adding a new record

4.4.14 *Full source code*

If you are using the source code *as is*, don't forget to include the Data Island called xmlPeople here, and then follow it with:

```
<P>Name:
<INPUT TYPE=TEXT DATASRC=#xmlPeople DATAFLD=NAME>
<P>ADDRESS:
  <INPUT class=regText DATASRC=#xmlPeople DATAFLD="ADDRESS">
<P>TEL:
  <INPUT class=regText DATASRC=#xmlPeople DATAFLD="TEL">
<P>FAX:
  <INPUT TYPE=TEXT class=regText DATASRC=#xmlPeople DATAFLD="FAX">
<P>EMAIL:
  <INPUT TYPE=TEXT DATASRC=#xmlPeople DATAFLD=EMAIL>
<BR>
<BR>
<INPUT ID="first" TYPE=button VALUE="<<" onClick="xml-
  People.recordset.moveFirst()">
<INPUT ID="prev" TYPE=button VALUE="<" onClick="if (xml-
  People.recordset.absoluteposition > 1) xmlPeople.recordset.movePrevi-
  ous()">
<INPUT ID="next" TYPE=button VALUE=">" onClick="if (xml-
  People.recordset.absoluteposition < xmlPeople.recordset.recordcount)
  xmlPeople.recordset.moveNext()">
<INPUT ID="last" TYPE=button VALUE=">>" onClick="xmlPeople.recordset.move-
  Last()">
<BR><BR>
<INPUT ID="add" TYPE=BUTTON VALUE="Add Employee"
  onClick="xmlPeople.recordset.addNew()">
```

4.4.15 *Getting an ADO recordset from XML Data Islands*

Once you have a Data Island, you can get an ADO recordset from it. Assuming you have an ADO recordset called rsPEOPLE and a Data Island called PEOPLE, then try this:

```
set rsPEOPLE = PEOPLE.recordset
```

Now that's pretty useful if you work with RDS! (RDS is a form of ADO that runs disconnected in the IE browser.)

4.5 *Getting the Microsoft XML objects onto your PC*

To download the Microsoft XML Parser Redistributable, go to http://msdn. microsoft.com/ downloads/tools/ xmlparser/xml- parser.asp

To use the code examples that use the Microsoft XML objects (such as DOM-Document), you first have to add a reference in your project to the "Microsoft XML 2.0" object. Naturally you must have these objects installed on the development and target distribution system where you will install your solution. There are two easy ways to get the Microsoft XML objects onto your systems. You can either install IE5, or you can extend IE4 with the XML redistributable, which you can download from the Microsoft website.

4.6 *Creating the objects*

ASP developers should use the following syntax to create a new XMLDOMDocument object programmatically. This is the same CreateObject() syntax for creating the other objects:

```
<%
Dim objXmlDoc
Set objXmlDoc = CreateObject("Microsoft.XMLDOM")
%>
```

VB programmers can either use the CreateObject() code above or add a reference in their project to the *Microsoft XML version 2.0* object, and then use:

```
Dim objXmlDoc As DOMDocument
Set objXmlDoc = new DOMDocument
```

This will create a new instance of the DOMDocument, which can be used immediately.

For these examples of working with XML files, throughout the book we will provide the code for manipulating these objects in either VB or ASP/VBScript.

As shown above, when changing the VB code to be used in VBScript, use the CreateObject() and then the Set statement. When changing ASP code to VB, remove the CreateObject(), add a reference to the object, and then use the DIM statement.

4.7 *Loading a file synchronously*

If you want your program and code execution to wait until the XML document has completely finished loading (into a DOMDocument), then load the document synchronously with this VB code:

```
Private Sub LoadXMLFile_Click()
  Dim objXmlDoc As DOMDocument

  'then load an XML document using the load method as follows:
  objXmlDoc.async = False
  objXmlDoc.Load ("http://mark/xmlcode/people.xml")

End Sub
```

4.8   *Loading a file asynchronously*

If you want to have your program working away on something (such as loading an animated image, showing a bar with a percentage complete sign, or background calculations) while the XML document is loading, then load the XML document asynchronously. This time you will use a `WithEvents` statement to allow access to the events of the DOMDocument to enable you to use the loading of the document asynchronous.

4.8.1   *Using WithEvents in VB*

To see how to use `WithEvents` in your code, try this code. Into the `General Declaration` section of a VB form, insert:

```
Dim WithEvents objXmlDoc As DOMDocument
```

Now, under a button on a form called `Command1`, place this code, which loads an XML file into the DOMDocument we created in the `General Declarations` section.

```
Private Sub Command1_Click()
Dim objXmlDoc As DOMDocument

  'create the instance of the DOMDocument
  Set objXmlDoc = New DOMDocument
  'then load an XML document using the load method as follows
  objXmlDoc.async = False
  objXmlDoc.Load ("http://mark/xmlcode/people.xml")

End Sub
```

Of course, now you need to be notified when the DOMDocument has completed loading the XML, which is where `WithEvents` comes in. In fact there are several other stages, such as when some of the xml is loaded or when the entire process is completed. For now let's only look at how to be notified when the loading is completed.

When you use the statement `WithEvents`, you can use the events for the object you are *sinking* events for. What this means is that the events that are occurring will occur in your program, and you can put code into these events.

In the example below, for the object `objXmlDoc`, we sink the DOMDocument's events by using the `WithEvents` statement. In the `onreadystatechange` event, we can query the DOMDocument property called `readyState` and check if the loading of the XML file is completed, or check for other variables or properties in our program code.

Open the code editor in VB for the form where you have instanced the object called DOMDocument. In the dropdown combo box that lists the controls you can code for, you will see the new `objXmlDoc` object. Select it and, in the list of

Open the code editor in VB for the form where you have instanced the object called DOMDocument. In the dropdown combo box that lists the controls you can code for, you will see the new `objXmlDoc` object. Select it and, in the list of events in the right-hand-side combo box, select the event you want to use. In this case we want to use the `onReadyStateChange()` event. When you select it, the event is created for you in your code.

Now, to write code that is connected to the `readystatechange()` event of the `objXmlDoc`, or to find out when the document has finished loading, do the following. In the new event, use the following VB code:

```
Private Sub objXmlDoc_onreadystatechange()
    'if the readyState is COMPLETE, then pop up a message box
    If (objXmlDoc.readyState = 4) Then
        MsgBox "Completed!"
    End If
End Sub
```

4.9 A roundtrip on using the DOM object with a TreeView

The next example is a simple VB project, where we will investigate populating a TreeView with data from an XML file using the DOM object. Then we will add and delete entries to the DOM object. This is a simple example, because we want to show you how to use the basic commands of the DOM object from beginning to end. Figure 4.9 shows the resulting view of this project.

After the form has loaded, click on the `Populate People` command button, which loads and displays the contents of the XML file. As you click on each person in the TreeView, the text box on the right-hand side fills with details relating to the element clicked on, using the DOM object to get the details.

We've included a web-browser control to the form so that you can see the changes happening to the XML file as you add and delete new elements. To add a new person, click on the `Clear Items for new Person` button, add your details to the text boxes, then click on the `Save New Person` button. This saves the new PER-SON element and adds it to the XML file.

To delete a person, click on a person in the TreeView. Click on the `Delete Person` button, which will automatically delete the selected person, removing him/her from the TreeView and DOM Object, as well as from the XML file.

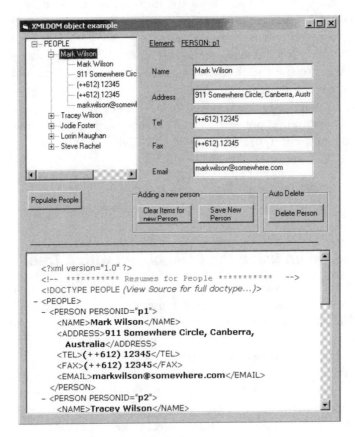

Figure 4.9   DOM sample screen-shot

4.9.1 *Preparing to run the example*

The DOM-
Document and
TreeView use
"Node" to specify
their objects, there-
fore we've tried to
explicitly differenti-
ate between the two
in our comments.

To run this project, download the source code from http://www.vbxml.com and then:

- Create a directory called "c:\dev"
- Copy the people2.xml and people2.dtd file into this directory we can't use the VB App.Path property, because we have to declare our DTD file in the XML file, which is a read-only property)
- Make sure that you have the Microsoft XML 2.0 dll installed

Now let's dig into the code.

4.9.2 *Module variables*

These go into the `General Declarations` of your project:

```
General_Declarations

Option Explicit

Private m_objDOMPeople As DOMDocument    ❶
Private m_blnItemClicked As Boolean    ❷

Const XMLPATH As String = "c:\dev\people2.xml"    ❸
```

❶ The member variable that will be used throughout the project.

❷ The member variable that will be used throughout the project.

❸ Constant used throughout the code for when we want to save the document.

4.9.3 *Populating the TreeView from the DOMDocument*

When you click on the `Populate People` button, the following code will populate the TreeView with the contents of the DOMDocument:

```
Private Sub cmdPopulate_Click()

    Dim objPeopleRoot As IXMLDOMElement
    Dim objPersonElement As IXMLDOMElement
    Dim tvwRoot As Node

    Set m_objDOMPeople = New DOMDocument
```

`ResolveExternals` stopts the m_objDOMPeople object from looking for external files, which in our case are the people2.dtd. Set this to `True` if you want the parser to find the external files:

```
m_objDOMPeople.resolveExternals = True
```

`ValidateOnParse` stops the `m_objDOMPeople` from validating the XML file against the people.dtd file. Set this to `True` if you want validation to occur:

```
m_objDOMPeople.validateOnParse = True
```

The XML file first needs to be loaded into the DOMDocument (m_objDOMPeople). We need to be aware of loading the file asynchronously; therefore: we set the property, `async`, to `False` before loading:

```
m_objDOMPeople.async = False
```

Load the XML into the DOMDocument using a string containing the XML location:

```
Call m_objDOMPeople.Load(XMLPATH)
```

Check that the load of the XML document was successful:

```
If m_objDOMPeople.parseError.reason <> "" Then
```

There has been an error with the loaded XML. Show the reason:

```
MsgBox m_objDOMPeople.parseError.reason
Exit Sub
  End If
```

Get to the root element of the XML, bypassing the comments, PIs:

```
Set objPeopleRoot = m_objDOMPeople.documentElement
```

Once we have obtained the root element (`documentElement`) of the DOMDocument, we can then start working with the data from the XML file. The first thing we want to add to the TreeView is the name of the root element of the XML file, which is `<PEOPLE>`. Then we need to start adding child Nodes to the TreeView.

Now let's populate the TreeControl from the DOMDocument.

Set the TreeView control properties:

```
tvwPeople.LineStyle = tvwRootLines
tvwPeople.Style = tvwTreelinesPlusMinusText
tvwPeople.Indentation = 400
```

Check if the TreeView has already been populated. If so, remove the root, which removes everything:

```
If tvwPeople.Nodes.Count > 0 Then
tvwPeople.Nodes.Remove 1
End If
```

Add a child to the root Node of the TreeView:

```
Set tvwRoot = tvwPeople.Nodes.Add()
```

Now all we need to do is iterate through these `childNodes` of the DOMDocument's `<PEOPLE>` elements, which is going to return five `<PEOPLE>` elements. This is done by the `For Each` loop, which lead us to the code in the `populateTreeWithChildren()` method.

Iterate through each `<PERSON>` element in the DOM to fill the tree, which in itself iterates through each child Node of that element (`objPersonElement`) to drill down into its child Nodes:

```
For Each objPersonElement In objPeopleRoot.childNodes
    populateTreeWithChildren objPersonElement
Next

webTarget.Navigate XMLPATH
cmdDelete.Enabled = True
cmdClear.Enabled = True

End Sub
```

Full source code

```
Private Sub cmdPopulate_Click()

  Dim objPeopleRoot As IXMLDOMElement
  Dim objPersonElement As IXMLDOMElement
  Dim tvwRoot As Node

  Set m_objDOMPeople = New DOMDocument

  m_objDOMPeople.resolveExternals = True

  m_objDOMPeople.validateOnParse = True

  m_objDOMPeople.async = False
  Call m_objDOMPeople.Load(XMLPATH)

  If m_objDOMPeople.parseError.reason <> "" Then
    MsgBox m_objDOMPeople.parseError.reason
    Exit Sub
  End If
  tvwPeople.LineStyle = tvwRootLines
  tvwPeople.Style = tvwTreelinesPlusMinusText
  tvwPeople.Indentation = 400

  If tvwPeople.Nodes.Count > 0 Then tvwPeople.Nodes.Remove 1
  End If

  Set tvwRoot = tvwPeople.Nodes.Add()

  For Each objPersonElement In objPeopleRoot.childNodes
    populateTreeWithChildren objPersonElement
  Next

  webTarget.Navigate XMLPATH
  cmdDelete.Enabled = True
  cmdClear.Enabled = True

End Sub
```

populateTreeWithChildren

This code is called from the `cmdPopulate` click event. For each `parentNode` created on the TreeView, drill down into the DOMElement that has been passed in and populate the TreeView with these DOMElement child Nodes.

The parameter objDOMNode is the current child Node from the `documentElement` property of the DOMDocument:

```
Dim objNameNode As IXMLDOMNode
Dim objAttributes As IXMLDOMNamedNodeMap
Dim objAttributeNode As IXMLDOMNode
```

```
Dim intIndex As Integer

Dim tvwElement As Node
Dim tvwChildElement As Node
```

We need to add a title to the current TreeView Node, such as `PERSON: Jodie Foster`, by adding the element's main child Node (`<NAME>`) as the heading for the Treeview of this section. Use the method `selectSingleNode()` to return the first Node with the `nodeName` of `NAME` that it finds:

```
Set objNameNode = objDOMNode.selectSingleNode("NAME")
```

Add the NAME element's parentNode nodeName and its value to the TreeView.

```
Set tvwElement = tvwPeople.Nodes.Add(1, tvwChild)
tvwElement.Text = objNameNode.parentNode.nodeName & ": " _
& objNameNode.nodeTypedValue
```

Add the ID of the Node to the TreeView Node's tag property. The element Node is holding the id attribute that we want to store in the tag as an identity reference. We therefore need to get a hold of this Node to get its value.

```
Set objAttributes = objDOMNode.Attributes
```

We know that we've named our id reference as `PERSONID`, so we should use the `getNamedItem()` method to tell the `NameNodeListMap` to get this Node. First we need to check if there are attributes:

```
If objAttributes.length > 0 Then

Set objAttributeNode = objAttributes.getNamedItem("PERSONID")
```

Store this value in the tag of the TreeView:

```
tvwElement.Tag = objAttributeNode.nodeValue
End If

tvwElement.EnsureVisible
intIndex = tvwElement.Index
```

We then need to populate the current TreeView Node, from the current DOM element Node (`objDOMNode`), by once again iterating through the childNodes (elements) of the `objDOMNode`. Therefore, iterate through the childNodes passed in DOMNode to this procedure to populate the TreeView with these child Node values:

```
For Each objPersonElement In objDOMNode.childNodes
    Set tvwChildElement = tvwPeople.Nodes.Add(intIndex, tvwChild)
    tvwChildElement.Text = objPersonElement.nodeTypedValue
  Next

End Sub
```

Full source code

```
Private Sub populateTreeWithChildren(objDOMNode As IXMLDOMElement)

    Dim objNameNode As IXMLDOMNode
    Dim objAttributes As IXMLDOMNamedNodeMap
    Dim objAttributeNode As IXMLDOMNode
    Dim intIndex As Integer

    Dim tvwElement As Node
    Dim tvwChildElement As Node

    Set objNameNode = objDOMNode.selectSingleNode("NAME")

    Set tvwElement = tvwPeople.Nodes.Add(1, tvwChild)
    tvwElement.Text = objNameNode.parentNode.nodeName & ": " _
                    & objNameNode.nodeTypedValue

    Set objAttributes = objDOMNode.Attributes

    If objAttributes.length > 0 Then

        Set objAttributeNode = objAttributes.getNamedItem("PERSONID")

        tvwElement.Tag = objAttributeNode.nodeValue
    End If

    tvwElement.EnsureVisible
    intIndex = tvwElement.Index

    For Each objPersonElement In objDOMNode.childNodes
        Set tvwChildElement = tvwPeople.Nodes.Add(intIndex, tvwChild)
        tvwChildElement.Text = objPersonElement.nodeTypedValue
    Next

End Sub
```

This completes our population of the TreeView from the DOMDocument.

Populating the text boxes from the DOMDocument

Now we will proceed to clicking on the TreeView and fetching the data from the DOMDocument to populate the text boxes on the right-hand side of the screen:

```
Private Sub tvwPeople_Click()

Dim objSelNode As Node
```

This code simply does a little bit of VB checking of unwanted event firing. For example, if this code has just come from the expand and collapse event, then don't run this code; simply ignore it.

```
If m_blnItemClicked = True Then
```

```
        m_blnItemClicked = False
        Exit Sub
End If

Set objSelNode = tvwPeople.SelectedItem
```

Call the procedure that handles populating the text boxes:

```
populatePeopleDetails objSelNode
```

```
End Sub
```

```
Private Sub populatePeopleDetails(objSelNode As Node)
```

This procedure populates the form's text boxes with details from the passed-in Node object (objSelNode) DOMDocument. The parameter objSelNode is the current Treeview Node that has been clicked on:

```
Dim objPersonElement As IXMLDOMElement
Dim objChildElement As IXMLDOMElement

If objSelNode Is Nothing Then Exit Sub
```

Ignore this TreeView selection if it has not been the PERSON Node that has been clicked on.

```
If Trim(objSelNode.Tag) <> "" Then
```

We need to find the TreeView Node that is being passed in, or its parents tag value, so that we can get the PERSONID attribute value. Then we can proceed to find the Node that has an attribute to the value of the stored TreeView Node's tag:

```
Set objPersonElement = m_objDOMPeople.nodeFromID(objSelNode.Tag)

lblElement.Caption = objPersonElement.nodeName & ": ID = " & _
                    objPersonElement.Attributes(0).nodeValue
```

With this found Node (objPersonElement), once again we will iterate through its child Nodes to populate the text boxes. We will use a Select Case to filter which element we will deal with:

```
For Each objChildElement In objPersonElement.childNodes
```

Check that the type of Node you are dealing with is an element Node, as it could also be other types of Nodes, such as PIs. Then populate the text box with the text from the DOM Node:

```
If objChildElement.nodeType = NODE_ELEMENT Then
Select Case UCase(objChildElement.nodeName)
Case "NAME"
txtName.Text = objChildElement.nodeTypedValue
Case "ADDRESS"
txtAddress.Text = objChildElement.nodeTypedValue
```

```
Case "TEL"
txtTel.Text = objChildElement.nodeTypedValue
Case "FAX"
txtFax.Text = objChildElement.nodeTypedValue
Case "EMAIL"
txtEmail.Text = objChildElement.nodeTypedValue
        End Select
 End If
Next objChildElement
End If

 Clear the object memory resources:
  Set objChildElement = Nothing
  Set objPersonElement = Nothing
End Sub
```

Full source code

```
Private Sub tvwPeople_Click()

  Dim objSelNode As Node

  If m_blnItemClicked = True Then
    m_blnItemClicked = False
    Exit Sub
  End If

  Set objSelNode = tvwPeople.SelectedItem
  populatePeopleDetails objSelNode

End Sub

Private Sub populatePeopleDetails(objSelNode As Node)

  Dim objPersonElement As IXMLDOMElement
  Dim objChildElement As IXMLDOMElement

  If objSelNode Is Nothing Then Exit Sub

  If Trim(objSelNode.Tag) <> "" Then

    Set objPersonElement = m_objDOMPeople.nodeFromID(objSelNode.Tag)

    lblElement.Caption = objPersonElement.nodeName & ": ID = " & _
                       objPersonElement.Attributes(0).nodeValue

    For Each objChildElement In objPersonElement.childNodes

      If objChildElement.nodeType = NODE_ELEMENT Then
        Select Case UCase(objChildElement.nodeName)
        Case "NAME"
            txtName.Text = objChildElement.nodeTypedValue
        Case "ADDRESS"
            txtAddress.Text = objChildElement.nodeTypedValue
        Case "TEL"
            txtTel.Text = objChildElement.nodeTypedValue
        Case "FAX"
            txtFax.Text = objChildElement.nodeTypedValue
        Case "EMAIL"
```

```
                txtEmail.Text = objChildElement.nodeTypedValue
          End Select
       End If
    Next objChildElement
 End If

 Set objChildElement = Nothing
 Set objPersonElement = Nothing
End Sub
```

Adding a new person to the DOMDocument

Here we need to fill the text boxes on the right-hand side with its contents, and then save the contents to the DOMDocument.

This is done in two parts: first we clear all the text boxes, then we save its contents. We know this is not *cool* coding, but it's just for ease of coding to show the basics of coding with the DOMDocument.

This clears the contents of the text boxes:

```
Private Sub cmdClear_Click()

    lblElement.Caption = ""
    txtName.Text = ""
    txtAddress.Text = ""
    txtTel.Text = ""
    txtFax.Text = ""
    txtEmail.Text = ""
    cmdAdd.Enabled = True
End Sub
```

After filling in the text boxes, click on the cmdAdd, to save the new PERSON to be added to the DOMDocument:

```
Private Sub cmdAdd_Click()
saveNewPerson
cmdAdd.Enabled = False
End Sub

Private Sub saveNewPerson()
```

The information on the screen shows that this method creates a new element and adds its children to the DOM object:

```
Dim objPerson As IXMLDOMElement
Dim objNewChild As IXMLDOMElement
```

Now we need to create a new PERSON child Node (objPerson) to the document-Element Node (PEOPLE):

```
Set objPerson = m_objDOMPeople.createElement("PERSON")
```

Before we can continue, we also need to give this PERSON Node a PERSONID attribute, which we will use with our getNewID() method to return this ID string. We must do this because the attribute has been set up as *Required* in the DTD file.

We use the `setAttribute()` method to add this attribute Node. Then we add this attribute Node to the element Node that requires it:

```
objPerson.setAttribute "PERSONID", getNewID
  m_objDOMPeople.documentElement.appendChild objPerson
```

To this new PERSON child, let's add its child Nodes (NAME, ADDRESS, etc). We have chosen to use the `createElement()` method to add the child Nodes. However, you can choose to use the `createNode()` method, which is just a choice of preference.

```
Set objNewChild = m_objDOMPeople.createElement("NAME").
objNewChild.Text = txtName.Text
```

We need to append (add) each child Node needs to the current PERSON Node before we can continue:

```
objPerson.appendChild objNewChild

Set objNewChild = m_objDOMPeople.createElement("ADDRESS")
objNewChild.Text = txtAddress.Text
objPerson.appendChild objNewChild

Set objNewChild = m_objDOMPeople.createElement("TEL")
objNewChild.Text = txtTel.Text
objPerson.appendChild objNewChild

Set objNewChild = m_objDOMPeople.createElement("FAX")
objNewChild.Text = txtFax.Text
objPerson.appendChild objNewChild

Set objNewChild = m_objDOMPeople.createElement("EMAIL")
objNewChild.Text = txtEmail.Text
objPerson.appendChild objNewChild
```

We re-use the `populateTreeWithChildren()` method to keep the TreeView in sync with the changes to the DOMDocument:

```
populateTreeWithChildren objPerson
```

You may add the new element to the DOMDocument, but it will not be added to the source until you save the document:

```
m_objDOMPeople.save XMLPATH

  webTarget.Refresh
  Set objPerson = Nothing
  Set objNewChild = Nothing

End Sub
```

Full source code

```
Private Sub cmdClear_Click()
```

```
        lblElement.Caption = ""
        txtName.Text = ""
        txtAddress.Text = ""
        txtTel.Text = ""
        txtFax.Text = ""
        txtEmail.Text = ""
        cmdAdd.Enabled = True
End Sub

Private Sub cmdAdd_Click()
        saveNewPerson
        cmdAdd.Enabled = False
End Sub

Private Sub saveNewPerson()

    Dim objPerson As IXMLDOMElement
    Dim objNewChild As IXMLDOMElement

    Set objPerson = m_objDOMPeople.createElement("PERSON")
    objPerson.setAttribute "PERSONID", getNewID
    m_objDOMPeople.documentElement.appendChild objPerson

    Set objNewChild = m_objDOMPeople.createElement("NAME")
    objNewChild.Text = txtName.Text
    objPerson.appendChild objNewChild

    Set objNewChild = m_objDOMPeople.createElement("ADDRESS")
    objNewChild.Text = txtAddress.Text
    objPerson.appendChild objNewChild

    Set objNewChild = m_objDOMPeople.createElement("TEL")
    objNewChild.Text = txtTel.Text
    objPerson.appendChild objNewChild

    Set objNewChild = m_objDOMPeople.createElement("FAX")
    objNewChild.Text = txtFax.Text
    objPerson.appendChild objNewChild

    Set objNewChild = m_objDOMPeople.createElement("EMAIL")
    objNewChild.Text = txtEmail.Text
    objPerson.appendChild objNewChild
    populateTreeWithChildren objPerson

    m_objDOMPeople.save XMLPATH

    webTarget.Refresh
    Set objPerson = Nothing
    Set objNewChild = Nothing

End Sub
```

Deleting a Person from the DOMDocument

Clicking the `Delete` button allows the user to delete a Node from the DOMDocument.

```
Private Sub cmdDelete_Click()
   deleteSelectedPerson tvwPeople.SelectedItem
End Sub
```

```
Private Sub deleteSelectedPerson(objSelNode As Node)
```

The following code deletes the selected TreeView Node, as well as the item from the DOMDocument. The parameter `objSelNode` is the TreeView Node that has been clicked on/opened.

```
Dim objPersonElement As IXMLDOMNode
```

If no TreeView Node has been selected, then exit the procedure:

```
If objSelNode Is Nothing Then Exit Sub
```

Once again we need to find the ID stored in the selected TreeView Node or its parentNode tag property, to be able to delete it:

```
If Trim(objSelNode.Tag) = "" Then
If Trim(objSelNode.Parent.Tag) <> "" Then
      Set objSelNode = objSelNode.Parent
   End If
End If
```

Once you have found this ID, use the `nodeFromID()` method of the DOM-Document to return the DOMDocument Node that needs to be deleted. Find the DOMDocument Node using the tag value found in the selected Node of the Tree-View tag property.

```
If Trim(objSelNode.Tag) <> "" Then
Set objPersonElement = m_objDOMPeople.nodeFromID(objSelNode.Tag)
```

If the DOMDocument Node exists, use the `removeChild()` method that can be done via the DOMDocument's `documentElement` property:

```
m_objDOMPeople.documentElement.removeChild objPersonElement
```

We need to save the DOMDocument to reflect the removal of its child Node. The TreeView also needs to be kept in sync with this deletion:

```
m_objDOMPeople.save XMLPATH
tvwPeople.Nodes.Remove objSelNode.Index
webTarget.Refresh
   End If

End Sub
```

Full source code

```
Private Sub cmdDelete_Click()
   deleteSelectedPerson tvwPeople.SelectedItem
```

```
End Sub

Private Sub deleteSelectedPerson(objSelNode As Node)

  Dim objPersonElement As IXMLDOMNode

  If Trim(objSelNode.Tag) = "" Then
    If Trim(objSelNode.Parent.Tag) <> "" Then
      Set objSelNode = objSelNode.Parent
    End If
  End If

  If Trim(objSelNode.Tag) <> "" Then

    Set objPersonElement = m_objDOMPeople.nodeFromID(objSelNode.Tag)

    m_objDOMPeople.documentElement.removeChild objPersonElement
    m_objDOMPeople.save XMLPATH
    tvwPeople.Nodes.Remove objSelNode.Index
    webTarget.Refresh
  End If

End Sub
```

4.10   *Saving an XML document to a file in ASP*

Once you have created an XMLDOMDocument, saving it to a file is easy. In your
project, add a reference to the `File System Object` (FSO) that is a part of the
Windows Scripting Host objects. In ASP you could use:

```
<%
```

First, create the DOMDocument object here.
Then load the DOMDocument object with the relevant strings.
Now you can load the XML into the string savedxml:

```
SAVEDXML = objDOMDocument.xml
```

Create an instance of the FileSystemObject:

```
Set FSO = CreateObject("Scripting.FileSystemObject")
```

Create a text file:

```
Set CUSTFILE = FSO.CreateTextFile(Server.MapPath("resume.xml"), True)
```

Now save the string to the XML file:

```
CUSTFILE.WriteLine (SAVEDXML)
```

Close the file:

```
CUSTFILE.Close
%>
```

With the `save()` method on the DOMDocument, you can also save the XML with one line of code (in either VB or VBScript):

```
objXmlDoc.save(Server.MapPath("resume.xml"))
```

4.11 Handling errors and debugging

The simplest way to debug is to display the XML property of a DOMDocument and see if you have managed to load your document. If this doesn't return or display anything, then there was an error loading. You must then view the last error.

Here we assume that you already have a DOMDocument called `objXmlDoc` and you have tried to load a document or string. To find the last error, access the `parseError` collection:

```
objXmlDoc.parseError.reason
```

4.12 Accessing the XML with ASP

If you want to get to the XML in your DOMDocument, then in ASP you can use:

```
Response.Write(objXmlDoc.xml)
```

In VB you can use:

```
MsgBox objXmlDoc.xml
```

4.13 Sending data back to the user

In most XML applications, you will extract data from a database and send it to the users. Exactly *how* you package it and send it is up to you.

There are many possibilities, but we will focus on the basics—where a VB or web page requests data and has it returned. The request is fired off to an ASP page, which accesses the database and replies with the data in the requested format.

The format that is returned could be XML, HTML, HTML with Data Islands, XML with XSL, ADO-persisted XML file, or other ingenious formats or alternatives we haven't listed here.

4.13.1   *Creating XML on the server from your relational database*

ASP files can be used to create XML data sources in the same way that they can be used to create HTML pages. The only major difference is that instead of the page's basic structure being that of an HTML page, its basic structure is that of an XML data source.

Without further delay, let's build an ASP file that returns a list of people who have resumes on our system. The return format will be XML. You open an ASP file (possibly passing extra information), then the ASP file talks to your database and returns an XML file containing a list of people who have resumes. See figure 4.10 for a possible design.

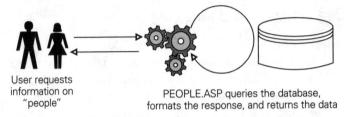

User requests information on "people"

PEOPLE.ASP queries the database, formats the response, and returns the data

Figure 4.10   Retrieving an XML pick list of people from a database

First, we declare that we are using VBScript on this ASP page:

```
<% @Language=VBScript %>
```

Now send back your XML heading information:

```
<?xml version="1.0"?>
```

Start your XML root Node:

```
<PEOPLE>
```

Now set up your database connection. This code assumes you have a valid ODBC connection called *VBXML*.

```
<%
    Set ObjConn = Server.CreateObject("ADODB.Connection")
    ObjConn.Open "VBXML"
```

Get the recordset. This code assumes you have a table named People that can be reached via the VBXML ODBC connection:

```
Set PEOPLE = ObjConn.Execute("select * from People")
```

Start looping through the records:

```
Do While Not PEOPLE.EOF
%>
```

Now construct the basic structure of the elements that will contain the data from your table. The People table has five fields: name, address, tel, fax, and email. In XML we want to see these fields as:

```
<NAME></NAME>
<ADDRESS></ADDRESS>
<TEL></TEL>
<FAX></FAX>
<EMAIL></EMAIL>
```

If we only return these fields, we won't structure the information so that anyone can tell where each person's details begin and end. We need to put in tags such as `<PERSON>` and `</PERSON>` around the above information. Our XML structure now looks like this:

```
<PERSON>
<NAME></NAME>
<ADDRESS></ADDRESS>
<TEL></TEL>
<FAX></FAX>
<EMAIL></EMAIL>
</PERSON>
```

Now to populate the XML file, we need to write VBScript code that will extract the data from the database and pop it into the XML format we identified.

This line of code will extract the NAME field from the PEOPLE recordset and then write it out between the XML tags `<NAME>` and `</NAME>`:

```
<NAME><%=People("Name")%></NAME>
```

The VBScript code to put in the ASP file to extract the data from the record and place it in XML tags looks like this:

```
<PERSON>
<NAME><%=People("Name")%></NAME>
<ADDRESS><%=People("Address")%></ADDRESS>
<TEL><%=People("Tel")%></TEL>
<FAX><%=People("Fax")%></FAX>
<EMAIL><%=People("Email")%> </EMAIL>
</PERSON>
```

With the people element constructed, you need only tell the ASP page to keep moving to the next entry in the table to complete the loop:

```
<% People.MoveNext
Loop
%>
```

Then close the root Node:

```
</PEOPLE>
```

Output of source code

Below is the exact output of the source code. This will be displayed in colors and with indentation in IE5, but if you view the source, it is all text that has been returned by your ASP file.

```
<?xml version="1.0" ?>
<PEOPLE>
<PERSON>
<NAME>Mark Wilson</NAME>
<ADDRESS>911 Somewhere Circle, Canberra, Australia</ADDRESS>
<TEL>(++612) 12345</TEL>
<FAX>(++612) 12345</FAX>
<EMAIL>Mark.Wilson@somewhere.com</EMAIL>
</PERSON>
<PERSON>
<NAME>Tracey Wilson</NAME>
<ADDRESS>121 Zootle Road, Cape Town, South Africa</ADDRESS>
<TEL>(++2721) 531 9090</TEL>
<FAX>(++2721) 531 9090</FAX>
<EMAIL>Tracey.Wilson@somewhere.com</EMAIL>
</PERSON>
<PERSON>
<NAME>Jodie Foster</NAME>
<ADDRESS>30 Animal Road, New York, USA</ADDRESS>
<TEL>(++1) 3000 12345</TEL>
<FAX>(++1) 3000 12345</FAX>
<EMAIL>Jodie.Foster@somewhere.com</EMAIL>
</PERSON>
<PERSON>
<NAME>Lorrin Maughan</NAME>
<ADDRESS>1143 Winners Lane, London, UK</ADDRESS>
<TEL>(++94) 17 12345</TEL>
<FAX>++94) 17 12345</FAX>
<EMAIL>Lorrin.Maughan@somewhere.com</EMAIL>
</PERSON>
<PERSON>
<NAME>Steve Rachel</NAME>
<ADDRESS>90210 Beverly Hills, California, USA</ADDRESS>
<TEL>(++1) 2000 12345</TEL>
<FAX>(++1) 2000 12345</FAX>
<EMAIL>Steve.Rachel@somewhere.com</EMAIL>
</PERSON>
</PEOPLE>
```

Full source code

To successfully create this sample code, you need:

- An ODBC data source of VBXML connected to a database
- A database with the table PEOPLE in it and the required fields

- A web server where you can place the ASP file (PWS 1.0a must have the ASP.EXE file installed to give it the ability to parse ASP files)
- A web server that can process ASP files
- Internet Explorer 5 (IE5) or an XML aware browser

The full code for this sample can then be typed into Notepad and saved into a directory on your web server. Assuming you can run ASP scripts on your server, it will return the following XML when it is opened.

```
<% @Language=VBScript %>
<?xml version="1.0"?>
<PEOPLE>
  <%
     Set ObjConn = Server.CreateObject("ADODB.Connection")
     ObjConn.Open "VBXML"
     Set PEOPLE = ObjConn.Execute("select * from People")
     Do While Not PEOPLE.EOF
  %>

<PERSON>
  <NAME><%=People("Name")%></NAME>
  <ADDRESS><%=People("Address")%></ADDRESS>
  <TEL><%=People("Tel")%></TEL>
  <FAX><%=People("Fax")%></FAX>
  <EMAIL><%=People("Email")%>  </EMAIL>
</PERSON>

     <% People.MoveNext
     Loop
     %>

</PEOPLE>
```

4.13.2 *Returning an ADO 2.1 recordset as XML*

When Microsoft introduced ADO 2.0, a new method was included on the recordset object—the `save()` method.

The `save()` method accepts two arguments, `FileName` and `PersistFormat`. At the time, the only `PersistFormat` you could use was `adPersistADTG`, which was a binary format.

If you want to, whip up this small VB application and we will show you the code to put under the two buttons (load and save). Figure 4.11 shows what your form should look like.

The code under the save button is:

```
Private Sub cmdSaveAdoFile_Click()
Dim PEOPLE As ADODB.Recordset
Dim ObjConn As New ADODB.Connection
```

```
'open an existing ODBC connection to your database
ObjConn.Open "VBXML"
'execute a select SQL statement
Set PEOPLE = ObjConn.Execute("select * from People")
'now save your records as a binary format
PEOPLE.Save "c:\adodemo.dat", adPersistADTG
End Sub
```

Figure 4.11   Saving ADO as XML application

For this demo, make sure your have added the "Microsoft ActiveX Data Object 2.1 Library" as a reference to your application. You can also use the "Microsoft ActiveX Data Object 2.0 Library" for this example, but not for the next example that uses XML.

The parameter `adPersistADTG` makes sure the format is binary. Open the `adoxml.dat` file and look at it. Do not save your changes!

The code for the loading button that loads the binary file back into an ADO recordset is:

```
Private Sub cmdLoadAdoFile_Click()
Dim myrecs As ADODB.Recordset
Set myrecs = New ADODB.Recordset

'open the binary file and load it
myrecs.Open "c:\adodemo.dat", "Provider=MSPersist"

'lets have a message box popup the number of records
MsgBox myrecs.RecordCount
End Sub
```

Well, that's enough of ADO 2.0. Let's have a look at the new goodies in ADO 2.1.

As you may have guessed, we now have another `PersistFormat`, called `adPersistXML`. So you can save your recordset as XML by using the following code:

For this demo, make sure you have referenced ADO 2.1 and not ADO 2.0. If you try to reference both, you will receive a naming conflict

```
Private Sub cmdSaveAdoFile_Click()
Dim PEOPLE As ADODB.Recordset
Dim ObjConn As New ADODB.Connection

'open an existing ODBC connection to your database
ObjConn.Open "VBXML"
'execute a select SQL statement against the database
Set PEOPLE = ObjConn.Execute("select * from People")
'save the recordset as an XML file
```

```
PEOPLE.Save "c:\adodemo.xml", adPersistXML
End Sub
```

Yes, the only change was the `adPersistXML` parameter. We also changed the file extension to .xml so that you can compare the previous `adodemo.dat` and this `adodemo.xml` file, if you want to.

If you haven't already tried this out, consider giving it a try. Open a recordset against a database you have handy and execute a query. Now use the code above to save your recordset as an XML file. Open the XML file in Windows Notepad and take a look at it. Don't be alarmed at how different it looks from the XML files you have seen until now. Don't change anything; otherwise, you probably won't be able to reload it back into another ADO 2.1 recordset again!

Now, to load that XML file from XML back into an ADO recordset, you can use this code for the load button:

```
Private Sub cmdLoadAdoFile_Click()
Dim PEOPLE As ADODB.Recordset
Set PEOPLE = New ADODB.Recordset

'open your XML file and load it
PEOPLE.Open "c:\adodemo.xml", "Provider=MSPersist"

'lets have a message box popup the number of records
MsgBox PEOPLE.RecordCount
End Sub
```

Did you notice that it is exactly the same code as before when we were loading the binary file?

So, there you have it! You have saved and loaded a recordset to a binary and an XML file in a few lines of code. The XML version is a very useful and portable text format for transferring your recordsets across the Internet (for example).

4.14 *Communicating with the server from VB using XMLHTTPRequest*

One of the cool things about XMLHTTP is the ability to post and receive XML data to or from an HTTP server.

This is an easy way to become server- and platform-independent, because the program doesn't mind who or what the HTTP server it's talking to is, or even what operating system it is running on. All the HTTP server needs to do is have the capability to receive HTTP calls such as POST or GET and then pass the call on to some form of program (ASP, CGI, Java Servlets, etc.).

This is not neces-sarily the case if you use custom extensions to your web server though.

So you can look at the combination of XML and HTTP calls as a kind of mid-dleware or glue to tie systems together.

In our case, we will open a connection to the host web server (the Personal Web Server 1.0a) on our PC and then use an ASP file that will give us a reply.

To make the connection, we will make use of an object that ships with IE5, called XMLHTTP. Basically, you open a POST() connection to your web server (which is all a web browser does anyway!). Then using this connection, you *talk* to the PEOPLEVB.ASP file, and it returns your pick list in XML format.

4.14.1 *Receiving an XML DOMDocument object in VB*

In the VB part of this example, the code to connect to the web server is:

```
'create the objects
Dim xmlHttp As new XMLHTTPRequest
Dim objXmlDoc As DOMDocument
Dim sRequest as string

'to avoid a bug in the HTTPRequest object, you must pass in a string variable
sRequest = "http://mark/xmlcode/demo.asp"
'open the POST (or GET) connection to the web server with a string variable
  as the second parameter
xmlHttp.Open "POST", sRequest, False
'establish the connection
xmlHttp.Send

'receive the response - note there are different types of responses, binary
  and text is also supported
Set objXmlDoc = xmlHttp.responseXML
```

On the web server side, we will use some ASP in the demo.asp file that is being called. Make sure your server-side ASP file sets the ContentType to text/xml. To send the XML back to the client, use:

```
<%
'make a variant object
Dim objXmlDoc

'place the DOMDocument into the objXmlDoc object
Set objXmlDoc = Server.CreateObject("MSXML.DOMDocument")

'load the XML document object here
objXmlDoc.load Server.MapPath("people.xml")

'set the content type to XML - note other types are supported
Response.contenttype = "text/xml"
```

```
'now send back the DOMDocument you have loaded above
response.write objXmlDoc
%>
```

Now you have a simple VB application that communicates with an ASP file on a web server and receives a DOMDocument as a response.

XSL—adding style to XML

What this chapter covers:

- Getting started with XSL
- XSL in your browser
- XSL, client- and server-side
- Advanced features and sample code

5.1   Overview

To participate in the standards building of XSL, join the email list majordomo@mulberrytech.com with subscribe XSL-List-Digest *in the body of the message. Thereafter you can send email to xsl-list@mulberrytech.com when participating in the discussions.*

In this chapter, we discuss using the Microsoft DOM and XSL to manipulate an XML document.

First, let's recap. There are currently movements within the W3C to *modularize* XSL. So far, we have XSL and XSLT. XSL is further broken up into XSL FO, which stands for XSL Formatting Objects. As this book goes to print, more modularization to XSL may emerge from the process. However, the good news is that it doesn't affect you when you create the code suggested in this book, because this book is not based on the W3C standards and their evolving methods and properties. We have based all our code on the Microsoft XML objects that shipped with IE5.

If you have an XML file, how would you put color and style into your boring XML text files? Perhaps you have thought about how to spruce up the way your XML looks. Perhaps you aren't interested in displaying your data using XSL (you may be quite happy with CSS), but you do need to rework your XML files in several other formats, perhaps including HTML or another XML format.

If you are familiar with CSS, then you will understand XSL reasonably easily. If not, then you will probably find the examples listed here tricky. You can do very impressive things with XSL, but it's not all that easy to learn.

XSL includes the CSS feature-set, and to add to the mix, it has the extensibility that makes XML so useful. XSL is an XML file, which means the DOM can manipulate it.

Note It's not over for the CSS aficionados! The CSS Object Model (CSS-OM) is an object model under development that will enable you to access the CSS rules, properties, values, and modules from a program. You can insert, change, or remove values, just like you do with the DOM.

5.2   What can XSL do?

XSL is very flexible. XSL (as defined by the W3C) provides *transformation* and *formatting* capabilities. You can use it to dynamically apply different characteristics to your XML file on the fly. You can:

- Transform XML into HTML, inserting option boxes, tables and images
- Transform XML into another XML (or HTML) format, which may be more suitable for high- or low-speed connections
- Use it to sort and filter (for example, you can limit the results to records matching a certain value)

- Use *pattern matching* to find records
- Include scripting (such as ECMAscript/Javascript/VBScript)

One thing that stands out in an XSL style sheet is the commonplace use of namespaces. In XSL there can be no reserved element names, so it's necessary to use some other mechanism to distinguish between elements that have XSL semantics and other elements. This is the problem that namespaces were designed to solve!

5.2.1 *What can the Microsoft XSL implementation do?*

Microsoft has implemented a substantial amount of useful features, which means that you can also query your data to extract only that which you actually want to display. Interestingly, some of the features in the Microsoft XSL objects are actually part of another W3C submission called XQL (eXtensible Query Language). You can use XSL to query via hierarchical relationships to find Nodes or elements with logical expressions, filters, patterns, and more.

5.2.2 *Where can I see a demo of XSL?*

If you want to have a look at the code behind the default style sheet in IE5, simply type res:// msxml.dll/DE-FAULTSS.XSL into your IE5 address bar and press enter. You can now see the code listing for the default XSL that IE5 uses on XML text. To view the plain XML, view the source for the page.

If you have not seen an XML file with an XSL stylesheet applied, then do the following:

- Open Windows Notepad and type in a simple XML file (there are many listed in this book)
- Save this file as myxml.xml (or any file name ending with .xml)
- Open this file in IE5

If you use an existing XML file, for this example make sure that the file does *not* reference an XSL file or, if it does, then edit the reference out. In other words, make sure there is *no* line similar to this one that references an XSL document in the XML file:

```
<?xml:stylesheet type="text/xsl" href="people.xsl"?>
```

When you opened the XML file in IE5, you were probably expecting the same listing of text that you saw in Notepad, since there is no stylesheet to change the look of the text. Instead, IE5 did a good job of displaying the document with colors and indentations. Even better, by clicking on the opening tags (such as `<PEOPLE>`), IE5 will display the elements contained within the PEOPLE element!

Welcome to your first XSL stylesheet. This is the default IE5 XSL formatting that is applied to XML documents that have no associated XSL stylesheet.

5.3   *Debugging your XML and XSL with IE5*

Browsing XML documents with IE5 also provides some other useful features, such as displaying XML files in color and as an expanding and collapsing tree. This provides a convenient way for you to check that your XML is well-formed. You can test that the XML and its external XSL, Schemas, and DTDs are well-formed and valid by opening the files in the browser. Errors are reported with line numbers to help you find and correct the error, making IE5 a good XML debugging tool. Figure 5.1 shows an example of IE5 reporting an error in one of our XML files.

As you can see in the above example, we had forgotten to close the > tag, and IE pointed out the error, the line it is on, the position it is at, and even quoted a bit of it. To be honest, sometimes the errors are not as easily digested when it involves webclasses and so on, but this is a very useful debugging tool to have.

We used Microsoft IE5 to debug all the XML code in this book.

XSL also separates the display from the data. In that way, the same data can be viewed in several different formats, or the same format can be applied to different XML documents.

Figure 5.1   IE5 debugging an XML error

In figure 5.2, you can see how the same XML document can be transformed into several different outputs by applying different XSL documents. How you do that is the subject of the next section.

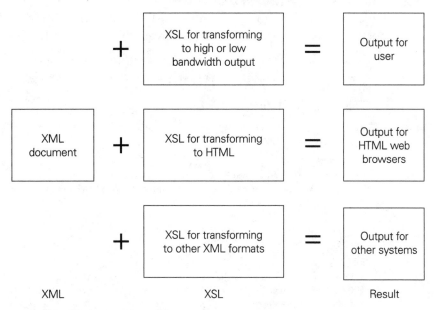

Figure 5.2   XSL adds style to XML

5.3.1   *Connecting up your XML and XSL files*

There are several ways to use an XSL file with your XML file. You can use `trans-formNode()` to transform any XML file with any appropriate XSL file:

```
xmlDOM.transformNode(xslDocument)
```

Or you can connect the XSL file to your XML file by inserting a reference to your XSL stylesheet into your XML.

In the example below, in the header of the XML file between the `<?xml version="1.0" ?>` and the opening of the root Node tag `<PEOPLE>`, we insert

```
<?xml-stylesheet type="text/xsl" href="people.xsl" ?>
```

Of course, this assumes we have saved the XSL file as people.xsl in the same local directory as the XML file. The header of the XML files looks like this:

```
<?xml version="1.0" ?>
<?xml-stylesheet type="text/xsl" href="people.xsl" ?>
<PEOPLE>
<PERSON>
etc...
```

5.3.2 *XML + XSL = HTML in a browser*

Let's have a look at how you can use XSL to transform XML data into an HTML document for display. To successfully create this sample code, you need:

- An XML-aware browser (such as Microsoft Internet Explorer 5)
- A text editor to create an HTML file

This is our XML file:

```
<?xml version="1.0" ?>
<PEOPLE>
<PERSON>
<NAME>Mark Wilson</NAME>
<ADDRESS>911 Somewhere Circle, Canberra, Australia</ADDRESS>
<TEL>(++612) 12345</TEL>
<FAX>(++612) 12345</FAX>
<EMAIL>Mark.Wilson@somewhere.com</EMAIL>
</PERSON>
<PERSON>
<NAME>Tracey Wilson</NAME>
<ADDRESS>121 Zootle Road, Cape Town, South Africa</ADDRESS>
<TEL>(++2721) 531 9090</TEL>
<FAX>(++2721) 531 9090</FAX>
<EMAIL>Tracey.Wilson@somewhere.com</EMAIL>
</PERSON>
<PERSON>
<NAME>Jodie Foster</NAME>
<ADDRESS>30 Animal Road, New York, USA</ADDRESS>
<TEL>(++1) 3000 12345</TEL>
<FAX>(++1) 3000 12345</FAX>
<EMAIL>Jodie.Foster@somewhere.com</EMAIL>
</PERSON>
<PERSON>
<NAME>Lorrin Maughan</NAME>
<ADDRESS>1143 Winners Lane, London, UK</ADDRESS>
<TEL>(++94) 17 12345</TEL>
<FAX>++94) 17 12345</FAX>
<EMAIL>Lorrin.Maughan@somewhere.com</EMAIL>
</PERSON>
<PERSON>
<NAME>Steve Rachel</NAME>
<ADDRESS>90210 Beverly Hills, California, USA</ADDRESS>
<TEL>(++1) 2000 12345</TEL>
<FAX>(++1) 2000 12345</FAX>
<EMAIL>Steve.Rachel@somewhere.com</EMAIL>
</PERSON>
</PEOPLE>
```

There is no reference to an XSL file in the preceding snippet of code.

Fortunately, the structure of this people.xml file is straightforward in that the same PERSON element is repeated five times with the same subelements. Equally happily, all we want is to generate an HTML table that has a heading and the five rows below it.

5.4 Building the HTML output

OK, so let's conceptually design our HTML file. What do we want? Well, we will want the output to have the normal HTML headers, and the first line of the table to act as our simplified header:

```
<HTML>
<BODY>
<TABLE BORDER="2">
<TR>
<TD>Name</TD>
<TD>Address</TD>
<TD>Tel</TD>
<TD>Fax</TD>
<TD>Email</TD>
</TR>
```

Now, we want the actual data for the fields to go below the header of the table. These rows will be repeated for each row in the XML file, so we should end up with five rows. Each row has <TR> (table row) and </TR> (end the table row) after it. Each column has <TD> and </TD> to mark it:

```
<TR>
<TD>"Name" information must appear here</TD>
<TD>"Address" information must appear here </TD>
<TD>"Tel" information must appear here </TD>
<TD>"Fax" information must appear here </TD>
<TD>"Email" information must appear here </TD>
</TR>
</TABLE>
</BODY>
</HTML>
```

The full HTML source that is required

This is the HTML output we want.

```
<HTML>
<BODY>
<TABLE BORDER="2">
<TR>
<TD>Name</TD>
<TD>Address</TD>
<TD>Tel</TD>
<TD>Fax</TD>
<TD>Email</TD>
```

```
</TR>
<TD>Mark Wilson</TD>
<TD>911 Somewhere Circle, Canberra, Australia</TD>
<TD>(++612) 12345</TD>
<TD>(++612) 12345</TD>
<TD>Mark.Wilson@somewhere.com</TD>
</TR>
<TR>
<TD>Tracey Wilson</TD>
<TD>121 Zootle Road, Cape Town, South Africa</TD>
<TD>(++2721) 531 9090</TD>
<TD>(++2721) 531 9090</TD>
<TD>Tracey.Wilson@somewhere.com</TD>
</TR>
<TR>
<TD>Jodie Foster</TD>
<TD>30 Animal Road, New York, USA</TD>
<TD>(++1) 3000 12345</TD>
<TD>(++1) 3000 12345</TD>
<TD>Jodie.Foster@somewhere.com</TD>
</TR>
<TR>
<TD>Lorrin Maughan</TD>
<TD>1143 Winners Lane, London, UK</TD>
<TD>(++94) 17 12345</TD>
<TD>++94) 17 12345</TD>
<TD>Lorrin.Maughan@somewhere.com</TD>
</TR>
<TR>
<TD>Steve Rachel</TD>
<TD>90210 Beverly Hills, California, USA</TD>
<TD>(++1) 2000 12345</TD>
<TD>(++1) 2000 12345</TD>
<TD>Steve.Rachel@somewhere.com</TD>
</TR>
</TABLE>
</BODY>
</HTML>
```

The XSL to output HTML from XML

Here is the XSL to create the HTML from your XML. After looking at this XSL,
we will go through it step-by-step.

```
<?xml version='1.0'?>
<xsl:stylesheet xmlns:xsl="http://www.w3.org/TR/WD-xsl">
<xsl:template match="/">
<HTML>
<BODY>
<TABLE BORDER="2">
<TR>
```

```
<TD>Name1</TD>
<TD>Address</TD>
<TD>Tel</TD>
<TD>Fax</TD>
<TD>Email</TD>
</TR>
<xsl:for-each select="PEOPLE/PERSON">
<TR>
<TD><xsl:value-of select="NAME"/></TD>
<TD><xsl:value-of select="ADDRESS"/></TD>
<TD><xsl:value-of select="TEL"/></TD>
<TD><xsl:value-of select="FAX"/></TD>
<TD><xsl:value-of select="EMAIL"/></TD>
</TR>
</xsl:for-each>
</TABLE>
</BODY>
</HTML>
</xsl:template>
</xsl:stylesheet>
```

The result illustrates how the basic transformation mechanism in XSL combines an XML file called people.xml with an XSL file called people.xsl to render an HTML document.

Description of the XSL code

Since an XSL stylesheet is an XML file itself, the file begins with the recommended xml declaration `<?xml version='1.0'?>`. The `<xsl:stylesheet>` element indicates that this document is a stylesheet file and provides a location for declaring the XSL namespace.

```
<HTML>
<BODY>
<TABLE BORDER="2">
<TR>
<TD>Name</TD>
<TD>Address</TD>
<TD>Tel</TD>
<TD>Fax</TD>
<TD>Email</TD>
</TR>
<xsl:for-each select="PEOPLE/PERSON">
<TR>
<TD><xsl:value-of select="NAME"/></TD>
<TD><xsl:value-of select="ADDRESS"/></TD>
<TD><xsl:value-of select="TEL"/></TD>
<TD><xsl:value-of select="FAX"/></TD>
<TD><xsl:value-of select="EMAIL"/></TD>
</TR>
</xsl:for-each>
</TABLE>
```

```
</BODY>
</HTML>
```

5.4.1   *xsl:for-each*

The `<xsl:for-each>` element locates a set of elements in the XML data and repeats a portion of the template for each one. In this case, the pattern PEOPLE/PERSON starts at the document root and drills down through the PEOPLE element to select the PERSON children. Since this sample contains five PERSON elements, five rows will be returned.

5.4.2   *xsl:value-of*

Now, to extract the actual values we are looking for, we can use `xsl:value-of`. The line

```
<xsl:value-of select="NAME"/>
```

extracts the value in the NAME element in the XML. Now you close the template with:

```
<xsl:stylesheet>
```

Really that's all there is to a simple XSL file that only does simple transformations. The syntax choices are bewildering, but that's also what makes XSL so valuable. It is flexible, simple, and as a result, powerful! Let's explore a bit further.

5.4.3   *Processing all the children*

But what if you simply want all of the children to pass through? Or what if you don't know which fields will be present? Let's look at another simple XSL file in table 5.1 that simply processes all the children Nodes below a specified level.

Table 5.1   XSL

XSL file	Description
<xsl:template match = "/">	The "/" in the beginning of the XSL declaration says that this Node applies to the root level of the XML document
<HTML>	Some "XML" that will pass through and be read as HTML
<BODY>	Some "XML" that will pass through and be read as HTML
<xsl:process-children/>	This indicates that all the children should be printed
</BODY>	Corresponding and closing XML tag for <BODY>
</HTML>	Corresponding and closing XML tag for <HTML>
</xsl:template>	Close the template

5.4.4 *Full source code*

You can see how easy it is to pass through HTML— but take care to send through closing HTML tags. A <P> must be matched by a closing </P>, or your output will fail well-formedness.

Here's the source code for the people.xml file that calls the people.xsl file:

XML source

```
<?xml version="1.0" ?>
<?xml:stylesheet type="text/xsl" href="people.xsl"?>
<PEOPLE>
<PERSON>
<NAME>Mark Wilson</NAME>
<ADDRESS>911 Somewhere Circle, Canberra, Australia</ADDRESS>
<TEL>(++612) 12345</TEL>
<FAX>(++612) 12345</FAX>
<EMAIL>Mark.Wilson@somewhere.com</EMAIL>
</PERSON>
<PERSON>
<NAME>Tracey Wilson</NAME>
<ADDRESS>121 Zootle Road, Cape Town, South Africa</ADDRESS>
<TEL>(++2721) 531 9090</TEL>
<FAX>(++2721) 531 9090</FAX>
<EMAIL>Tracey.Wilson@somewhere.com</EMAIL>
</PERSON>
<PERSON>
<NAME>Jodie Foster</NAME>
<ADDRESS>30 Animal Road, New York, USA</ADDRESS>
<TEL>(++1) 3000 12345</TEL>
<FAX>(++1) 3000 12345</FAX>
<EMAIL>Jodie.Foster@somewhere.com</EMAIL>
</PERSON>
<PERSON>
<NAME>Lorrin Maughan</NAME>
<ADDRESS>1143 Winners Lane, London, UK</ADDRESS>
<TEL>(++94) 17 12345</TEL>
<FAX>++94) 17 12345</FAX>
<EMAIL>Lorrin.Maughan@somewhere.com</EMAIL>
</PERSON>
<PERSON>
<NAME>Steve Rachel</NAME>
<ADDRESS>90210 Beverly Hills, California, USA</ADDRESS>
<TEL>(++1) 2000 12345</TEL>
<FAX>(++1) 2000 12345</FAX>
<EMAIL>Steve.Rachel@somewhere.com</EMAIL>
</PERSON>
</PEOPLE>
```

XSL source code

```
<?xml version='1.0'?>
<xsl:stylesheet xmlns:xsl="http://www.w3.org/TR/WD-xsl">
<xsl:template match="/">
```

```
<HTML>
<BODY>
<TABLE BORDER="2">
<TR>
<TD>Name</TD>
<TD>Address</TD>
<TD>Tel</TD>
<TD>Fax</TD>
<TD>Email</TD>
</TR>
<xsl:for-each select="PEOPLE/PERSON">
<TR>
<TD><xsl:value-of select="NAME"/></TD>
<TD><xsl:value-of select="ADDRESS"/></TD>
<TD><xsl:value-of select="TEL"/></TD>
<TD><xsl:value-of select="FAX"/></TD>
<TD><xsl:value-of select="EMAIL"/></TD>
</TR>
</xsl:for-each>
</TABLE>
</BODY>
</HTML>
</xsl:template>
</xsl:stylesheet>
```

5.4.5 *Using XSL as a Data Island*

The code below shows an HTML file, people.htm, that references two external local Data Islands, people.xml and people.xsl.

There is also a snippet of script, which runs when the page has loaded. This script loads the two Data Islands and then transforms the XML into HTML using the transformNode() function that is exposed by the Data Island.

First, we open the HTML document header:

```
<HTML>
<HEAD>
<TITLE>Using XSL as a Data Island!</TITLE>
</HEAD>
```

Now we create two Data Islands. The source DSO points to the XML file, and the style DSO points to the XSL file.

```
<XML id="source" src="people.xml"></XML>
<XML id="style" src="people.xsl"></XML>
```

This script will be run when the *window* fires the onload event. The script will then transform the XML into XSL and store the results in the xslPEO-PLE.innerHTML object:

```
<SCRIPT FOR="window" EVENT="onload">
xslPEOPLE.innerHTML = source.transformNode(style.xmlDocument)
</SCRIPT>
```

Open the HTML BODY tag:

```
<BODY>
```

Now we will use the `DIV` tag to display the `xslPEOPLE` object, which is where our transformed XML has been stored:

```
<DIV id="xslPEOPLE"></DIV>
```

Now let's close the BODY and HTML tags:

```
</BODY>
</HTML>
```

That's it!

Output of source code

As you may have guessed, as shown in figure 5.3, the output in IE5 is the same as the XSL example given above!

Namel	Address	Tel	Fax	Email
Mark Wilson	911 Somewhere Circle, Canberra, Australia	(++612) 12345	(++612) 12345	Mark.Wilson@somewhere.com
Tracey Wilson	121 Zootle Road, Cape Town, South Africa	(++2721) 531 9090	(++2721) 531 9090	Tracey.Wilson@somewhere.com
Jodie Foster	30 Animal Road, New York, USA	(++1) 3000 12345	(++1) 3000 12345	Jodie.Foster@somewhere.com
Lorrin Maughan	1143 Winners Lane, London, UK	(++94) 17 12345	++94) 17 12345	Lorrin.Maughan@somewhere.com
Steve Rachel	90210 Beverly Hills, California, USA	(++1) 2000 12345	(++1) 2000 12345	Steve.Rachel@somewhere.com

Figure 5.3 XSL as a Data Island

Full source code

```
<HTML>
<HEAD>
<TITLE>Using XSL as a Data Island!</TITLE>
</HEAD>

<XML id="source" src="people.xml"></XML>
<XML id="style" src="people.xsl"></XML>

<SCRIPT FOR="window" EVENT="onload">
xslPEOPLE.innerHTML = source.transformNode(style.xmlDocument);
</SCRIPT>

<BODY>
<DIV id="xslPEOPLE"></DIV>
```

```
</BODY>
</HTML>
```

5.4.6 *Switching styles with TransformNode*

Now let's try something a bit more challenging. Let's make an HTML file that can switch styles without submitting the HTML back to the server. In other words, the styles will change without waiting for the page to reload.

There are many ways to achieve this. To be consistent in these examples, we will present several Data Islands, each containing an alternative XSL stylesheet. Unfortunately, this is a Microsoft IE5-only solution, as we are using Data Islands again, but the transformNode() function is available in ASP and VB.

Let's also provide a button for three different stylesheets, and if the user clicks on one of the buttons, that stylesheet will be applied. Just to make it even more interesting, the third stylesheet will order the table by the NAME column!

Since all the action with the stylesheets will take place on the client, this document can be an HTML page. Your web pages only really need to be ASP pages when they will contain script, which will be executed on the server. In our people.htm page, we provide the normal HTML header tags:

```
<HTML>
<HEAD>
<TITLE>Using XSL as a Data Island!</TITLE>
```

Now in the <HEAD> tag, we insert some script. Although scripting can be placed anywhere within an HTML file, it is normally placed within the <HEAD> and </HEAD> tags.

We declare the language we are using as VBScript:

```
<SCRIPT LANGUAGE="VBScript">
```

We create four functions that will be executed from various command buttons in their onclick() events:

```
FUNCTION btnTable_onclick()
    xslPEOPLE.innerHTML = source.transformNode(Style-
    Table.xmlDocument)
END FUNCTION
```

Now, in each onclick() event, we place into the xslPEOPLE.innerText the results of the transformation of the XML and XSL stylesheet that is contained in the StyleTable Data Island:

```
FUNCTION btnPlain_onclick()
xslPEOPLE.innerText = source.documentElement.xml
END FUNCTION
```

However, in the plain display, we are a little sneaky and don't use a stylesheet. We just display the underlying XML from the source object:

```
FUNCTION btnSortByName_onclick()
xslPEOPLE.innerHTML = source.transformNode(Sort-
  ByName.xmlDocument)
END FUNCTION
```

This time we are transforming using the XSL stylesheet contained in the Sort-
ByName Data Island and storing the results in the xslPEOPLE object to be displayed in the DIV tag. Now, close the script tag:

```
</SCRIPT>
```

This script will run when the window has opened:

```
<SCRIPT FOR="window" EVENT="onload">
 xslPEOPLE.innerText = source.documentElement.xml
</SCRIPT>
```

Let's create our three Data Islands. For the sake of not repeating the same code
over and over, we will begin referencing them as external files. There is a code listing
at the end for the sortbyname.xsl stylesheet, because it contains a new piece of XSL
code to sort the columns:

```
<XML id="source" src="people.xml">
</XML>
<XML id="StyleTable" src="people.xsl">
</XML>
<XML id="SortByName" src="sortbyname.xsl">
</XML>
```

These are the Data Islands. Note how they point to external XML and XSL
files. Now let's close the HTML head and open the HTML body tags:

```
</HEAD>
<BODY>
```

Create the three HTML buttons that call the three functions listed above:

```
<P>Choose which style sheet you want applied:</P>
<P><INPUT id=button1 name=btnPlain type=button value="Plain text"> 
<INPUT id=button2 name=btnTable style="LEFT: 90px; TOP: 53px" type=button
  value=Table> 
<INPUT id=button3 name=btnSortByName style="LEFT: 90px; TOP: 15px"
  type=button value="Table - sort by name"> </P>

<P>Current stylesheet:</P>
```

Now use a DIV tag (called xslPEOPLE) in which the three functions store their
transformed results:

```
<DIV id="xslPEOPLE"></DIV>
```

Let's close the HTML tags and we are done:

```
</BODY>
</HTML>
```

As you saw on page 95, separate from the HTML file above are the three Data Islands. The three Data Island snippets of code were not included in order to limit the amount of code in that example. However, one interesting point was that the third Data Island was an XSL file that sorts our table by the NAME column.

By now you are probably familiar with the way an XSL file is laid out, so let's just jump to where the action is! It's in the `<xsl:for-each select="PEOPLE/PER-SON">` line. This line now expands to include the XSL keywords `order-by=`, and that is followed by the column you want to order by.

Don't forget, one of the tricks in this nifty example is how we used the xslPEO-PLE (which is the name for a DIV HTML tag) to display the transformed results. That's a neat trick to list your code, or text, or whatever in a low-code way. As the source of xslPEOPLE changes from the different `transformNode()` actions, the contents of the DIV HTML element change visually. If it saves us lines of code, then we like it!

Output of source code

Figure 5.4 shows what the results of the code look like on startup.

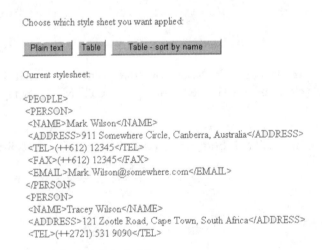

Choose which style sheet you want applied:

| Plain text | Table | Table - sort by name |

Current stylesheet:

```
<PEOPLE>
<PERSON>
 <NAME>Mark Wilson</NAME>
 <ADDRESS>911 Somewhere Circle, Canberra, Australia</ADDRESS>
 <TEL>(++612) 12345</TEL>
 <FAX>(++612) 12345</FAX>
 <EMAIL>Mark.Wilson@somewhere.com</EMAIL>
</PERSON>
<PERSON>
 <NAME>Tracey Wilson</NAME>
 <ADDRESS>121 Zootle Road, Cape Town, South Africa</ADDRESS>
 <TEL>(++2721) 531 9090</TEL>
```

Figure 5.4   A plain text style

This happens without submitting the page back to the server and waiting for the next web page to be returned— which is a real timesaver!

When you click the Table button, the StyleTable stylesheet is applied. Figure 5.5 shows an example of this stylesheet.

Choose which style sheet you want applied:

| Plain text | Table | Table - sort by name |

Current stylesheet:

Namel	Address	Tel	Fax	Email
Mark Wilson	911 Somewhere Circle, Canberra, Australia	(++612) 12345	(++612) 12345	Mark.Wilson@somewhere.com
Tracey Wilson	121 Zootle Road, Cape Town, South Africa	(++2721) 531 9090	(++2721) 531 9090	Tracey.Wilson@somewhere.com
Jodie Foster	30 Animal Road, New York, USA	(++1) 3000 12345	(++1) 3000 12345	Jodie.Foster@somewhere.com
Lorrin Maughan	1143 Winners Lane, London, UK	(++94) 17 12345	++94) 17 12345	Lorrin.Maughan@somewhere.com
Steve Rachel	90210 Beverly Hills, California, USA	(++1) 2000 12345	(++1) 2000 12345	Steve.Rachel@somewhere.com

Figure 5.5 Choosing the table stylesheet

Why did the display change? It changed because the results of the transformation are stored in xslPEOPLE, which is displayed in the DIV HTML tag.

Full source code

```
<HTML>
<HEAD>
<TITLE>Using XSL as a Data Island!</TITLE>

<SCRIPT LANGUAGE="VBScript">

  FUNCTION btnPlain_onclick()
xslPEOPLE.innerText = source.documentElement.xml
END FUNCTION

FUNCTION btnTable_onclick()
xslPEOPLE.innerHTML = source.transformNode(Style-
  Table.xmlDocument)
END FUNCTION
```

```
FUNCTION btnSortByName_onclick()
xslPEOPLE.innerHTML = source.transformNode(Sort-
  ByName.xmlDocument)
END FUNCTION

</SCRIPT>

<SCRIPT FOR="window" EVENT="onload">
  xslPEOPLE.innerText = source.documentElement.xml
</SCRIPT>

<XML id="source" src="people.xml">
</XML>

<XML id="StyleTable" src="people.xsl">
</XML>

<XML id="SortByName" src="sortbyname.xsl">
</XML>

</HEAD>

<BODY>

<P>Choose which style sheet you want applied:</P>
<P><INPUT id=button1 name=btnPlain type=button value="Plain text"> 
<INPUT id=button2 name=btnTable style="LEFT: 90px; TOP: 53px" type=button
  value=Table> 
<INPUT id=button3 name=btnSortByName style="LEFT: 90px; TOP: 15px"
  type=button value="Table - sort by name"> </P>

<P>Current stylesheet:</P>

<DIV id="xslPEOPLE"></DIV>

</BODY>
</HTML>
```

Here's the source for the sortbyname.xsl stylesheet:

```
<?xml version='1.0'?>
<xsl:stylesheet xmlns:xsl="http://www.w3.org/TR/WD-xsl">
<xsl:template match="/">
<HTML>
<BODY>
<TABLE BORDER="2">
<TR>
<TD>Name</TD>
<TD>Address</TD>
<TD>Tel</TD>
<TD>Fax</TD>
```

```
<TD>Email</TD>
</TR>
<xsl:for-each select="PEOPLE/PERSON" order-by="NAME">
<TR>
<TD><xsl:value-of select="NAME"/></TD>
<TD><xsl:value-of select="ADDRESS"/></TD>
<TD><xsl:value-of select="TEL"/></TD>
<TD><xsl:value-of select="FAX"/></TD>
<TD><xsl:value-of select="EMAIL"/></TD>
</TR>
</xsl:for-each>
</TABLE>
</BODY>
</HTML>
</xsl:template>
</xsl:stylesheet>
```

5.5 Patterns

Let's investigate some more advanced XSL. We will work our way through sorting, querying, using operators, filtering, and using expressions such as booleans.

5.5.1 Sorting

Using `order-by="NAME"` will by default present the NAME field in ascending order. However, if you place a minus (−) sign before the sort key, then the NAME field will be in descending order. The plus (+) sign is used as an alternative to relying on the default setting of ascending order.

> *Note* The W3C makes use of an XSL:Sort syntax in their documents, so you should be aware that it is likely that the Microsoft IE5 syntax for sorting will change in future releases.

5.5.2 Context

In an XSL stylesheet, the context for a query is the source Node being currently processed by an `<xsl:template>` or `<xsl:for-each>` element. In the example above, the line of code

```
<xsl:for-each select="PEOPLE/PERSON" order-by="NAME">
```

applies an order sequence to each person in the people xml.

The context was `PEOPLE/PERSON`. A basic XSL pattern describes a path through the XML hierarchy starting from the root, downward through the slash-separated list of child element names.

5.5.3   *Pattern operators*

Table 5.2 lists operators we can use in an XSL query.

Table 5.2   XSL query operators

Operator	Description
/	Use the root Node or the root of the DOMDocument as the context
./	Explicitly use the current context
//	A search across any number of levels of the hierarchy from the root of the document
.//	A search across any number of levels of the hierarchy from the current context
*	This is equivalent to finding all
@	Indicates the attribute you are working with
=	Equal to

Table 5.3 shows some of those operators in action! This is the good stuff.

Table 5.3   Code examples of XSL operator

Example	Explanation
PERSON/*	Find all element children of PERSON elements
PERSON/NAME	Matches NAME elements that are children of PERSON elements
PERSON/ NAME[@FIRST-NAME]	Although you have not seen this before in our examples, this finds NAME elements that are children of PERSON elements and have a "first-name" attribute
PERSON[0]	Find the first PERSON element (note, this is zero-based)
PERSON[EMAIL][4]	Find the fourth PERSON element that has an EMAIL child Node
PERSON[end()]	Find the last PERSON Node
/*/NAME	Find all NAME elements that are grandchildren of the root
/	Find all grandchildren of the current context
@*	Find all attributes in the current context
//NAME	Find all NAME elements anywhere in the current DOMDocument
COUNTRY/PERSON[end()]	Although this is not in the examples, if you wanted to find the last PERSON in each COUNTRY Node, this is what you would use!

5.5.4 *Filtering and logical operators*

The Microsoft MSXML supports some extra extensions to patterns. These extensions have been proposed in the XQL submission to the W3C.

But if that isn't enough, then look at this! Filter patterns can contain expressions such as boolean expressions, AND, OR, and NOT expressions.

Table 5.4 lists the expressions you can use.

Table 5.4   XSL Logical operators

Example	Explanation
AND	logical and
OR	logical or
NOT()	negation
=	equal
!=	not equal
>	greater than
<	less than
>=	greater than or equal to
<=	less than or equal to

Table 5.5 lists some more examples of logical operators:.

Table 5.5   XSL examples of logical operators

Example	Explanation
PERSON[NAME and EMAIL]	Find all PERSON elements that contain at least one NAME and one EMAIL element
PERSON[(EMAIL or ADDRESS) and NAME]	Find all PERSON elements that contain at least one EMAIL or ADDRESS and at least one NAME element
PERSON[TELEPHONE and not(ADDRESS)]	If you wanted to telephone all your customers whose ADRRESS was missing from your data, this would be the syntax for you!
PERSON[NAME != "Mark Wilson"]	Find all PERSON where the NAME childElement is not equal to "Mark Wilson"
PERSON[index() <= 2]	Find the first three PERSON elements (0, 1, 2)
PERSON/NAME[@FIRST-NAME != "Mark"]	If you wanted to find all the NAME elements under PERSON where the attribute "first-name" was not Mark, this is the correct syntax

Table 5.6 lists some commonly requested XSL statements. Of course, like the examples in table 5.5, you have to rework these for your own examples.

Table 5.6   XSL commonly used examples of logical operators

Example	Explanation
FRIEND[NAME = /EMPLOYEE/NAME]	This is useful! If you want to find (from the same context) matching NAME details for the FRIEND and EMPLOYEE Nodes, you could use this code
PERSON[BIRTHDATE < date("1985-01-01")]	Another very useful one! Find all PERSON where the BIRTHDATE is before January 1, 1985
PERSON[BIRTHDATE < date(@BEFORE)]	If you cannot hard-code the date, then dynamically insert the date as an element and use this code. Find all PERSON where the BIRTHDATE is less before the date held in the attribute called BEFORE
ancestor(PERSON)	Find the nearest PERSON ancestor of the current element. NOTE: This is probably only useful if you have a deep hierarchy and need to quickly move up some levels

Some of the syntax in these examples has been put forward as a part of the XQL proposal. It may not be W3C XSL syntax.

Not too difficult, especially if you have used SQL before! Be careful though—some of this syntax is not W3C XSL syntax. Microsoft has extended the syntax in advance of their other proposals (like XQL) being accepted. But since Microsoft has shipped the objects with support for all these statements (and a whole lot more!), and this is a book about the Microsoft XML objects, you can rest assured your code will work.

5.5.5   *Using patterns*

Perhaps you came to the end of the previous section and thought that was easy enough, but how do you actually *use* XSL? If you wanted to use a boolean expression or a filter, where exactly would you *put* the expression?

Let's say we have an XSL file called PEOPLEINFO.XSL, as shown below. Note the following:

- The XML example file references an XSL file called PEOPLEINFO.XSL
- The XML example file has an extra level, where the address details have subelements

```
<?xml version="1.0" ?>
<?xml-stylesheet type="text/xsl" href="peopleinfo.xsl" ?>
<PEOPLE>
<PERSON>
<NAME>Mark Wilson</NAME>
<ADDRESS>
<STREET>911 Somewhere Circle</STREET>
```

```
<CITY>Canberra</CITY>
<COUNTRY>Australia</COUNTRY>
<TEL>(++612) 12345</TEL>
<FAX>(++612) 12345</FAX>
</ADDRESS>
<EMAIL>Mark.Wilson@somewhere.com</EMAIL>
</PERSON>
<PERSON>
<NAME>Tracey Wilson</NAME>
<ADDRESS>
<STREET>121 Zootle Road</STREET>
<CITY>Cape Town</CITY>
<COUNTRY>South Africa</COUNTRY>
<TEL>(++2721) 531 9090</TEL>
<FAX>(++2721) 531 9090</FAX>
</ADDRESS>
<EMAIL>Tracey.Wilson@somewhere.com</EMAIL>
</PERSON>
<PERSON>
<NAME>Jodie Foster</NAME>
<ADDRESS>
<STREET>30 Animal Road</STREET>
<CITY>New York</CITY>
<COUNTRY>USA</COUNTRY>
<TEL>(++1) 3000 12345</TEL>
<FAX>(++1) 3000 12345</FAX>
</ADDRESS>
<EMAIL>Jodie.Foster@somewhere.com</EMAIL>
</PERSON>
<PERSON>
<NAME>Lorrin Maughan</NAME>
<ADDRESS>
<STREET>1143 Winners Lane</STREET>
<CITY>London</CITY>
<COUNTRY>UK</COUNTRY>
<TEL>(++94) 17 12345</TEL>
<FAX>++94) 17 12345</FAX>
</ADDRESS>
<EMAIL>Lorrin.Maughan@somewhere.com</EMAIL>
</PERSON>
<PERSON>
<NAME>Steve Rachel</NAME>
<ADDRESS>
<STREET>90210 Beverly Hills</STREET>
<CITY>LA</CITY>
<COUNTRY>USA</COUNTRY>
<TEL>(++1) 2000 12345</TEL>
<FAX>(++1) 2000 12345</FAX>
</ADDRESS>
<EMAIL>Steve.Rachel@somewhere.com</EMAIL>
</PERSON>
```

```
</PEOPLE>
```

Next, let's look at the XSL that the above XML references:

```
<?xml version='1.0'?>
<xsl:stylesheet xmlns:xsl="http://www.w3.org/TR/WD-xsl">
```

These are the standard opening statements for an XSL stylesheet:

```
<people>
  <xsl:for-each order-by="+ name" select="person"
xmlns:xsl="http://www.w3.org/TR/WD-xsl">
```

This element says: for the person children of the root Node, process those children in ascending order according to the value of the name element.

Within that `xsl:for-each` element are the directives on how to process each `person` element:

```
<person>
  <xsl:attribute name="">
    <xsl:value-of select="@bookID"/></xsl:attribute>
```

These directives serve to generate the same XML that exists in the original *patient* element. Now we pass through each of the values we want in the new output text stream:

```
    <name><xsl:value-of select="name"/></name>
    <address>
        <street><xsl:value-of select="address/street"/></street>
        <apt><xsl:value-of select="address/apt"/></apt>
        <city><xsl:value-of select="address/city"/></city>
        <state><xsl:value-of select="address/state"/></state>
        <zip><xsl:value-of select="address/zip"/></zip>
    </address>
    <birthdate><xsl:value-of select="birthdate"/></birthdate>
    </person>
  </xsl:for-each>
</people>
```

Do you see where we use the patterns, filters, and operators?

Filtering is done through the select attribute. In fact, the above stylesheet does filter the data. This is not obvious, though, because no patient elements get left out. However, if we change the `xsl:for-each` start tag to read as:

```
<xsl:for-each order-by="+ name" select="patient[name>'M']"
xmlns:xsl="http://www.w3.org/TR/WD-xsl">
```

we will process only those people children that have a name element with a value less than M. Now our original XML document will be transformed into an XML document that contains information about people whose names start with letters between A and M.

5.6 *How to make a hyperlink*

OK, here is a question that is frequently asked. How do you make a hyperlink (in your output HTML) with XSL?

The XSL for this would be:

```
<?xml version='1.0'?>
<xsl:stylesheet xmlns:xsl="http://www.w3.org/TR/WD-xsl">
<xsl:template match="/">
<HTML>
<BODY>
<TABLE BORDER="2">
<TR>
<TD>View</TD>
</TR>
<xsl:for-each select="PEOPLE/PERSON">
<TR>
<TD>
<A>
<xsl:attribute name="href"><xsl:value-of select="LINK"/></xsl:attribute>
<xsl:value-of select="NAME"/>
</A>
</TD>
</TR>
</xsl:for-each>
</TABLE>
</BODY>
</HTML>
</xsl:template>
</xsl:stylesheet>
```

The XSL above assumes you have a valid document for each of your links and an XML file such as:

```
<?xml version="1.0" ?>
<?xml-stylesheet type="text/xsl" href="7_2 hyperlink.xsl" ?>
<PEOPLE>
<PERSON>
<NAME>Mark Wilson</NAME>
<LINK>Mark.htm</LINK>
</PERSON>
<PERSON>
<NAME>Tracey Wilson</NAME>
<LINK>Tracey.htm</LINK>
</PERSON>
<PERSON>
```

```
<NAME>Jodie Foster</NAME>
<LINK>Jodie.htm</LINK>
</PERSON>
<PERSON>
<NAME>Lorrin Maughan</NAME>
<LINK>Lorrin.htm</LINK>
</PERSON>
<PERSON>
<NAME>Steve Rachel</NAME>
<LINK>Steve.htm</LINK>
</PERSON>
</PEOPLE>
```

5.7 Summary

As you can see, XSL is an extremely powerful tool to manipulate your data, XML files, or the look and feel of your documents. In fact, XSL will be used beyond these examples. Applications, office documents, and other solutions will increasingly rely on XML and XSL to render the user interfaces that are appropriate at the time rather than only providing one *user experience* all the time.

Building XML solutions

6

6.1 Overview

In this chapter, you will see how all the technology we have discussed can be put together to form various solutions. We will use the following objects and technologies that can be found on most VB6 systems that have IE5 installed:

- The Microsoft IE5 XML object called HTTPRequest for communicating with a webserver
- The FileSystemObject for interacting with the file system on the PC
- The XML object called a DOMDocument
- IE5 used extensively for displaying XML
- A webclass created in VB6

These are all the key COM objects and VB or ASP features you will most likely use in your projects in the future.

So we have built two solutions to demonstrate how ASP, VB, or a combination of both in VB webclasses could be used as a front end to your applications. We also demonstrate how to use HTTPRequest as the connection from your front end to the web server, and then we explore the middle tier, where the Microsoft XML DOM objects are encapsulated in an object-oriented way. Finally, the solution interacts with the database, also in an object-oriented way.

UML and XML have a great deal in common. They are both technology independent and vendor- and platform-neutral.

The first solution is a simpler solution than the second. It uses ASP and a webclass to connect to a middle tier on the server. In addition to this, the second solution attempts to demonstrate XML and HTTPRequest being used between the front end and the server from a VB application.

You may notice that we have provided high level diagrams to help you understand the flow of the program you are reading about. Mostly we do not use advanced diagrams or concepts in these code examples. We do use class diagrams and flow diagrams to show you what the different parts of the code solution look like and how they relate to each other.

The diagrams and concepts we use are UML (Unified Modeling Language). This is, of course, not a UML book and also not a book intended to teach anyone how to program in an object-oriented way. The UML and OO notation used here is simple and intuitive enough for the average programmer to understand and hopefully will encourage developers to investigate further.

Note This is, of course, not a UML book and also not a book intended to teach anyone how to program in an object-oriented way. If you would like to know more about UML, we suggest reading a book called *UML Distilled* by Martin Fowler.

6.2 *What do we want to achieve in these examples?*

In the previous sections of this book, we outlined some ASP, VB, and XML concepts, technology, and code. Now we will create a solution out of it all to show what can be done.

If some of the major benefits of XML are that it is platform-independent, an open specification, flexible, and stored in a text format, then it is surely a great candidate for being used to plumb the data in your distributed applications.

This could mean many things to many people, so let's explore some ideas.

6.2.1 *Data brokering*

A data broker sells information to others who require it. In the future a huge industry will pop up where you will transparently buy and sell your information over the Internet.

It has been said that in this modern *soft* economy, the true value of companies is their employees, and many companies are actually simply selling information, knowledge, and concepts.

Increasingly, stock exchanges, insurance companies, banks, and other massive institutions are realizing that they are simply transforming, repackaging, or shifting massive amounts of valuable information around. In between, they are using software programs and calculations on this data in order to create a profit.

Although this is not a book on economic theory, it seems to us that companies that best use their knowledge are the most successful. Another competitive advantage is getting feedback from your customers and promptly taking action based on that feedback.

eCommerce can be more than just selling your goods via the Internet. In time, you will expose your data directly to your partners and transparently and dynamically interact with them.

Fortunately for these companies, the Internet is also potentially an excellent avenue for selling your data! This is called being a *data broker*. A news organization gathers information worldwide and distributes it again, for a price. Your company may be gathering information, but once you have used it you may not be reselling it. This could be a major source of income that is being bypassed.

Just in case you were wondering, automatically shoving your data up onto your website in HTML doesn't really cut it, because you cannot create your own tags in HTML and clients cannot get customized information. You could pop a download onto your website when your data changes—but still that's not as responsive as a customized solution.

Speaking of protocols, check out the WEBDAV extensions to web servers. Search for it at the Microsoft website or at a search engine such as http://www.askjeeves.com

What we need is a way to expose your data to a consumer. In fact, we need several different ways to expose your data. Actually, we need several different ways to get to the same information, and we need the information in several different formats!

Ideally, the solutions should be based on Internet protocols and be open and flexible. If your internal systems or data structures change, the outside consumer of the data should be able to adjust without causing more support phone calls.

The ideal format of that data would be—wait for it—XML (surprise!). It is the ideal intermediary data structure (as we continually discover in this book).

However, the difference is that the consumer would most likely be an application or an object in this scenario. In this chapter, we will see several ways to automatically expose your data to outside applications that will use your data.

6.2.2 *Communications between objects*

In VB5 when you built objects that communicated complex amounts of data, you were pretty much forced to stuff your data into arrays and pass them between objects. On a network, this was usually done via DCOM (Distributed Component Object Model). This works well on Windows-only networks or where the data isn't traveling over the Internet.

Now in VB6 you can pass objects as parameters, and you can also use the CreateObject() *function to instantiate an object on someone else's computer.*

Now in VB6 you can pass objects as parameters, for example between classes. You can also use the CreateObject() function to instantiate an object on someone else's computer, which is also very useful. Sadly, we had to wait until VB6 to be able to do this. However, even with these new features, what happens if your data is rapidly changing? Do you want to keep on registering the new version of the object? Or what if you are swapping data to systems where the object you are passing is not or cannot be registered? Even worse, what if you are moving data between operating systems where the types or nature of objects are completely different?

If we pass XML between our objects, rather than passing objects or arrays, these are no longer issues. The consumer only needs to understand XML and be able to retrieve the DTD as a guide to the structure of the XML file. This provides far more flexibility in many situations.

6.2.3 *Beyond the network, into the Internet*

Even if we passed XML around, connecting objects over the Internet using VB was not all that easy. Until now. Using CGI (Common Gateway Interface) or other languages, we can return custom HTML pages and more. Other technologies, such as Cold Fusion, are excellent solutions as well.

The latest version of DCOM works across the Internet!

As a developer in ASP or VB, you mostly only had access to the web browser control and to third-party ActiveX controls. However, even then these controls focused on automating FTP and similar solutions. Like me, you probably found that the web browser control and these other controls can't meet your more advanced communications needs, like transferring data across the Internet between applications.

Now with IE5, we have access to a very exciting array of objects and methods that we can use to access web servers and business objects data across the Internet. In the examples to come, we will see how to use some of these objects.

6.2.4 *Simplifying frameworks*

Software development companies that create large applications usually attempt to reuse the same database functionality, such as adding records to tables and so on. Within these companies, the object-oriented crowd usually strives to create a *framework* to provide reusability for the code common to all the database calls.

For an interesting example of systems exposing their structure, check out ADO's OpenSchema() *method, which returns a record-set with the database metadata of your SQL Server 6.5 or 7.*

In this situation, if you include the framework into your applications, then you can reuse the same code. This is usually done by passing around arrays with columns in them. The columns indicate if the data is *dirty* (changed) or not. If it is dirty, then it is returned to the server to be unpacked and stored back in the database.

One of the hidden costs to a framework is maintaining it and the issue of ensuring that any new program that needs to use the framework knows exactly what information is provided by which component and in what format. Customers are educated on how to extend it, and new developers are trained to use it.

With XML you can provide a format- and language-neutral framework. Frameworks can become simplified by exposing their data in an XML- and probably RDF-centric way.

6.2.5 *Disconnected programs and data*

Check out RDS. It is a disconnected version of ADO that runs in the IE browser on the client.

With the advent of the Internet, the issue of having your programs run without a hitch in a disconnected (from a database) situation is important. Making programs that are bound to databases will not happen as much in the future, as our programs will have to work over the Internet and from web pages. Because XML can *carry* its own structure, it is the perfect data format for disconnected programs.

Let's have a look at two examples of using XML (with the full source code), Examples A and B.

Example A is a fairly simple solution where a VB front end:

- Communicates with a web server
- Communicates with a business object (DLL)
- We can see how to persist an ADO recordset and reload it back into an ADO recordset

These are the basic code techniques we will use in the rest of the examples, so it is important to fully understand the code listed. Once you have understood Example A, we will move on to the moderately difficult Example B.

Example B is where we demonstrate:

- A VB application communicating in several different ways with many different server-side objects
- The data is packed on the server and returned, where it is unpacked into the format required, such as VB6 class collections

Finally, we look at a rudimentary data manipulation framework. We explore some ideas of how the XML documents in Example B could be extended. We also look at how to create business objects and improved packing and unpacking.

6.3 *A quick overview of the examples*

The UML is now the vindustry standard for modeling applications and a whole lot more. For example, we have seen a book for modeling networks in UML.

In this chapter, we will present a lot of source code in VB and ASP. The source code will be more complex than the code you have seen in the previous chapters of this book. This time we will demonstrate using XML in webclasses, classes, and DLLs.

Now, let's take a high-level look at the applications that we are about to build. Figure 6.1 shows the application flow between the five major objects (or components) that we will build in our sample projects.

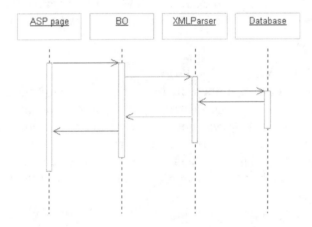

Figure 6.1   Sample UML sequence diagram

In figure 6.1, the application flow is as follows:

The application calls the communications object, which makes contact with the ASP page on the web server. The ASP pages interact with the business objects, which in turn access the database. Once the database has been queried, the business objects may format the data and return the result to the ASP page. The ASP page replies with the requested data, and the client-side communications objects supply the calling application with the requested information in the required format.

You can see that the communication interactions between the five components (or objects) in this three-tier distributed application are quite easily demonstrated by a *sequence* diagram. It may be easier to think of these objects as layers in the program. Each of these layers could represent several objects, classes, or even VB forms.

In order for you to understand the program at a code level, we still will need a clearer view of the flow between components, showing their methods and properties in order for you to be able to see just how useful XML is within a common solution such as this.

Figure 6.2 is a class diagram that shows the first and second layers, the application and communication layers. In these two layers, we have five objects. Four of these objects are forms, and one is a class that takes care of the communications.

In figure 6.2, you can see that the MDI Form's name is frmParent, and it uses three child forms. The `frmHTTP` form then uses a class. In each of the forms and the class, you can see the properties and methods. You will see the code for these forms and classes shortly.

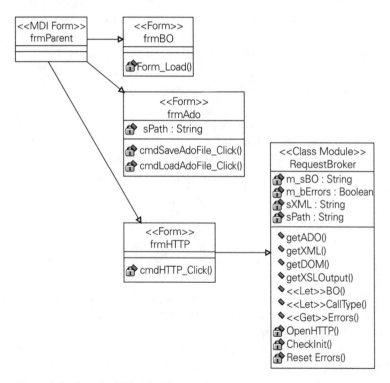

Figure 6.2   Sample UML three tier services model

In UML, there are several other types of arrows that show relationships. For example, inherited relationships will show slightly different lines.

In case you were wondering, the line between `frmHTTP` and the class `Request-Broker` is usually the result of a VB line of code such as:

```
Dim objRequest as new RequestBroker
```

Let's look at the entire solution now. In the overall picture, we group all the objects into three tiers (or levels): the Data Services tier, the Business Services tier, and the User Services tier. The Data Services usually hold the objects that access the data source, such as a database. The Business Services hold the objects that have business rules or logic in them.

In our case, the Business Services will hold the server XML formatting and manipulation. The User Services hold the client-side objects (including forms and normal VB objects). In our case, the User Services objects may be receiving XML from the Business Services and will need to use the XML in the application itself.

So, take a more detailed look at all the objects in the three tiers in figure 6.3.

Let's take a look at the three tiers that we will build in these solutions. The form `frmHTTP` calls the class `RequestBroker`, which in turn calls the ASP file, which calls our middle-tier business object, `PeopleBO`, which is a class. The `PeoplBO` class inherits its structure by implementing two classes called `IBO` and `IXML`, which are called interface classes. We will discuss `Implements` and how to use them a bit later.

Note　Interface classes: they provide an interface or structure for the *PeopleBO* class. What that means is that if several classes implement the same interface classes, you can be assured that every one of those classes will have all the methods that the interface classes have. This is an easy way to standardize your classes.

Don't be concerned if the diagrams appear to differ in small ways from the source code. The diagrams are provided to help you get an overview of the flow of the program that you are looking at.

We can also see that between the business object `PeopleBO` and the `DBManager` we have the `XMLParser`. `DBManager` actually does the accessing of the database, while the `XMLParser` converts the ADO record into XML and formats it the required way.

Try to become comfortable and even familiar with this diagram and its objects, as it is the basis of all our discussion from here onward. One by one we will discuss all the objects and their source code.

In figure 6.3, on the left, we can see that the MDIForm uses three child forms. The top one is `frmAdo`, which connects directly to the database. The second one down is the `frmBO`, and the link goes to the business object. The business object talks to a class called the XML Parser, which communicates with the database.

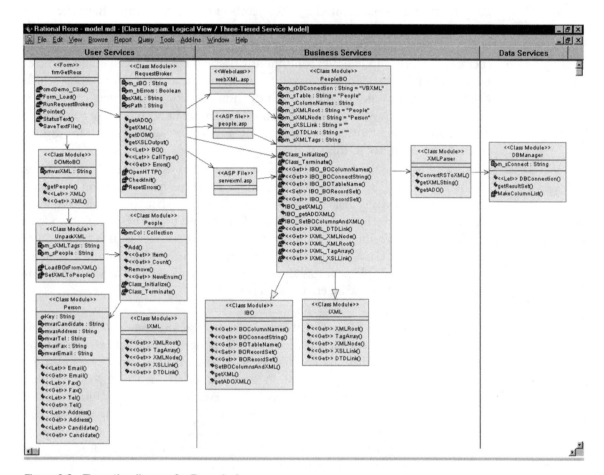

Figure 6.3 Three-tier diagram for Example A

6.4 *Implements*

Notice that the business object has slightly different arrows pointing at the two bottom classes. What this means is that the business object implements these classes.

When the `PeopleBO` class implements `IBO` and `IXML`, it must create a copy of all the methods of `IBO` and `IXML`. Even if there will be no code for some of those methods, they must still exist in `PeopleBO`.

This is a very useful feature of object orientation. Imagine that you and your team are creating one business object for each table in your database. You can imagine that there will be a huge number of business objects. To make the system easy to use, each class created by the members of the team must have the same methods, such as `start()`, `create()`, `save()`, `load()`, and so on.

If you are the team leader, how can you achieve this? You could email everyone, check their work, and basically continuously hassle them. Sure, you could also create an add-in for the VB6 environment that creates these standard methods, which would be nice as well. Of course, the next time someone uses a new copy of VB without the add-ins, your security is gone. The danger in both of these solutions is if there are inconsistencies by the time the application ships. Errors and future extensibility are at risk in this situation.

Or, you can use the Implements feature. For the object-oriented crowd, this is old hat—but for VB5 developers, this was a welcome new extension to Visual Basic. VB6 didn't really make it any easier to use, sadly. What you can do is create a class which only has the signature for the methods and properties, with no code in it. This is called an interface or abstract class. This abstract class is then implemented it in other class. This provides a structure the other classes must adhere to. All the classes that implement this abstract class will have to have the same methods and properties, otherwise an error will occur.

Implements were introduced in VB5.

Note If you have VB or Visual Interdev open, add a reference to the Microsoft XML 2.0 libraries and then press F2 to open the object browser. In the dropdown that says <All libraries>, choose MSXML. Now look in the list of objects that have loaded. In there you will see the DOMDocument that we often work with in this book. However, if you look a bit further down, you will see *IXMLDOMDocument*. Take a close look at the two and you will see that the methods of DOMDocument include the methods from *IXMLDOMDocument*. *IXMLDOMDocument* is only an interface that other libraries can implement to ensure consistency!

The classes that must implement IXML and IBO will place this code in their general declarations area:

```
Implements IXML
Implements IBO
```

Now, you must place all of the implemented methods into your class. Fortunately, this is not as hard as it sounds. All the methods are in the declarations dropdown; just select them and their code will appear.

If you look closely, PeopleBo has the same methods as the IXML and IBO classes. It has to, because it has stated it will implement the methods of those interfaces.

There is one more reason why Implements are useful to developers. If you look at the documentation for the method called `save()` for the DOMDocument object, you will see it can be saved to a text file, another DOMDocument, and to the ASP Response object. No surprises there; however, if you read on a bit more you will find that it can also be saved to any COM object that supports the `IStream`, `IPersistStream`, or `IpersistStreamInit` interfaces.

6.5 *Techniques for reusing business objects*

There is another major benefit of using the Implements keyword in your classes. If you want to ensure reusability, then make sure that the objects that are interchangeable (such as our business objects) implement the same interface.

Now your code can iterate through a series of business objects in a `FOR...NEXT` loop and manipulate each business object—without your code being concerned about changing methods and properties!

We think of this solution as a conveyor belt that sends various objects toward your code. Your code is a machine that simply works with objects. As long as the object has the required methods, takes the same parameters, and so on, the conveyor belt will run smoothly.

There are a few ways to iterate through a large number of objects. You could use the following code:

```
Dim objectvariable as object
Set objectvariable = CreateObject("progID", ["servername"])
```

Keep on changing the contents of `objectvariable` to the next object you want to work with.

You could also create all the objects (or instances of them) and load them into a collection. Now your code can work with one collection of objects—and of course, since you implemented an interface, you can be sure all the objects have the same methods.

Another useful approach that increases your flexibility with objects is the `Call-ByName()` function, which is provided by VB6. The `CallByName()` function is used to get or set a property or invoke a method at runtime using a string name.

Here, we use `CallByName()` to set the `MousePointer` property of a text box:

```
CallByName Text1, "MousePointer", vbLet, vbCrosshair
```

Now let's return the value of the `MousePointer` property:

```
Result = CallByName (Text1, "MousePointer", vbGet)
```

Finally, we can use the `Move()` method to move to the next text box:

```
CallByName Text1, "Move", vbMethod, 100, 100
```

6.6 *Creating the projects*

We have created two projects. In the pages to come, you will see several classes and a substantial amount of code. Okay, this is what you have been waiting for—let's get the hard hats out, people! Let's look at how our two projects are designed.

Note   Make sure you go to http://www. vbxml.com or
http://www. thespot4.com to the get the latest source code!

6.7 *SimpleUI—just the basics*

The first project is called SimpleUI and demonstrates the basics of communicating with a web server, communicating with a DLL, and persisting an ADO recordset.

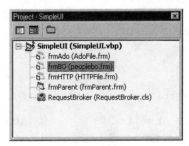

Figure 6.4   The SimpleUI project

Throughout all of this, we are passing XML around. Figure 6.4 demonstrates how this project will be implemented.

We will demonstrate various functionality:

- We will create some code to demonstrate how to communicate over the Internet HTTP protocol

- We will show how to build a small solution that links to a business object and requests our list of people from the business object

This simple VB application shows different tricks and features in different forms:

- Form `frmAdo` shows how to save ADO recordsets to a persisted XML format and then reload the records again. The form uses an ODBC DSN to access the database table.

- Form `frmHTTP` demonstrates how to open an HTTP connection to a web server (using `RequestBroker`), pass parameters, read the parameters in ASP files, and retrieve XML.
- Form `frmBO` calls a business object DLL (the "DBToXML" project above) directly without going via HTTP and demonstrates how to distribute your code and logic so that it is reusable.

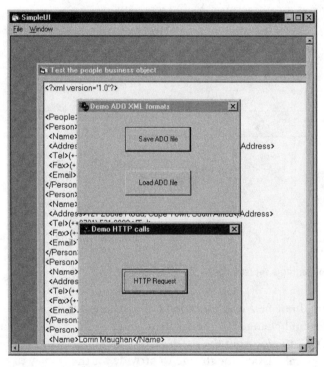

Figure 6.5   The SimpleUI application

Make sure you go to http://www. vbxml.com or http://www. thespot4.com to the get the latest source code!

In figure 6.5, you can see the three separate forms open inside an MDIForm. The two on top are for the ADO examples and HTTP communication with the server. The code behind the buttons on the forms demonstrates the use of ADO and HTTPRequest, respectively. The form in the background has already communicated with a business object (a DLL) and received and displayed its XML.

We require several different objects in this application. Figure 6.6's sequence diagram is a good way to show how each of the three forms interact with objects.

6.7.1 *frmAdos and the objects*

Using an ADO-only approach has costs and benefits. The benefits are mainly the ease and quick development cycle. The costs though are more serious. For one thing, this solution doesn't work across the Internet. Secondly, if you change your table structures in the database, all your programs must be recompiled. Also, what if you want the data to be returned in a specific format? The ADO-only approach is restrictive, as it only returns ADO recordsets.

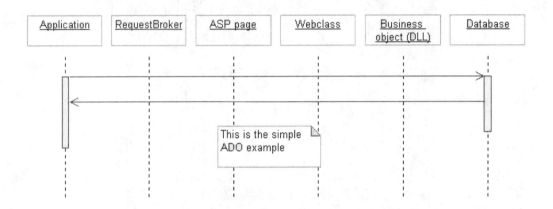

Figure 6.6 Sequence diagrams for frmAdo

This would not be a good solution for anything but the simplest application. It cannot withstand changes to the database and cannot return anything more complex than SQL queries from the database or other data sources. There is hardly any manipulation, calculation, or change to provide for the display of the data.

6.7.2 *frmBO and the objects*

In figure 6.7, the sequence diagram for the business object, we see that the issue of the inevitable changes to the database structure has been resolved by *masking* the data by putting a business object in front of it. Now if you change the database you only need to recompile the business object. The business object can also retrieve information from several data sources (using ADO, for example, it can retrieve emails or project management information, etc.) and then combine this information into one response.

That's better, but what about working across the Internet? The VB6 `CreateObject()` function is extremely powerful, but not across the Internet. (Although the new version of DCOM does work across the Internet.) Have you ever tried adding a reference to an object that resides on another computer or on a computer on another machine across the Internet?

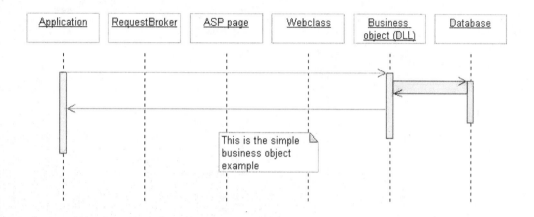

Figure 6.7   The business object sequence diagram

A good solution, but we can do much better.

In figure 6.8, the ASP (or webclass) sequence diagram, we expose the business object via a single ASP (or webclass) page. The webclass approach is very similar to the ASP approach, where the call is made to a VB created webclass rather than an ASP page.

Note   Upgrading, debugging, or otherwise changing ASP code is a far simpler task than changing webclass code. ASP text can be changed on the fly, whereas a webclass can only be changed when the web server is stopped.

That's a pretty good solution, because now we can create a connection to the web server and pass parameters to the webclass or ASP page, which will then open various business objects and perform manipulations on the results of the business object before sending the data back.

6.7.3   *How the ADO-only approach works*

Although the sequence diagram shown in figure 6.9 only shows the form and a database being accessed, we have added some code in to save the ADO recordset to a file and then load it again.

As you can see, there is not very much to it on the surface: an MDIForm, a child form, and two buttons on the child form. Each button does something dif-

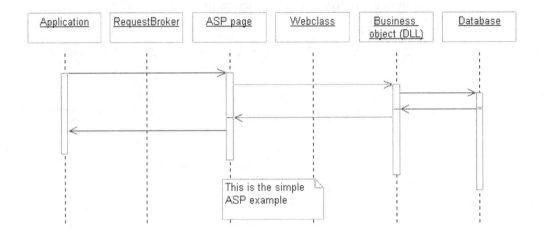

Figure 6.8 The ASP or Webclass sequence diagram

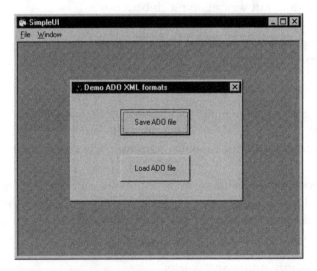

Figure 6.9 The ADO example

ferent. The first one connects to the database and then saves the ADO recordset to an XML file. The Load ADO file button reads that XML file and turns it back into a recordset.

There are two parts to this section of the project:

- The `Save ADO file` button
- The `Load ADO file` button

The SimpleUI project setup

Figure 6.10 displays the project window for the SimpleUI project. This project must have references to the following objects:

- Microsoft XML version 2.0
- Microsoft Scripting Runtime (for the Microsoft FilesSystemObject)
- Microsoft ActiveX Data Objects 2.1 Library
- DBToXML (either the project in a group, or the compiled DLL)

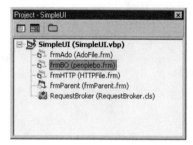

Figure 6.10   The basic SimpleUI project functionality

The code behind the Save ADO file button

In the following code, we see how to connect to a database using the VBXML ODBC DSN. We access a table called People and retrieve the fields. This record-set is then saved to a file, or *persisted* in an XML format. All file operations are handled by making use of the FileSystemObject object. (This object is found in the Microsoft Scripting Runtime dll, SCRRUN.dll, that we must reference in this project.)

```
Private Sub cmdSaveAdoFile_Click()

        Dim rstPeople As ADODB.Recordset
        Dim adoCon As New ADODB.Connection
        Dim objFSO As New FileSystemObject

        'use an error handler
        On Error GoTo ErrorHandler
        'switch on the hourglass
        Me.MousePointer = vbHourglass
```

```
          'store the path of the xml file
          m_strPath = App.Path & "\adodemo.xml"
          'check to see if the file exists and if it does, delete it
          If objFSO.FileExists(m_strPath) Then objFSO.DeleteFile (m_strPath)
          'open the ODBC adoConection
          adoCon.Open "VBXML"
          'retrieve the records using the ADO adoConection command
          Set rstPeople = adoCon.Execute("select * from People")
          'save the ADO recordset as a persisted XML file
          rstPeople.Save m_strPath, adPersistXML
          'announce that we have received the records and display them
          MsgBox "The ADO recordset has been persisted to the file:
              " & m_strPath
          'set the hourglass back to normal
          Me.MousePointer = vbNormal

      Exit Sub

  ErrorHandler:

      MsgBox "There is an error at source " & Err.Source & " with a description
      of " & Chr(13) & Err.Description & Chr(13) & "with the errorcode of "
      & Err.Number
      Exit Sub

  End Sub
```

The code behind the Load ADO file button

```
  Private Sub cmdLoadAdoFile_Click()

      Dim adoRS As New ADODB.Recordset
      Dim objFSO As New FileSystemObject

      'use an error handler
      On Error GoTo ErrorHandler

          'set up the path of the file
          m_strPath = App.Path & "\adodemo.xml"
          'check if the file exists
          If Not (objFSO.FileExists(m_strPath)) Then
              MsgBox "There is no file at the location: " & Chr(13)
                  & m_strPath & Chr(13) & "First save an ADO recordset,
                  then you can load one."
              Exit Sub
          End If
          'switch on the hourglass
          Me.MousePointer = vbHourglass
          'open the file directly into an ADO recordset
          adoRS.Open m_strPath, "Provider=MSPersist"
          'lets have a message box popup a confirmation
```

```
MsgBox "An ADO recordset has loaded from the file: " &
    m_strPath
'switch the hourglass off
Me.MousePointer = vbNormal

    Exit Sub

ErrorHandler:

    MsgBox "There is an error at source " & Err.Source & " with
    a description of " & Chr(13) & Err.Description & Chr(13)
    & "with the errorcode of " & Err.Number
    Exit Sub

End Sub
```

Summary

Well, that was pretty easy. We connected to a database and saved the resulting recordset to a file. Then we loaded the file and presented the user with a confirmation message box. Since most of the code we used here is built by Microsoft (the ADO, the ODBC, and so on), we don't really have to do much at all!

6.7.4   *How the business object approach works*

The sequence diagram in figure 6.11 shows the form connecting to the business object that in turn connects to a database. The results are returned to the front end and displayed in a text box on the form.

As you can see, it is the same MDIForm with a child form in it, and on the child form is a text box.

It doesn't look like much—but welcome to the wonderfully murky world of business objects, Implements, and classes. (Nice to see you again if you have visited before!)

What happens in this example is that on loading, the form contacts our compiled DLL (which is in the VB project references, to keep it simple) and requests the XML. The business object contacts the database and then sends the resulting ADO to another class called XML Parser that happily waits for recordsets, which it can turn into XML (it doesn't use the ADO save() method).

XML Parser can be used by several different applications or components or even called using CreateObject from ASP. As a result, it is the ideal candidate for being a reusable class, rather than code that is hard-coded in each calling application.

In the three-tier diagram you saw earlier, the business object is the PeopleBO class. Since the design is intended to be reusable, any business object could be in the sequence diagram shown in figure 6.12, provided it supplies the expected public methods. That's why we use `Implements`!

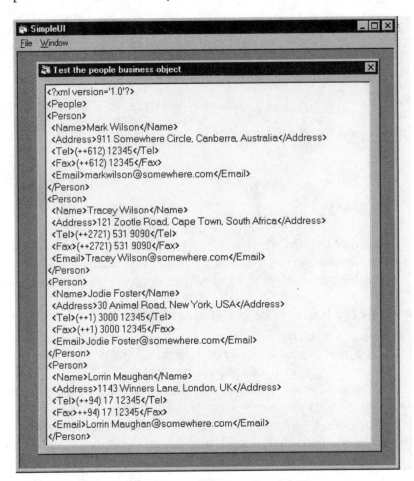

```
SimpleUI                                    _ □ ✕
File  Window
    Test the people business object              ✕
    <?xml version='1.0'?>
    <People>
    <Person>
     <Name>Mark Wilson</Name>
     <Address>911 Somewhere Circle, Canberra, Australia</Address>
     <Tel>(++612) 12345</Tel>
     <Fax>(++612) 12345</Fax>
     <Email>markwilson@somewhere.com</Email>
    </Person>
    <Person>
     <Name>Tracey Wilson</Name>
     <Address>121 Zootle Road, Cape Town, South Africa</Address>
     <Tel>(++2721) 531 9090</Tel>
     <Fax>(++2721) 531 9090</Fax>
     <Email>Tracey Wilson@somewhere.com</Email>
    </Person>
    <Person>
     <Name>Jodie Foster</Name>
     <Address>30 Animal Road, New York, USA</Address>
     <Tel>(++1) 3000 12345</Tel>
     <Fax>(++1) 3000 12345</Fax>
     <Email>Jodie Foster@somewhere.com</Email>
    </Person>
    <Person>
     <Name>Lorrin Maughan</Name>
     <Address>1143 Winners Lane, London, UK</Address>
     <Tel>(++94) 17 12345</Tel>
     <Fax>++94) 17 12345</Fax>
     <Email>Lorrin Maughan@somewhere.com</Email>
    </Person>
```

Figure 6.11   The business object example

Simply, the form or ASP page (or whatever calls the business object) initiates a sequence of communication. The business object talks to the XML Parser that requests the data from the database. The database returns the recordset; the XML Parser chops it up into XML and gives the XML back to the caller, which is the business object. The business object now hands it back to the ASP page or form or whatever called the business object in the beginning.

Each time a call is made, only one method is called, and perhaps a parameter is passed. In this way, the code is highly reusable. Any business object (not just the `PeopleBO`) can be used, and the XML Parser will deal with any caller (not just the `PeopleBO`).

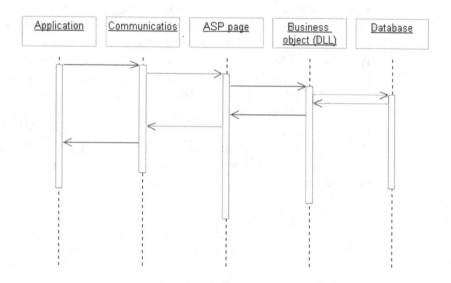

Figure 6.12   Business object sequence diagram

Source code

The business object source code contains the following six parts:

- The calling form
- The `PeopleBO` class
- The `XMLParser` class
- The `DBManager`
- The `IXML` class
- The `IBO` class

The calling form code

This form only has a few lines of code in it:

```
Private Sub Form_Load()
    'instantiate the business object
    Dim objPeople As New PeopleBO
```

```
'place the results of the business object into the text box
txtResults = objPeople.IBO_getXML

End Sub
```

The solution is wonderfully simple and reusable. A business object is called and the reply is placed into the textbox called `txtResults`. Almost all the complexity is placed into the classes, and because of this design, you can call the same code in those classes from several different programs.

When you read the next pieces of code, refer to the sequence diagram or the two-tier diagram for this example. The form above calls the `PeopleBO` class. The `PeopleBO` class inherits some methods from the `IBO` class and also uses the `XML-Parser` class to do the data accessing and packing. By packing, we mean that it takes the recordset and puts it into a text file that contains XML. We do not use the ADO XML persist format, because (although being valid) it looks like a mess to a human (even though it makes wonderfully clear sense to another ADO recordset).

The DBToXML project setup

These classes would normally be on the server and in a separate project from the front end form. In example B, a webclass or an ASP page is called, which in turn calls this DLL on the server.

This project is referenced by the `frmBO` form. Figure 6.13 shows the project window, which shows the classes that are found in this project.

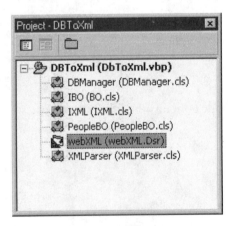

Figure 6.13 The DBToXml VB project

This project must have references to the following objects:

- Microsoft XML version 2.0
- Microsoft Scripting Runtime (for the Microsoft FilesSystemObject)
- Microsoft ActiveX Data Objects 2.1 Library

- DBToXML (either the project in a group, or the compiled DLL)
- Microsoft Active Server Pages Object Library (for the webclass)
- Microsoft webclass Library v1.0

The PeopleBO class code

The source code for the business object DLL called PeopleBO is listed here. You can see that the ActiveX DLL implements two interfaces, IXML and IBO, which ensure this code will have the same methods and public properties as other DLLs that implement the same interfaces:

```
Option Explicit

Implements IXML
Implements IBO
```

We also create a few constants in this business object. Each business object will have its own constants, such as different tables to access and different XML column names and the corresponding table column names.

```
' DSN name
Const m_strDBConnection As String = "VBXML"

' IBO interface variables
' Main Table name for the business object
Const m_strTable As String = "People"

' String Array of column names from table in db
Private m_strColumnNames()    As String
Private m_adoRS As ADODB.Recordset

' IXML interface variables
' DTD name for the converting in XML parser
Const m_strXMLRoot As String = "People"
Const m_strXMLNode As String = "Person"
Const m_strXSLPI As String = "http:/mark/xmlcode/people.xsl"
Const m_strDTDEntry As String = "http:/mark/xmlcode/people.dtd"

Private m_strXMLTags() As String

Private m_objBO As IBO
Private m_objXML As IXML

Private Sub Class_Initialize()
    'when the XMLParser is called, oBO and oXML will pass this class (Me)
    and that will enable the called class to access properties in this
    class, namely the IBO and IXML interface
    Set m_objBO = Me
    Set m_objXML = Me
End Sub
```

```
Private Sub Class_Terminate()
    'clear the object memory
    Set m_adoRS = Nothing
    Set m_objBO = Nothing
    Set m_objXML = Nothing
End Sub

Private Property Get IBO_BOColumnNames() As String()
    'this returns the string array of column names set in the
        function IBO_SetBOColumnsAndXML()
    IBO_BOColumnNames = m_strColumnNames
End Property

Private Property Get IBO_BOConnectString() As String
    'this returns the string which is the DB Connection which is set in the
        general declarations
    IBO_BOConnectString = m_strDBConnection
End Property

Private Property Get IBO_BOTableName() As String
    'this returns the string which is the table name that is set in the
        general declarations
    IBO_BOTableName = m_strTable
End Property

Private Property Set IBO_BORecordSet(RHS As ADODB.Recordset)
    'DB Manager sets the recordset here via the XMLParser class in function
        getXML()
    Set m_adoRS = RHS
End Property

Private Property Get IBO_BORecordSet() As ADODB.Recordset
    Set IBO_BORecordSet = m_adoRS
End Property

Public Function IBO_getXML() As String
    'create an instance of the XMLParser
    Dim objXmlParser As New XMLParser
    'call the XMLParser method, pass Me and then return that to
        the caller
    IBO_getXML = objXmlParser.getXMLString(m_objBO, m_objXML)
    Set objXmlParser = Nothing
End Function

Public Function IBO_getADOXML() As String
    'create an instance of the XMLParser
    Dim objXmlParser As New XMLParser
    'call the XMLParser method and then return that to the caller
    IBO_getADOXML = objXmlParser.getADO(m_objBO, m_objXML)
    Set objXmlParser = Nothing
End Function
```

In SetBOColumnsAndXML we set up the column names and corresponding table column names:

```
Private Sub IBO_SetBOColumnsAndXML()

    'Match the DB column names to XML tags for the elements
    'e.g. if the columnname for 'lastname' from the db must match with
        'name' for the element tag, then they must be the
        same array number in the two arrays.

    ReDim m_strColumnNames(4)
    ReDim m_strXMLTags(4)

    m_strColumnNames(0) = "Name"
    m_strColumnNames(1) = "Address"
    m_strColumnNames(2) = "Tel"
    m_strColumnNames(3) = "Fax"
    m_strColumnNames(4) = "Email"

    m_strXMLTags(0) = "Name"
    m_strXMLTags(1) = "Address"
    m_strXMLTags(2) = "Tel"
    m_strXMLTags(3) = "Fax"
    m_strXMLTags(4) = "Email"

End Sub
```

DTDEntry, XMLNode, XMLRoot, TagArray, and XSLPI are set before the getADO() or getXML() method of this business object is called.

Because this class implements the methods of the IXML interface, the methods have exactly the same method names as the IXML class—in this case IXML_DTDEntry() and so on. There are ways of masking these names (by placing another class with *friendly* method names between these two classes), but we do not show how to do that here.

```
Private Property Get IXML_DTDEntry() As String
    'it returns the string which is the table name that is set in the general
        declarations
    IXML_DTDEntry = m_strDTDEntry
End Property

Private Property Get IXML_XMLNode() As String
    'it returns the string which is the table name that is set in the general
        declarations
    IXML_XMLNode = m_strXMLNode
End Property

Private Property Get IXML_XMLRoot() As String
    'it returns the string which is the table name that is set in the
        general declarations
```

```
        IXML_XMLRoot = m_strXMLRoot
End Property

Private Property Get IXML_TagArray() As String()
    'it returns the string array of column names set in the function
        IBO_SetBOColumnsAndXML()
    IXML_TagArray = m_strXMLTags
End Property

Private Property Get IXML_XSLPI() As String
    'it returns the string which is the table name that is set in the general
        declarations
    IXML_XSLPI = m_strXSLPI
End Property
```

The XMLParser class code

The XMLParser is a class that interacts with the database and then converts the resulting recordset to XML. It does not use the persistence of ADO 2.1 to do this; it merely parses the recordset into a set of XML Nodes or elements.

```
Option Explicit

Public Function ConvertRSToXML(adoRS As ADODB.Recordset, objXML As IXML)
  As String
'This function coverts ADO recordsets to XML files
'It does not use the ADO 2.1 persistence feature

    Dim strTab As String
    Const strOpen As String = "<"
    Const strClose As String = ">"
    Const strEndOpen As String = "</"

    Dim strXML As String
    Dim strVersion As String
    Dim strDTD As String
    Dim strXSL As String
    Dim strTags() As String
    Dim i As Integer

    Dim adoField As ADODB.Field
```

Here we build string-holding references to the DTD or an XSL file, if there is one:

```
    'if the BO specified a DTD
    If objXML.DTDEntry <> "" Then strDTD = "<!DOCTYPE RESUME " & Chr(34) &
        objXML.DTDEntry & Chr(34) & ">" & vbCrLf
    'if the BO specified an XSL
    If objXML.XSLPI <> "" Then strXSL = "<?xml:stylesheet type=" & Chr(34)
        & "text/xsl" & Chr(34) & " href=" & Chr(34) & objXML.XSLPI & Chr(34)
        & "?>" & vbCrLf
```

```
        'get the BO specified tag array
        strTags = objXML.TagArray
        strTab = CStr(Space(2))
```

Here we start building the XML file:

```
'start with title of xml version
strVersion = "<?xml version='1.0'?>" & vbCrLf


'xml root
strXML = strOpen & objXML.XMLRoot & strClose & vbCrLf
```

Now we loop through the recordset, filling in the XML file:

```
If adoRS.RecordCount > 0 Then
        adoRS.MoveFirst

        While Not (adoRS.EOF)
            'write the xml node
            strXML = strXML & strOpen & objXML.XMLNode & strClose & vbCrLf

            'loop through the fields in the row
            For i = 0 To adoRS.Fields.Count - 1
                'Tag header
                strXML = strXML & strTab & strOpen & strTags(i) & strClose

                'Result
                strXML = strXML & adoRS.Fields(i).Value

                'Tag ending
              strXML = strXML & strEndOpen & strTags(i) & strClose & vbCrLf
            Next
          strXML = strXML & strEndOpen & objXML.XMLNode & strClose & vbCrLf
            adoRS.MoveNext
        Wend

        'end of xml file, close the xml root
        strXML = strXML & strEndOpen & objXML.XMLRoot & strClose
    End If

    'send the string back
    ConvertRSToXML = strVersion & strDTD & strXSL & strXML

End Function
```

The `getXMLString()` function is used to access the database (using DB-Manager) and return a string:

```
Public Function getXMLString(objBO As IBO, objXML As IXML) As String
'this function receives the calling class as a variable in objBO and as objXML

    Dim objDBManager  As DBManager

    'create the DB Manager
    Set objDBManager = New DBManager
```

```
'in the calling class (for example PeopleBO) set up the columns and XML
        tags
objBO.SetBOColumnsAndXML
'set the DB Manager's connections
objDBManager.DBConnection = objBO.BOConnectString
'pass the column names and table name to the DB Manager and return the
        resulting ADO recordset
Set objBO.BORecordSet = objDBManager.getResultSet(objBO.BOColumnNames,
        objBO.BOTableName)
'pass the new recordset and IXML interface to the BO object (for example
        PeopleBO)
'and return the resulting XML string
getXMLString = ConvertRSToXML(objBO.BORecordSet, objXML)

End Function
```

Provide the DBManager with a connect string (which would be an ODBC connection, any passwords, and so on):

```
'create the DB Manager
Set objDBManager = New DBManager
'in the calling class (for example PeopleBO) set up the columns and XML
        tags
objBO.SetBOColumnsAndXML
'set the DB Manager's connections
objDBManager.DBConnection = objBO.BOConnectString
'pass the column names and table name to the DB Manager and return the
        resulting ADO recordset
```

We pass to the DBManager the column names array and the table from which the business object specifies that the column names must come from:

```
Set objBO.BORecordSet = objDBManager.getResultSet(objBO.BOColumnNames,
        objBO.BOTableName)
'pass the new recordset and IXML interface to the BO object (for example
        PeopleBO)
'and return the resulting XML string
```

Pass the recordset to ConvertRSToXML():

```
getXMLString = ConvertRSToXML(objBO.BORecordSet, objXML)

End Function
```

The getADO() function is used to access the database (using DBManager) and return an ADO recordset in persisted format.

Before diving into the getADO() function code, we should note that the business object is passed as a parameter to this function getADO() as PeopleBO, but received in this function getADO() as IBO. This is an important issue.

```
Public Function getADO(objBO As IBO, objXML As IXML) As String
```

Say we received the `objBO` object parameter as the `PeopleBO` class, for example:

```
Public Function getADO(objBO As PeopleBO, objXML As IXML) As String
```

Then when you type `objBO`, you will see that the list methods that pop up are the methods belonging to the class `PeopleBO`. However, we received it as `IBO`, not as `PeopleBO`. So when we type into our code the following letters, `objBO`, then the list methods of the `IBO` interface pop up.

You see we can send the `objBO` object parameter as a parameter of the type `PeopleBO`, but since it implements `IBO`, we can receive the parameter as `IBO`–which is the interface it implemented.

Why is this useful? If you don't know which business object you will receive (`CustomerBO`, `PeopleBO`, or `EmployeeBO`) then you need only to implement `IBO` in all those classes, and then you can receive them as `IBO`–regardless of which business object is passed.

This is a vital benefit of using interfaces to achieve reusability.

The `getADO()` function continues as follows:

```
Dim objDBManager As DBManager
Dim objDOMDocument As DOMDocument
Dim strPath As String

strPath = App.Path & "\" & "adoxml.xml"
'set up the columns in the calling business object
objBO.SetBOColumnsAndXML
'initialize the DBManager
Set objDBManager = New DBManager
objDBManager.DBConnection = objBO.BOConnectString
'retrieve the DBManager's recordset
Set objBO.BORecordSet = objDBManager.get-
  ResulSet(objBO.BOColumnNames, objBO.BOTableName)
```

Here we persist the ADO recordset as an XML file:

```
objBO.BORecordSet.Save strPath, adPersistXML
```

and then load the XML into a DOMDocument:

```
'load the file into a DOMDocument
objDOMDocument.Load strPath
'delete the file
Kill strPath
'send the XML back
getADO = objDOMDocument.xml

End Function
```

The DBManager class code

The DBManager conveniently outsources the accessing of the database into a class that can be used from any other classes:

```
Option Explicit

Private m_strConnect As String
```

The calling application or class put a valid connect string into this property, the DBConnection property:

```
Public Property Let DBConnection(sValue As String)
    m_strConnect = sValue
End Property
```

The columns are passed in as an array of strings, concatenated together and eventually used in a select statement:

```
Private Function MakeColumnList(sColumnNames() As String) As String

    'concatenate the array of column names in a string,
    'separated by a comma
    MakeColumnList = Join(sColumnNames, ", ")

End Function
```

The calling application or class then can call:

```
Public Function getResultSet(sColumnNames() As String, sTable As String)
 As ADODB.Recordset
  Dim strSQL As String
  Dim adoCon As ADODB.Connection
  Dim adoRst As ADODB.Recordset

  'Prepare the SQL query by creating a string from the array parsed in,
  'for the columns and the table name.
  'The array 'sColumnNames' constists of the column names in the order
  'that they must be selected from the database.
  strSQL = "SELECT " & MakeColumnList(sColumnNames) & " FROM " & sTable

  'prepare ADO objects
  Set adoCon = New ADODB.Connection
  Set adoRst = New ADODB.Recordset

  'Open database connection
  adoCon.ConnectionString = m_strConnect
  adoCon.CursorLocation = adUseClient
  adoCon.Open
  Set adoRst.ActiveConnection = adoCon
```

Open the recordset and send it back to the caller (which in this case is a class that will turn it into an XML file):

```
'get resultset
adoRst.Open strSQL, , adOpenForwardOnly, adLockReadOnly, adCmdText
Set getResultSet = adoRst

End Function
```

The IXML class code

The IXML class is one of two interface classes. In the IXML class, the following is defined:

```
Option Explicit

'This provides an interface for an XML file.
'It is used with the business object classes,
'as well as when defining tags and elements for an XML file

'Provide the XMLRoot name
Public Property Get XMLRoot() As String

End Property
```

Notice that no code is placed in these methods. That is because the code for the methods is placed in the class that implements this interface. This class, IXML, is therefore only an INTERFACE to the other classes:

```
'String array of the tags for the XML and DTD.
'This must coincide with the column
'names of the business object
Public Property Get TagArray() As String()

End Property

'Provide the XML Node name
Public Property Get XMLNode() As String

End Property

'Provide the link to the XSL Stylesheet
Public Property Get XSLPI() As String

End Property

'Provide the link to the DTD
Public Property Get DTDEntry() As String

End Property
```

The IBO class code

This is the second interface that is used in this application as it is currently designed. Again see how no code is put into these methods, since the methods are purely an interface to be implemented in a class, where the code will be placed against these methods:

```
Option Explicit

'For each business object, implement this interface.
'It stores the underlying information of the business object, which
'is mainly the database information, such as the table name
'and columns.

'The following 'Get' methods do not have associated 'Let' methods
'as in the Business object classes, their data is held in local
'variables (see the general declaration of the PeopleBO class)

'A string array of the column names from the main table
'which need to be displayed in the XML file.  The order arrays
'of this array needs to coincide with the string array, 'TagArray',
'found in the IXML interface
Public Property Get BOColumnNames() As String()

End Property

'what is the ODBC connect string?
Public Property Get BOConnectString() As String

End Property

'what is the main table name from the database for this BO?
Public Property Get BOTableName() As String

End Property

'recordset for the BO once the DBManager class has taken the info from
'this interface to get the recordset (see DBManager function getResult-
  set())
Public Property Get BORecordSet() As ADODB.Recordset

End Property

Public Property Set BORecordSet(adoRS As ADODB.Recordset)

End Property

'in the BO class, this is where the BOColumnNames string array
'and the IXML TagArray array is set.
Public Sub SetBOColumnsAndXML()

End Sub

'a wrapper method for getting the XML from the XMLParser
'class
```

```
Public Function getXML() As String

End Function

Public Function getADOXML() As String

End Function
```

Summary

We have moved from directly accessing the database to masking the database with a business object. We also introduced how to implement classes to force consistency across different DLLs, which helps achieve a high degree of reuse. We saw why creating an object such as XML Parser is useful when some functionality is used several times by different objects.

6.7.5 *How the ASP approach works*

We are back on familiar territory here—ASP files with VBScript in them. Most of this code was created and explained earlier in the book. The sequence diagram in figure 6.14 shows how the form connects to the ASP page, and the ASP page in turn connects to a database.

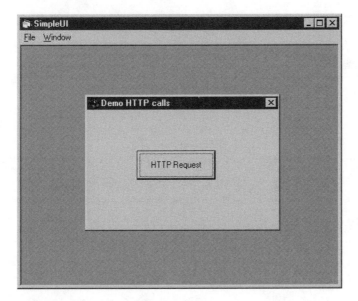

Figure 6.14   The ASP example

As you can see, the ASP example doesn't look like much: an MDIForm, a child form, and one button on the child form. When you click the button, the project opens an HTTPRequest connection with the server and then it calls an ASP page, passing a parameter to the ASP page. The ASP page in turn talks to the business object, which talks to the database.

The code behind the HTTPRequest form

The code under the button opens an HTTP GET() connection to the web server and sends two parameters to the ASP page. The code in the ASP page then parses the parameters and returns the requested information.

You can make several other types of connections to a web server, such as a PUT(), which passes an HTML form. The receiving ASP page then parses the HTML form. However, since we are calling the ASP page from code, it is easier to use the GET() type and pass parameters as in the following code:

```
Option Explicit

Private Sub cmdHTTP_Click()

    Dim httpOB As New XMLHTTPRequest
    Dim strXML As String
    Dim strURL As String
    Dim strPath As String
    Dim strMsg As String
    Dim objDOMDocument As DOMDocument

On Error GoTo ErrorHandler

    'switch on the hourglass
    Me.MousePointer = vbHourglass

    'in this example, to keep it simple, we will only ask for XML and
    'only for PEOPLE information
    'set the URL to be called into a string, because the first release
    'of this object has a bug that crashes if the strURL parameter is
    'not a string
    strURL = "http://mark/xmlcode/servexml.asp?ReplyType=eXML&useBO=PEOPLE"

    'make the call
    Call httpOB.Open("GET", strURL, False)
    Call httpOB.send

    'get the response back
    strXML = httpOB.responseText

    'tell the user it was successful and show the XML in a message box
```

```
        strMsg = "We have successfully retrieved an XML document from the
              webserver" & Chr(13) & Chr(13) & "The XML displayed below may
              be truncated by the message box" & Chr(13) & Chr(13) & strXML
        MsgBox strMsg

        'switch off the hourglass
        Me.MousePointer = vbDefault

    Exit Sub

ErrorHandler:

    MsgBox "There is an error at source " & Err.Source & " with a description
      of " & Chr(13) & Err.Description & Chr(13) & "with the errorcode of "
      & Err.Number
    Exit Sub

End Sub
```

The ASP page code

In the ASP page, use

```
response.buffer = true
```

to stop the headers of the HTML page from being sent back before you have completely finished building the page:

```
<% response.buffer = true %>
```

State the scripting language to be used:

```
<% LANGUAGE="VBScript" %>
```

In the first version of the Microsoft IE5 XML object HTTP-Request, when opening a connection to the web server, one of the parameters is the URL to open. This URL should be in a string and not explicit, otherwise the program will crash when compiled.

Get the passed parameters, passed as QueryStrings, and put them into local variables:

```
<% mytype = Request.QueryString("ReplyType") %>
<% BO = Request.QueryString("useBO") %>
```

Check if the user wants straight XML returned with PEOPLE in it:

```
<% if mytype = "eXML" and BO = "PEOPLE" then %>
<?xml version="1.0" ?>
```

Open the root Node:

```
<PEOPLE>
```

Open the database connection and loop through the records, placing them into the XML elements:

```
<%
    Set ObjConn = Server.CreateObject("ADODB.Connection")
    ObjConn.Open "VBXML"
    Set PEOPLE = ObjConn.Execute("select * from People")
    Do While Not PEOPLE.EOF
```

```
%>
<PERSON>
  <NAME><%=People("Name")%></NAME>
  <ADDRESS><%=People("Address")%></ADDRESS>
  <TEL><%=People("Tel")%></TEL>
  <FAX><%=People("Fax")%></FAX>
  <EMAIL><%=People("Email")%>  </EMAIL>
</PERSON>
    <% People.MoveNext
    Loop
    %>
```

Close the root Node:

```
</PEOPLE>
```

Check if the user wants a client-side XSL transformation with PEOPLE in it:

```
<% elseif mytype = "eXSLHTML"  and BO = "PEOPLE" then %>
<?xml version="1.0" ?>
```

Insert the stylesheet link:

```
<?xml:stylesheet type="text/xsl" href="http://mark/xmlcode/people.xsl"?>
<PEOPLE>
```

The rest of this code is the same as in the ASP page sample code section above:

```
<%
    Set ObjConn = Server.CreateObject("ADODB.Connection")
    ObjConn.Open "VBXML"
    Set PEOPLE = ObjConn.Execute("select * from People")
    Do While Not PEOPLE.EOF
  %>
<PERSON>
  <NAME><%=People("Name")%></NAME>
  <ADDRESS><%=People("Address")%></ADDRESS>
  <TEL><%=People("Tel")%></TEL>
  <FAX><%=People("Fax")%></FAX>
  <EMAIL><%=People("Email")%>  </EMAIL>
</PERSON>
    <% People.MoveNext
    Loop
    %>
</PEOPLE>

<% end if %>
```

At this point, you have completed building the page, so the buffering stops and the page is now returned.

The webclass code

Calling a webclass instead of calling an ASP from a VB application is trivial. Most of the code is the same. Certainly the call to the ASP page via HTTPRequest is the same; however, the webclass is created in VB and not in Microsoft Visual Interdev or Microsoft FrontPage. Here is the equivalent webclass code that you can build in VB:

We do not make any use of HTML Template Web-Items or Custom WebItems; we simply write VB code in the Start() *method, receive the parameters in the Request object, and return the string in the* Response *object.*

```
Option Explicit

Private Sub WebClass_Start()

    Dim objPeople As New PeopleBO
    Dim strXML As String
    Dim strRequest As String
    Dim strBO As String
    Dim objConn As ADODB.Connection
    Dim rstPeople As Recordset
    Dim objDOMDocument As DOMDocument
    Dim xslDoc As DOMDocument
    Dim objFSO As New FileSystemObject

    On Error GoTo ErrorHandler
```

In webclasses, you can create VB code using all your familiar constructs and references to objects. As you saw in the ASP code, if this webclass is called from a GET() HTTPRequest call, we can pass parameters, which are accessed from your code using the Request object with the QueryString property:

```
'put the QueryStrings into local strings
    strRequest = Request.QueryString("ReplyType")
    strBO = Request.QueryString("useBO")
```

Now we simply look at the parameters to decide if the caller is asking for XML, XML transformed on the server-side, XML with an XSL PI in it, or a persisted ADO recordset; or should the code access a business object.

Of course, if you are a VB developer, you will look at this code and think of millions of uses. In the business object example, you can see some code calls to the classes we described earlier in the book:

```
'check if the user wants XML back
If strRequest = "eXML" Then
    'begin building an XML file
    strXML = "<?xml version=" & Chr(34) & "1.0" & Chr(34) & " ?>"
    'open the root Node
    strXML = strXML & "<PEOPLE>"

    'open the ADO connection
    Set objConn = Server.CreateObject("ADODB.Connection")
    'make sure you have a valid ODBC DSN here
```

```
objConn.Open "VBXML"
'get the recordset
Set rstPeople = objConn.Execute("select * from People")
'loop through the recordset
Do While Not rstPeople.EOF
      'put the recordset into the XML elements
      strXML = strXML & "<PERSON>"
      strXML = strXML & "<NAME>" & rstPeople("Name") & "</NAME>"
      strXML = strXML & "<ADDRESS>" & rstPeople("Address") & "</
          ADDRESS>"
      strXML = strXML & "<TEL>" & rstPeople("Tel") & "</TEL>"
      strXML = strXML & "<FAX>" & rstPeople("Fax") & "</FAX>"
      strXML = strXML & "<EMAIL>" & rstPeople("Email") & "</EMAIL>"
      strXML = strXML & "</PERSON>"

      'keep moving through the recordset
      rstPeople.MoveNext
Loop

'close the root Node
strXML = strXML & "</PEOPLE>"

'check if the user wants XML transformed into HTML on the server side
ElseIf strRequest = "eXSLHTML" Then
   'load the XML file
   Set objDOMDocument = Server.CreateObject("Microsoft.XMLDOM")
   objDOMDocument.Load (Server.MapPath("people.xml"))
   'load the XSL file
   Set xslDoc = Server.CreateObject("Microsoft.XMLDOM")
   xslDoc.Load (Server.MapPath("people.xsl"))
   'transform the XML and put it into a string for sending back
   strXML = objDOMDocument.transformNode(xslDoc)

'check if the user wants XML with an XSL included—client-side trans-
       formation
ElseIf strRequest = "eXMLXSL" Then
   'create the XML headers
   strXML = "<?xml version=" & Chr(34) & "1.0" & Chr(34) & " ?>"
   'put in a link to the XSL file
   strXML = strXML & "<?xml:stylesheet type=" & Chr(34) & "text/xsl" &
         Chr(34) & " href=" & Chr(34) & "http://mark/xmlcode/peo-
         ple.xsl" & Chr(34) & "?>"

   'the rest of this is the same as the XML example above
   strXML = strXML & "<PEOPLE>"

   Set objConn = Server.CreateObject("ADODB.Connection")
   objConn.Open "VBXML"
   Set rstPeople = objConn.Execute("select * from People")
   Do While Not rstPeople.EOF
```

```
         strXML = strXML & "<PERSON>"
         strXML = strXML & "<NAME>" & rstPeople("Name") & "</NAME>"
         strXML = strXML & "<ADDRESS>" & rstPeople("Address") & "</
            ADDRESS>"
         strXML = strXML & "<TEL>" & rstPeople("Tel") & "</TEL>"
         strXML = strXML & "<FAX>" & rstPeople("Fax") & "</FAX>"
         strXML = strXML & "<EMAIL>" & rstPeople("Email") & "</EMAIL>"
          strXML = strXML & "</PERSON>"

      rstPeople.MoveNext
   Loop

   strXML = strXML & "</PEOPLE>"

'check if the user wants a DOMDocument
ElseIf strRequest = "DOMDocument" Then
   'load the XML file
   Set objDOMDocument = Server.CreateObject("Microsoft.XMLDOM")
   objDOMDocument.Load (Server.MapPath("people.xml"))
   'set the content type of the ASP response object to XML
   Response.ContentType = "text/xml"
   'put the XML into the string for sending back
   strXML = objDOMDocument.xml

'check if the user wants an ADO 2.1 persisted recordset back
ElseIf strRequest = "ADO" Then
   'make the connection
   Set objConn = Server.CreateObject("ADODB.Connection")
   'make sure you have a valid ODBC DSN here!
   objConn.Open "VBXML"
   'get the recordset
   Set rstPeople = objConn.Execute("select * from People")

   'delete the file if it exists
   If objFSO.FileExists(Server.MapPath("adodemo.xml")) Then
         objFSO.DeleteFile (Server.MapPath("adodemo.xml"))
   'save the ADO recordset as a persisted ADO XML recordset
   rstPeople.Save (Server.MapPath("adodemo.xml")), adPersistXML

   'create the DOMDocument
   Set objDOMDocument = Server.CreateObject("Microsoft.XMLDOM")
   'load the XML into the DOMDocument
   objDOMDocument.Load (Server.MapPath("adodemo.xml"))
   'set the content type of the ASP response object to XML
   Response.ContentType = "text/xml"
   'put the XML into the string for sending back
   strXML = objDOMDocument.xml

'check if the user wants to retrieve the XML from a business object
ElseIf strRequest = "BO" Then
```

```
          'if the business object to retrieve is the PEOPLE one, then
          If strBO = "People" Then
              'call the PEOPLE business object (DLL) and get the XML back as
                    a string
              strXML = objPeople.IBO_getXML
          End If

      End If

      'now send the response string back!
      Response.Write strXML

  Exit Sub

  ErrorHandler:

  'Just exit the process on the server
  'Raising an error wouldn't make sense as this runs on the server
  'Consider logging the error
  'If you set this DLL to run unattended, it will automatically log the mes-
    sages

  Exit Sub
```

If you want to see this code running, type it into your VB webclass designer; place it into the `Private Sub WebClass_Start()` method. You do not need to make any further changes to the default webclass that is created by the wizard.

However, when you first run the webclass, VB will offer to create an ASP file that your code can call. You may have noticed that all our code examples called webXML.asp, which is the ASP file VB created to provide access to this DLL.

6.8 *XMLDemo—a more complete example*

The second project we have is the full client-side demonstration of accessing a web server using ASP or webclasses and passing data around using XML. This application brings all the code and ideas in this book together into a flexible and reusable three-tier solution. It should show off all the code in this book and demonstrate the usefulness of VB, webclasses, ASP, and XML.

Figure 6.15 shows what the user interface of this project looks like.

On the left is a selection of choices that the user can make, and on the right is IE5, which will display the output. For example, the user may choose the ASP file to PEOPLE table and Client-side XSL to HTML in IE5 on the left. When the user clicks the Demo button, the application will call the various classes and objects, the database will be queried, and XML will be returned with an XSL file. The XML and XSL combination will display as a client-side table in IE5, which is on the right-hand side of this form.

As you can see, there are many different choices in the user interface. As a developer or team leader, you may be able to find several different pieces of code or solutions within this project that will be useful to you.

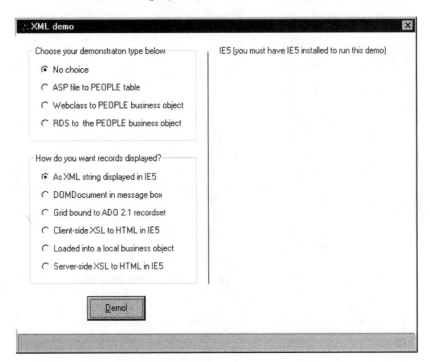

Figure 6.15   Example B user interface

Table 6.1 will help you find the code you may be looking for.

Table 6.1   Source code listing for projects

Type	Returned as	Solution style applied
No choice	N/A	This choice is only there to show all the choices visually; no action is taken
ASP	XML	Returns XML directly from a database by using an ASP HTPRequest call
ASP	DOM	N/A
ASP	ADO	N/A
ASP	Client XSL	Returns XML with an XSL PI, directly from a database, by using an ASP HTTPRequest
ASP	Business object	N/A
ASP	Server XSL	N/A
Webclass	XML	Returns XML directly from a database by using an ASP HTPRequest call
Webclass	DOM	Returns XML from an .xml file by using an ASP HTPRequest call; then at the client, the XML is loaded into a DOMDocument
Webclass	ADO	Returns ADO persisted as XML, then converts XML back to ADO and binds a grid to the ADO
Webclass	Client XSL	Returns XML direct from a database by using an ASP HTPRequest call
Webclass	Business object	Accesses a business object (PeopleBO) and returns XML (the rebuilding on the client-side into a class collection is not built yet)
Webclass	Server XSL	Returns HTML—by transforming an XML file with an XSL file— directly from a database by using an ASP HTPRequest call

Figure 6.16 shows what the project looks like in VB6.

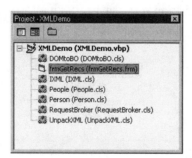

Figure 6.16   Example B XML Demo

For convenience, the collection of classes we use here is the standard output of the class wizard that is in the VB5 and VB6 environment. There are more advanced ways of building collection classes, but we will not discuss them.

In this project, you can see that the classes and the forms are all client-side and contain the files needed to request the data from the web server. Once the data is returned, another class called DOMtoBO will then be used to unpack the XML and—if the application requires it—place the XML into a collection of classes (the People and Person classes).

Also, note that there is a copy of the interface class called IXML on the client. As you saw before, implementing an interface has substantial benefits for standardizing the methods your programs use across the project.

If you build this project, make sure your project has references to the following objects:

- Microsoft XML version 2.0 (or higher)
- Microsoft Scripting Runtime (for the FilesSystemObject)
- Microsoft ActiveX Data Objects 2.1 Library
- Microsoft Internet controls (for the web browser)

Now let's look at the code for the getRecs form.

6.8.1 *The code for getRecs*

The getRecs form is the user interface to this sample project. It provides the user with a series of choices of how they want the sample application to retrieve and display the XML around.

Below, the General Declarations for this form include an enum. An enum is really useful as it ensures that you have a choice of parameters for member list dropdowns when VB6 uses Intellisense to auto-complete your code for you. We also create two objects, objRequestBroker and objDOMtoBO.

```
Option Explicit

'use an enumeration for the option control
'the enumeration number should correspond to the value of the option controls
Private Enum eReturn
    eXML = 0
    eDOM = 1
    eADO = 2
    eXSL = 3
    eBO = 4
    eXSLHTML = 5
End Enum

'use an enumeration for the option control
'the enumeration number should correspond to the value of the option controls
Private Enum eType
    eASP = 0
    eWebclass = 1
```

```
        eRDS = 2
        eNoChoice = 3
End Enum

Private m_objRequestBroker As New RequestBroker
Private m_objDOMtoBO As New DOMtoBO
```

The code below is for the command button called `cmdDemo`, which is on the form `getRecs`. When the users clicks the button, based on the choices they have made, the `objRequestBroker` is requested to return the records in the correct form. The format could be as client-side XSL or any of the other choices.

On the click event of the button `cmdDemo`, the option type that the user has chosen is evaluated, then the object `m_objRequestBroker` is initialized with the correct variables. Then `RunRequestBroker` is called:

```
Private Sub cmdDemo_Click()

    On Error GoTo ErrorHandler

    'set the mouse pointer to true
    Pointer True
    'set the xml displayers to invisible
    grdADODemo.Visible = False
    webTarget.Visible = False

    'if the display button was clicked, but with NONE chosen, do nothing
    If optType(eType.eNoChoice).Value = True Then
        MsgBox "'No choice' is used only to display all the return
            types."
        Pointer False
        Exit Sub
    End If

    'set the status text
    StatusText ("Initializing the RequestBroker")

    'initialize the RequestBroker with the source
    m_objRequestBroker.BO = "PEOPLE"

    'initialize the RequestBroker with the call type
    If optType(eType.eASP).Value = True Then
        m_objRequestBroker.CallType = eCTAsp

    ElseIf optType(eType.eWebclass).Value = True Then
        m_objRequestBroker.CallType = eCTWebClass

    Else  'RDS
        m_objRequestBroker.CallType = eCTRDS
    End If
```

```
'initialize the RequestBroker with the return type
If optReturn(eReturn.eXML) Then
    m_objRequestBroker.ReturnType = eXML

ElseIf optReturn(eReturn.eDOM) Then
    m_objRequestBroker.ReturnType = eDOM

ElseIf optReturn(eReturn.eADO) Then
    m_objRequestBroker.ReturnType = eADO

ElseIf optReturn(eReturn.eXSL) Then
    m_objRequestBroker.ReturnType = eXSL

ElseIf optReturn(eReturn.eBO) Then
    m_objRequestBroker.ReturnType = eBO

Else     'eReturn.eXSLHTML
    m_objRequestBroker.ReturnType = eXSLHTML
End If

'start the RequestBroker
Call RunRequestBroker

Exit Sub

ErrorHandler:

MsgBox "There is an error at source " & Err.Source & " with a description
of " & Chr(13) & Err.Description & Chr(13) & "with the errorcode of "
& Err.Number

Exit Sub

End Sub
```

The load procedure for the form `getRecs` makes sure the web browser embedded in the form doesn't try to connect to the Internet or the local intranet as it starts up. It also pops up a welcome message:

```
Private Sub Form_Load()

On Error GoTo ErrorHandler

    'make sure the browser doesn't try to start up an Internet connection
    webTarget.Offline = True
    'welcome the user - this is not a useful msgbox and can be removed
    MsgBox "This program demonstrates the usefulness of XML for:" &
    Chr(13) & Chr(13) & "1.) The ideal inter-program exchange format
    where the DTD provides the structure for the document.  On any given
    day the structure can change - provided the DTD changes as well,
    any programs using the data will not be risked" & Chr(13) & Chr(13)
```

```
        & "2.) Companies can make their live data available via the Internet
        for sale" & Chr(13) & Chr(13) & "3.)  Data can be retrieved from
        almost any data source"
        'disable the Return option boxes
        Call EnableReturnOptions(False)


    Exit Sub

ErrorHandler:
    MsgBox "There is an error at source " & Err.Source & " with a description
    of " & Chr(13) & Err.Description & Chr(13) & "with the errorcode of "
    & Err.Number
    Exit Sub


End Sub
```

The `RunRequestBroker()` procedure builds a string containing a path to the server and the name of the XML file on the server. Based on the type of return required by the user in `optReturn`, it then calls and receives the XML output back from the already initialized `m_objRequestBroker`. Also depending on the user's choice, either the web browser is used, a grid is used, or a confirmation message is displayed:

```
Private Sub RunRequestBroker()

    Dim adoRst As ADODB.Recordset
    Dim xmlDOM As DOMDocument
    Dim strXML As String
    Dim objPeople As New People
    Dim strPath As String
    Dim strMsg As String

    On Error GoTo ErrorHandler

        strPath = App.Path & "\" & "xmlfromserver.xml"

            'Business object request
            If optReturn(eReturn.eBO).Value = True Then
              'get and then place the XML into the objDOMtBO
              m_objDOMtoBO.XML = m_objRequestBroker.getXML
              'start the conversion to the local business object
              Call m_objDOMtoBO.getPeople(objPeople)
              'check the rudimentary error notification system
              If m_objRequestBroker.Errors = True Then
                  MsgBox "The Request Broker reports that there were errors"
              Else
                 Beep
                 'tell the user it was successful - we cannot display the
                     object
                 grdADODemo.Visible = False
                 webTarget.Visible = False
              End If
            'ADO request
```

```
ElseIf optReturn(eReturn.eADO).Value = True Then
        Set adoRst = m_objRequestBroker.getADO
        'check the rudimentary error notification system
        If m_objRequestBroker.Errors = True Then
           MsgBox "The Request Broker reports that there were errors"
      Else
           'tell the user it was successful and offer to display
             the results bound to a grid
           MsgBox "We have successfully retrieved an ADO recordset from the
             webserver."
           Set grdADODemo.DataSource = adoRst
           grdADODemo.ZOrder
           grdADODemo.Visible = True
      End If

  'DOM request
  ElseIf optReturn(eReturn.eDOM).Value = True Then
      Set xmlDOM = m_objRequestBroker.getDOM
      'check the rudimentary error notification system
      If m_objRequestBroker.Errors = True Then
         MsgBox "The Request Broker reports that there were errors"
        Else
          Beep
            'tell the user it was successful and offer to display the
              results in IE5
            strMsg = "We have successfully retrieved a DOMDocument from
              the webserver" & Chr(13) & Chr(13) & "NOTE: The XML
              displayed below may be truncated" & Chr(13) & Chr(13) & xml-
              DOM.XML
         MsgBox strMsg
        End If

  'XML using XSL request
  ElseIf optReturn(eReturn.eXSL).Value = True Then
      strXML = m_objRequestBroker.getXMLXSLDoEvents
      'check the rudimentary error notification system
      If m_objRequestBroker.Errors = True Then
         MsgBox "The Request Broker reports that there were errors"
       Else
          'tell the user it was successful and offer to display
            the results in a web browser
          Beep
          StatusText ("XML received from server")
          'create temp file
          SaveTextFile strXML, strPath
          DoEvents
          'get browser to display the file
          webTarget.Navigate strPath
          DoEvents
          webTarget.Visible = True
      End If
```

```
'XML request
ElseIf optReturn(eReturn.eXML).Value = True Then
    strXML = m_objRequestBroker.getXML
    'check the rudimentary error notification system
    If m_objRequestBroker.Errors = True Then
        MsgBox "The Request Broker reports that there were errors"
      Else
        'tell the user it was successful and offer to display the
             results in IE5
            Beep
            StatusText ("XML received from server")
            'create temp file
            SaveTextFile strXML, strPath
            'get browser to display the file
            webTarget.Navigate strPath
            webTarget.Visible = True
      End If

'XSL to HTML request
ElseIf optReturn(eReturn.eXSLHTML).Value = True Then
    strXML = m_objRequestBroker.getXSLHTML
    'check the rudimentary error notification system
    If m_objRequestBroker.Errors = True Then
        MsgBox "The Request Broker reports that there were errors"
      Else
        'tell the user it was successful and offer to display the
             results in IE5
            Beep
            StatusText ("XML received from server")
            'create temp file
            SaveTextFile strXML, strPath
            'get browser to display the file
            webTarget.Navigate strPath
            webTarget.Visible = True
      End If
 End If

Pointer False

    StatusText ("Complete")

  Exit Sub

ErrorHandler:

    MsgBox "There is an error at source " & Err.Source & "
    with a description of " & Chr(13) & Err.Description &
    Chr(13) & "with the errorcode of " & Err.Number

  Exit Sub

End Sub
```

This is a simple procedure that can be called from anywhere to set the cursor pointer to an hourglass or default cursor:

```
Private Sub Pointer(PointerOn As Boolean)

    On Error GoTo ErrorHandler

        'manage the mouse pointer
        If PointerOn = True Then
            Me.MousePointer = vbHourglass
        Else
            Me.MousePointer = vbNormal
        End If

    Exit Sub

ErrorHandler:

    MsgBox "There is an error at source " & Err.Source & " with a descrip-
    tion of " & Chr(13) & Err.Description & Chr(13) & "with the errorcode
    of " & Err.Number

    Exit Sub

End Sub
```

This is a simple procedure that can be called from anywhere to set the status bar text to a status message provided by the calling procedures:

```
Private Sub StatusText(Status As String)

    On Error GoTo ErrorHandler

        'set the mousepointer
        Me.stsDemo.SimpleText = Trim(Status)

    Exit Sub

ErrorHandler:

    MsgBox "There is an error at source " & Err.Source & " with a descrip-
    tion of " & Chr(13) & Err.Description & Chr(13) & "with the errorcode
    of " & Err.Number

    Exit Sub

End Sub
```

This function saves the results to a text file so that the browser can be directed to this file and display it:

```
Public Function SaveTextFile(Content As String, FilePath As String) As
  Boolean

    Dim objFSO As New Scripting.FileSystemObject
    Dim objTS As Scripting.TextStream

    On Error GoTo ErrorHandler

        'create a text file using the FileScriptingObject which should in
            the references for this VB project
        Set objTS = objFSO.CreateTextFile(FilePath, True)
        'write the string which has been passed
        objTS.Write Content
        'close the text file
        objTS.Close

        'return true
        SaveTextFile = True

    Exit Function

ErrorHandler:
        MsgBox "There is an error at source " & Err.Source & " with a descrip-
            tion of " & Chr(13) & Err.Description & Chr(13) & "with the errorcode
        of " & Err.Number

    Exit Function

End Function
```

This is a simple procedure to set various choices as visible or hidden, depending on the selection the user has made:

```
Private Sub SetReturnVisible(CallType As eType)

    If CallType = eCTAsp Then
        optReturn(eReturn.eADO).Visible = False
        optReturn(eReturn.eBO).Visible = False
        optReturn(eReturn.eDOM).Visible = False
        optReturn(eReturn.eXML).Visible = True
        optReturn(eReturn.eXSL).Visible = True
        optReturn(eReturn.eXSLHTML).Visible = False
        'set this as the choice
        optReturn(eReturn.eXML).Value = True
        'enable the Return option boxes
        EnableReturnOptions (True)
         ElseIf CallType = eCTRDS Then
        optReturn(eReturn.eADO).Visible = False
        optReturn(eReturn.eBO).Visible = False
        optReturn(eReturn.eDOM).Visible = False
        optReturn(eReturn.eXML).Visible = False
```

```
        optReturn(eReturn.eXSL).Visible = False
        optReturn(eReturn.eXSLHTML).Visible = False
        'enable the Return option boxes
        EnableReturnOptions (True)

        ElseIf CallType = eCTWebClass Then
        optReturn(eReturn.eADO).Visible = True
        optReturn(eReturn.eBO).Visible = False
        optReturn(eReturn.eDOM).Visible = True
        optReturn(eReturn.eXML).Visible = True
        optReturn(eReturn.eXSL).Visible = True
        optReturn(eReturn.eXSLHTML).Visible = True
        'set this as the choice
        optReturn(eReturn.eXML).Value = True
        'enable the Return option boxes
        EnableReturnOptions (True)

    Else  'eNONE
        optReturn(eReturn.eADO).Visible = True
        optReturn(eReturn.eBO).Visible = False
        optReturn(eReturn.eDOM).Visible = True
        optReturn(eReturn.eXML).Visible = True
        optReturn(eReturn.eXSL).Visible = True
        optReturn(eReturn.eXSLHTML).Visible = True
        'disable the Return option boxes
        EnableReturnOptions (False)
    End If

End Sub
```

This is a simple procedure to set various choices as visible when the user clicks the option box:

```
Private Sub optType_Click(Index As Integer)

    'pass the index which also corresponds to the enumeration number
    SetReturnVisible (Index)

End Sub
```

This is a simple procedure to set various choices as enabled or disabled depending on the selection the user has made:

```
Private Sub EnableReturnOptions(Choice As Boolean)

    'enable all Return option boxes
    optReturn(eReturn.eADO).Enabled = Choice
    optReturn(eReturn.eBO).Enabled = Choice
    optReturn(eReturn.eDOM).Enabled = Choice
    optReturn(eReturn.eXML).Enabled = Choice
    optReturn(eReturn.eXSL).Enabled = Choice
    optReturn(eReturn.eXSLHTML).Enabled = Choice

End Sub
```

6.8.2 *The DOMtoBO class code—populating the client-side business object*

In the GUI, for the business object, the code in the RequestBroker() method is:

```
Private Sub RunRequestBroker()

Dim adoRst As ADODB.Recordset
Dim xmlDOM As DOMDocument
Dim strXML As String
Dim objPeople As New People
Dim strPath As String
Dim strMsg As String

On Error GoTo ErrorHandler

strPath = App.Path & "\" & "xmlfromserver.xml"

'business object request
If optReturn(eReturn.eBO).Value = True Then
'get and then place the XML into the objDOMtBO
m_objDOMtoBO.XML = m_objRequestBroker.getXML  ❶
'start the conversion to the local business object
Call m_objDOMtoBO.getPeople(objPeople)  ❷
'check the rudimentary error notification system
If m_objRequestBroker.Errors = True Then
MsgBox "The Request Broker reports that there were errors"
Else
Beep
'tell the user it was successful - we cannot display the object
grdADODemo.Visible = False
webTarget.Visible = False
MsgBox "There are " & objPeople.Count & " BO's returned from
  this XML."
End If
..........
```

❶ The first thing we are doing here is setting the XML string for the DOMtoBO object, which we have received from the server.

❷ Populates this xml string into the local business objects, which are going to use the DOMDocument.

In the following example, we demonstrate how to populate the business objects using the getPeople() method. As this is only an example demonstrating how to implement these business objects, we will not do anything after the business objects are retrieved. In the RequestBroker class, the RunRequestBroker() method calls the DOMtoBO class:

```
Option Explicit
```

```
'local variable(s) to hold property value(s)
Private m_strXML As String
Private m_objDOMPeople As New DOMDocument

Public Sub getPeople(ByVal objPeople As People)

    Dim objPeopleRoot As IXMLDOMElement
    Dim objPersonElement As IXMLDOMElement
    Dim objChildNode As IXMLDOMElement
    Dim strName As String
    Dim strAddress As String
    Dim strTel As String
    Dim strFax As String
    Dim strEmail As String

    Dim i As Integer   'to count in loop & used as key

    On Error GoTo ErrorHandler

    'this can stop the m_objDOMPeople object from looking
    'for external files, which in our case are the people.dtd and the peo-
        ple.xsl
    'files - set this to true if you want the parser to look for the external
        files
    m_objDOMPeople.resolveExternals = False

    'this can stop the m_objDOMPeople from validating the XML file
    'against the people.dtd file - set this to true if you want 'validation
    to occur
    m_objDOMPeople.validateOnParse = True

    'load the XML into the DOMDocument, using a string containing
    'the XML
    Call m_objDOMPeople.loadXML(m_strXML)

    If m_objDOMPeople.parseError.reason <> "" Then
        ' there has been an error with the loaded XML - show the reason
        MsgBox m_objDOMPeople.parseError.reason
    End If

    'get the root element of the XML - bypassing the comments, PI's etc
    Set objPeopleRoot = m_objDOMPeople.documentElement

    'check that there are children for the root node
    If objPeopleRoot.hasChildNodes Then
        'iterate through each element(person)
        'of the root(People)
        For Each objPersonElement In objPeopleRoot.childNodes

            'iterate through each child element(name, address, etc. of
            'the current element(person)
```

```
                    For Each objChildNode In objPersonElement.childNodes
                        Select Case objChildNode.nodeName
                            Case "NAME"
                                strName = objChildNode.nodeTypedValue
                            Case "ADDRESS"
                                strAddress = objChildNode.nodeTypedValue
                            Case "TEL"
                                strTel = objChildNode.nodeTypedValue
                            Case "FAX"
                                strFax = objChildNode.nodeTypedValue
                            Case "EMAIL"
                                strEmail = objChildNode.nodeTypedValue
                        End Select
                    Next
                    'add this info to a new business object
                    objPeople.Add CStr(i), strName, strAddress, strTel, strFax, _
                            strEmail, CStr(i)
                    i = i + 1
                Next
            Else
                MsgBox "There is no data for this XML file"
            End If

    'set reference of all used object to Null
    Set objPeopleRoot = Nothing
    Set objPersonElement = Nothing
    Set objChildNode = Nothing

    Exit Sub
    ErrorHandler:
        MsgBox "There is an error at source " & Err.Source & " with a description
        of " & Chr(13) & Err.Description & Chr(13) & "with the errorcode of "
        & Err.Number
        Exit Function

    End Sub
    Public Property Let XML(ByVal vData As String)
        m_strXML = vData
    End Property

    Public Property Get XML() As String
        XML = m_strXML
    End Property

    Public Property Get PeopleDOM() As DOMDocument
        Set PeopleDOM = m_objDOMPeople
    End Property
```

Loading data into the DOMDocument

```
'this can stop the m_objDOMPeople object from looking
'for external files, which in our case are the people.dtd and the peo-
    ple.xsl
'files - set this to true if you want the parser to look for the external
    files
m_objDOMPeople.resolveExternals = False

'this can stop the m_objDOMPeople from validating the XML file
'against the people.dtd file - set this to true if you want 'validation
    to occur
m_objDOMPeople.validateOnParse = True

'load the XML into the DOMDocument, using a string containing
'the XML
Call m_objDOMPeople.loadXML(m_strXML)
```

We have turned off the `resolveExternals` property because version 2 of the Microsoft XML DOM had a bug when there were external files associated with the `loadXML()` method.

To load the string of XML data from the server, we need to use the `loadXML()` method. If you have a file anywhere, such as passing across the Internet or on the server, then you should use the `load()` method and pass its URI name or file name as a string.

Getting to the XML data

```
'get the root element of the XML - bypassing the comments, PI's etc
Set objPeopleRoot = m_objDOMPeople.documentElement
```

In the code above, the object `objPeopleRoot` has been declared as a `IXML-DOMElement` object, which will contain a collection of `childNodes` for each `<PERSON>...</PERSON>`element in the following XML file:

```
<PERSON>
  <NAME>Mark Wilson</NAME>
  <ADDRESS>911 Somewhere Circle, Canberra, Australia</ADDRESS>
  <TEL>(++612) 12345</TEL>
  <FAX>(++612) 12345</FAX>
  <EMAIL>Mark.Wilson@somewhere.com</EMAIL>
</PERSON>
```

Therefore we will iterate through each `<PERSON>` element to get to the data.

Iterating through the elements

```
'check that there are children for the root node
If objPeopleRoot.hasChildNodes Then
    'iterate through each element(person)
```

```
                      'of the root(People)
                      For Each objPersonElement In objPeopleRoot.childNodes

                          'iterate through each child element(name, address, etc. of
                          'the current element(person)
                          For Each objChildNode In objPersonElement.childNodes
                              Select Case objChildNode.nodeName
                                  Case "NAME"
                                      strName = objChildNode.nodeTypedValue
                                  Case "ADDRESS"
                                      strAddress = objChildNode.nodeTypedValue
                                  Case "TEL"
                                      strTel = objChildNode.nodeTypedValue
                                  Case "FAX"
                                      strFax = objChildNode.nodeTypedValue
                                  Case "EMAIL"
                                      strEmail = objChildNode.nodeTypedValue
                              End Select
                          Next
```

We only have two levels of elements here, the `<PERSON>` elements and one level of child Nodes (`<NAME></NAME>`, `<ADDRESS></ADDRESS>`, etc.). Therefore we only require two loops for extracting the data using the `For Each()` method:

```
For Each objPersonElement In objPeopleRoot.childNodes
```

The object `objPersonElement` has been defined as an `IXMLDOMElement` object, which iterates through the `objPersonElement.childNodes` property, which is the iterating interface called `IXMLDOMNodeList`. Therefore, we can use this `For Each` loop.

The same applies for the `objChildNode` object. Here we iterate through each child Node of the element Node. We simply hard-code the values from each Node into a string, which will populate the business objects.

6.8.3 *The People and Person class*

Before we can explain how to create the business object, we must first explain the People and Person class. These classes were created using the VB add-in *Class Builder Utility*.

Figures 6.17 and 6.18 show the Collection builder in the Class Builder Utility and Class Builder Utility Add-in, respectively. In VB, open the add-in and click on the *Add new collection* icon. This displays a screen asking you to insert all the relevant details for the class, like:

`People` for the collection name
`Person` for the new class

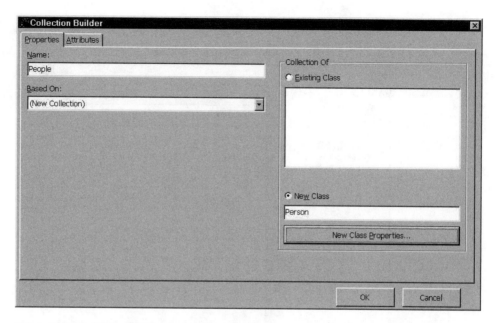

Figure 6.17 **Collection builder in the Class Builder Utility**

After pressing *OK*, you will be back in the Class Builder screen. Now to your Person class, add its properties and method.

Now your business object classes have been created. Let's proceed to how we add our business objects once we have the XML string.

Creating a new business object

After we have added our properties to our Person object, we must add this object to the People class. This is done in the following way:

```
'add this info to a new business object
objPeople.Add CStr(i), strName, strAddress, strTel, strFax,
 strEmail, CStr(i)
```

Inside the collection class, Person, this Add() method has been created, which will create a new Person business object.

The object objPeople is passed in by reference. Therefore any changes made to it will be changed in the front end. This changed object is therefore returned back to the frmGetRecs.

There you go; your business objects are created and returned from an XML file.

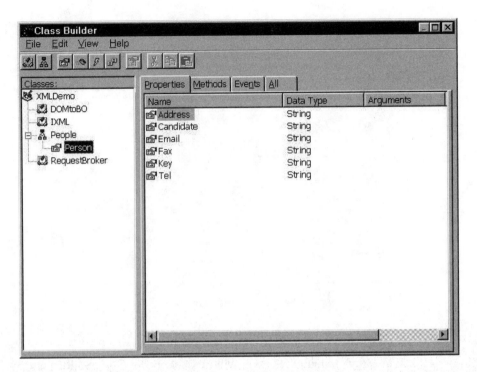

Figure 6.18   Class Builder Utility

6.9 *Summary*

As we mentioned earlier, we are not dealing with attribute or entities here, so there is still quite a bit of scope that can be added to this code.

Creating these business objects using collection classes seems to be the recognized way to create business objects in VB. We wanted to show you this recognized method of collection classes for creating business objects, but IMHO is not the most reusable method. If you compare this collection class code to the server code in the DBToXML project, you will see that the DBToXML project makes use of generic and reusable code by using interfaces (i.e., the implementation of IBO and IXML).

Personally we would use the same interfaces (IXML and IBO) in this project, which would need to be refined to suit the client side, and still use the DOMDocument to extract the data. We would then create an Iterator (enumeration) class, which would allow us to easily iterate (loop) through the business objects. Perhaps we would store the DOMDocument in the iterator, as it has useful methods of easily finding the data. For example, the DOMDocument's `nodeFromID()` method finds a Node with an id when we have used attributes for storing our ID's. This would replace storing the business objects in a collection when looping through the iterator. The `IBO` interface would be used in the Iterator class code so that it could work with any business object that has implemented this interface.

The Microsoft DOM
objects in detail

What this chapter covers:

- Descriptions of the Microsoft XML objects
- Sample code for most of the methods and properties
- Easy-reference table guide to the objects

7.1 Overview

Microsoft has shipped some very useful objects with IE5 that can be used from any programming language that can make use of COM objects. In this part of the book, we will focus on the XML DOM objects using VB or VBScript.

To better under-
stand code or
descriptions of the
DOMDocument,
try to think of an
XML document
as a tree. Another
useful analogy is
to think of
parents and
their children.

To better understand code or descriptions about the DOM, try to think of an XML document as a tree. Another useful analogy is to think of parents and their children. We start with the actual root of the document, then it meanders down to each processing instruction, the document root element, attributes, etc. These objects in the DOM are known by there own type (e.g., Element, Attribute, etc.), but each type is generally called a *Node*. The DOM gives us collections objects as well, known as `NodeLists` when a parent has many children that need to be grouped. Figure 7.1 describes how the tree structure is implemented:

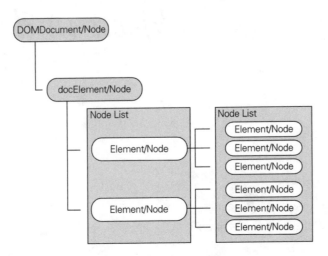

Figure 7.1   Nodes and NodeLists in the DOM Object

This chapter,
while comprehen-
sive, should not be
used as a com-
plete reference.

The XML DOM Object implements the XML DOM interfaces. These interfaces make reusability throughout the DOM practical. Because these two objects share the same interfaces, the code becomes easier to understand and work with, which we will see in a short while.

7.2 DOM objects

First we need to explain the various, common DOM objects that you will use with the MSXML DOM Object.

We will focus on the examples of these XML DOM objects shown in table 7.1.

Table 7.1   XML DOM Objects

Object name	Description
DOMDocument	This object represents the root of the XML file.
XMLDOMElement	This object represents each element in the DOM-Document, namely the root, root element, and each other element.
XMLDOMNode	This object represents a single Node in the document tree and includes support for data types, namespaces, DTDs, and XML Schemas.
XMLDOMNodeList	Use this object to access (by name) and iterate through the XMLDOMNode collection.
XMLDOMNamedNodeMap	Use this object to access and iterate through the attributes in an element.
XMLDOMCDATASection	This object represents a section in the value of an element that is closed in the CDATA section brackets, which are characters that cannot be parsed by the XML.
XMLDOMAttribute	This object represents a single attribute Node for a given element.
XMLDOMDocumentType	This object represents the Document Type (DTD) in an XML file.
XMLDOMEntity	This object represents an entity in the DTD section of the XML file.
XMLDOMProcessingInstruction	This object represents a processing instruction found in the XML file.
XMLDOMParseError	This object returns detailed information about the last error, including the line number, character position, and a text description.
XMLHTTPRequest	This object enables you to establish a connection to a web server from your code and send put, get, and other standard HTML requests.

In our examples, we will refer to these objects using the names listed in table 7.2.

Table 7.2   XML object naming conventions

XML object interface	Our naming convention
DOMDocument	objDOMDocument
XMLDOMNode	objXMLDOMNode
XMLDOMNodeList	objXMLDOMNodeList

Table 7.2 XML object naming conventions (continued)

XMLDOMNodeListMap	objXMLDOMNodeListMap
XMLDOMParseError	objXMLDOMParseError
XMLDOMElement	objXMLDOMElement
XMLDOMAttribute	objXMLDOMAttribute

7.2.1 DOMDocument

The DOMDocument object represents the root of the XML file. As the file is loaded into the DOMDocument, the XML file and its external references, such as DTDs, get validated by the DOMDocument.

The DOMDocument is the first *port of call* to the XML file. This is the only object that can be created. All the other objects, like the elements, can only be created or accessed from the DOMDocument object.

Example

This example loads an XML file into a DOMDocument object:

```
Dim objDOMDocument As DOMDocument

Set objDOMDocument = New DOMDocument
objDOMDocument.async = False
objDOMDocument.Load "http://mark/xmlcode/people2.dtd"
```

7.2.2 XMLDOMElement

This object represents each element in the XML tree. The XMLDOMElement includes support for manipulating the element and the attributes associated with the element.

The attributes associated with an element are added and manipulated via the XMLDOMElement object.

Example

The following example returns the root element of the XML file from a DOMDocument:

```
Dim objDOMDocument As DOMDocument
Dim objXMLDOMElement As IXMLDOMElement
Set objDOMDocument = New DOMDocument
objDOMDocument.async = False
objDOMDocument.Load "http://mark/xmlcode/people2.dtd"

Set objXMLDOMElement = objDOMDocument.documentElement
```

7.2.3 *XMLDOMNode*

This is one of the base objects of the DOM. Most of the other DOM objects inherit this object; therefore, you will see a lot of properties and methods repeated in each of these objects.

These objects are:

- DOMDocument
- XMLDOMAttribute
- XMLDOMCDATASection
- XMLDOMComment
- XMLDOMDocumentFragment
- XMLDOMDocumentType
- XMLDOMElement
- XMLDOMEntity
- XMLDOMEntityReference
- XMLDOMNotation
- XMLDOMProcessingInstruction
- XMLDOMText
- XTLRuntime

Although all these objects inherit methods and properties from the XMLDOMNode object, they will all also have properties and methods that are unique to their function. For example, the XMLDOMElement object has extra methods for obtaining attribute information. The XMLDOMNode interface provides just the basic information, like the name of the Node, its text, etc.

To know which type of Node is currently being accessed, the nodeType property returns which type of Node you are referencing when using the XMLDOMNode object, which is explained in detail later in this chapter under the nodeType property.

Also, see the docType property for more information on *Dual interfaces*. This explains how to cast from one type of object to the other.

Example

The following example is the same as the example from the XMLDOMElement, except it now uses the XMLDOMNode object to return the root element of the XML file from a DOMDocument.

```
Dim objDOMDocument As DOMDocument
Dim objXMLDOMElement As IXMLDOMNode

Set objDOMDocument = New DOMDocument
objDOMDocument.async = False
```

```
objDOMDocument.Load "http://mark/xmlcode/people2.dtd"
```

```
Set objXMLDOMNode = objDOMDocument.documentElement
```

7.2.4 *XMLDOMNodeList*

The `XMLDOMNodeList` object is a collection of Nodes. Its methods allow us to iterate through all the children Nodes of a Node. You can use the `For Each … Next` loop for this iteration. However, you can also choose to iterate through these Nodes using its method of `nextNode()`.

This object is returned in the property, such as `childNodes`, or methods such as `getElementsByTagName()` and `selectNodes()`.

Example

The following example uses the `childNodes` property of the DOMDocument to return the children Nodes of the root element of the DOMDocument. (For more details see the `childNodes` property, which also shows an example of how to iterate through the `XMLDOMNodeList` collection.)

```
Dim objDOMDocument As DOMDocument
Dim objXMLDOMNodeList As IXMLDOMNodeList

Set objDOMDocument = New DOMDocument
objDOMDocument.async = False
objDOMDocument.Load "http://mark/xmlcode/people2.dtd"
```

```
Set objXMLDOMNodeList = objDOMDocument.documentElement.childNodes
```

7.2.5 *XMLDOMNamedNodeMap*

This is the other collection object in the DOM. It is used to iterate through the attributes for a specific element. It also allows you to manipulate the attribute collection for an element. To name a few, methods include `getNamedItem()`, `removeNamedItem()`, etc. The `XMLDOMNamedNodeMap` also supports namespaces as well.

Example

The following example returns the number of attributes found in the root element of a DOM object.

```
Dim objDOMDocument As DOMDocument
Dim objXMLDOMNamedNodeMap As IXMLDOMNamedNodeMap

Set objDOMDocument = New DOMDocument
objDOMDocument.async = False
objDOMDocument.Load "http://mark/xmlcode/people2.dtd"
Set objXMLDOMNamedNodeMap = objDOMDocument.documentElement.Attributes
MsgBox "The number of attribute are " & objXMLDOMNamed-
  NodeMap.length
```

7.2.6 *XMLDOMCDATASection*

The XMLDOMCDATASection object represents the content that is inserted in your XML between the CDATA section brackets, ![...]].

An XML example is:

```
<ADDRESS><![CDATA[#911 Somewhere Circle, Canberra, Australia]]></ADDRESS>
```

The XMLDOMCDATASection object inherits methods and properties from the XMLDOMText object; therefore, you will find the XMLDOMCDATASection object as a child Node of an XMLDOMText object. The parent XMLDOMText object will parse the contents of the CDATA section and return the full element text without the brackets. (See the nodeType property later in this chapter for more details on and examples of the CDATA section.)

7.2.7 *XMLDOMAttribute*

The XMLDOMAttribute object represents an attribute for an element. Attributes are properties of an element, thus not really children of an element. As mentioned in the XMLDOMNamedNodeMap object, the collection of attributes for an element are returned in the XMLDOMNamedNodeMap object, which returns an XMLDOMAttribute object (or an XMLDOMNode object, as it inherits the XMLDOMNode interface).

The attributes are usually defined in the DTD or Schema of the XML file.

Example

In the following example we get an attribute object from the first child of the root element object, using the attributes name (which was defined in the DTD) to return the attribute object.

```
Dim objDOMDocument As DOMDocument
Dim objXMLDOMElement As IXMLDOMElement
Dim objXMLDOMAttribute As IXMLDOMAttribute

Set objDOMDocument = New DOMDocument
objDOMDocument.async = False
objDOMDocument.Load "http://mark/xmlcode/people2.dtd"

Set objXMLDOMElement = objDOMDocument.documentElement.firstChild
Set objXMLDOMAttribute = objXMLDOMElement.getAttribute-
  Node("PERSONID")
```

7.2.8 *XMLDOMDocumentType*

The XMLDOMDocumentType object contains information on all the entities and notations in a declared DTD of the XML file. This object is only found as a property, called the docType, of the DOMDocument object. This object and its properties are read-only. Therefore, you cannot add a DTD to a DOMDocument; it has to already have been declared in the XML file. You cannot add anything to the declared DTD for the XML file either.

Example

On our website, vbxml.com, there were quite a few discussions on how to add a DTD to a DOMDocument. With the current version of the msxml.dll, there was a bug if you added a DTD in a string and then used the loadXML() method.

The following example returns an XMLDOMDocumentType from the DOMDocument. We have added another line of code, `objDOMDocument.resolveExternals = True`, which is needed in order to instruct the DOMDocument to notice any external files associated with this XML file.

```
Dim objDOMDocument As DOMDocument
Dim objXMLDOMDocumentType As IXMLDOMDocumentType

Set objDOMDocument = New DOMDocument
objDOMDocument.async = False
objDOMDocument.resolveExternals = True
objDOMDocument.Load "http://mark/xmlcode/people2.xml"

Set objXMLDOMDocumentType = objDOMDocument.doctype
```

7.2.9 *XMLDOMEntity*

In your DTD file, you declare entities for *constants* that you want to use in your XML file.

For more information on entities, see chapter 2, "XML boot camp."

In XML, five built-in entities (known as predefined entities) exist that all parsers can decipher (see table 7.3). Many parsers can automatically read more entities than these five, but the DOMDocument object currently only recognizes these five. The rest need to be defined in your DTDs.

Table 7.3 Built-in entities that the DOMDocument automatically parses

Entity reference	Character that is represented
&amp;	& – ampersand
&apos;	' – apostrophe
&gt;	> – greater than
&lt;	< – less than
&quot;	" – double quote

The `XMLDOMEntity` object represents an entity in the `childNodes` property of the `docType` (DTD) property of the DOMDocument. So, if you want to find out what has been declared as entities in the DTD, just search through the child Nodes of the `XMLDOMDocument` object.

As mentioned above for the XMLDOMDocumentType object, you cannot add an entity declaration to the DTD in an XML file, as the XMLDOMDocumentType object is read-only.

7.2.10 *XMLDOMProcessingInstruction*

Any processing instruction found in an XML file is returned as an XMLDOMProcessingInstruction object. Therefore, it's good practice to check the type of Node that you are working with, in case one of these PIs or comments pop up. For example, this PI has been added in between an element:

```
<PERSON id="p1">
  <?realaudio version="4.0"?>
  <NAME>Mark Wilson</NAME>
  <ADDRESS>911 Somewhere Circle, Canberra, Australia</ADDRESS>
  <TEL>(++612) 12345</TEL>
  <FAX>(++612) 12345</FAX>
  <EMAIL>markwilson@somewhere.com</EMAIL>
</PERSON>
```

The same issue applies to comments in your XML file. They are represented as Nodes as well.

As the XMLDOMProcessingInstruction object is writable, you can add a PI to a DOMDocument (see the nodeType property later in this chapter).

7.2.11 *XMLDOMParseError*

If the DOMDocument finds any errors when it parses the XML file or string, the XMLDOMParseError object returns the last parse error details. The details that are passed are the line number where the error occurred, the character position on the line, the reason, etc.

The XMLDOMParseError object is the only object that the DOMDocument inherits. Therefore, you never really need to access it, because it's part of the DOMDocument properties.

Example

The following example checks whether there have been any errors after an XML file has been loaded into a DOMDocument:

```
Dim objDOMDocument As DOMDocument
Dim objXMLDOMElement As IXMLDOMElement

Set objDOMDocument = New DOMDocument
objDOMDocument.async = False
objDOMDocument.Load "http://mark/xmlcode/people2.dtd"

If objDOMDocument.parseError.reason <> "" Then
```

```
' there has been an error with the loaded XML - show
the reason
   MsgBox objDOMDocument.parseError.reason
End If
```

7.2.12 *XMLHTTPRequest*

The XMLHTTPRequest object provides methods that enable you to establish a connection to a file or an object on a web server, such as an ASP page. The two major methods are open() to make the connection and send() to send your request. There are also properties that can be used to read the response: responseText, responseStream, responseXML, and responseBody.

Example

The following example makes a connection with an ASP page. The web page then prepares the XML and returns it. The XMLHTTPRequest property called reposonseXML can be used to access that XML.

```
Dim objXMLHttp As New XMLHTTPRequest
Dim objDOMDocument As DOMDocument

objXMLHttp.Open "POST", "http://mark/xmlcode/demo.asp", False  ❶

objXMLHttp.Send  ❷
Set objDOMDocument= objXMLHttp.responseXML  ❸
```

❶ Open the POST (or GET) connection to the web server.

❷ Establish the connection.

❸ Receive the response.

7.3 *DOM object properties*

These are some of the properties we think would be useful in the context of this book. The descriptions below are limited to our needs and, while being detailed they may not fully describe the capabilities of each object. More complete descriptions can be read from the documentation or on the Microsoft website.

The listing below is a list of all the properties for all of the XMLDom objects. Use this chart when you need to find a property in one of the interfaces that could be useful for something that you are trying accomplish. The properties that are bolded in table 7.4 are the ones that we will explain. As mentioned before, they have been selected because they are properties and methods we think would be useful in the context of this book.

Table 7.4 DOMDocument properties

Properties	DOMDocument	XMLDOMNode	XMLDOMNodeList	XMLDOMNamedNodeMap	XMLDOMAttribute	XMLDOMCDATASection	XMLDOMComment	XMLDOMDocumentFragment	XMLDOMDocumentType	XMLDOMElement	XMLDOMEntity	XMLDOMEntityReference	XMLDOMImplementation	XMLDOMNotation	XMLDOMParseError	XMLDOMProcessingInstruction	XMLDOMText	XTLRuntime	XMLHTTPRequest
async																			
attributes		✓			✓	✓	✓	✓	✓	✓	✓	✓		✓		✓	✓	✓	
baseName	✓	✓			✓	✓	✓	✓	✓	✓	✓	✓		✓		✓	✓	✓	
childNodes	✓	✓			✓	✓	✓	✓	✓	✓	✓	✓		✓		✓	✓	✓	
data					✓	✓										✓	✓		
dataType	✓	✓			✓	✓	✓	✓	✓	✓	✓	✓		✓		✓	✓	✓	
definition	✓	✓			✓	✓	✓	✓	✓	✓	✓	✓		✓		✓	✓	✓	
doctype	✓																		
document-Element	✓																		
entities									✓										
errorCode															✓				
filepos															✓				
firstChild	✓	✓			✓	✓	✓	✓	✓	✓	✓	✓		✓		✓	✓	✓	
implementation	✓																		
item			✓	✓															
lastChild	✓	✓			✓	✓	✓	✓	✓	✓	✓	✓		✓		✓	✓	✓	
length			✓	✓	✓	✓												✓	
line															✓				
name					✓				✓										
namespace-URI	✓	✓			✓	✓	✓	✓	✓	✓	✓	✓		✓		✓	✓	✓	
nextSibling	✓	✓			✓	✓	✓	✓	✓	✓	✓	✓		✓		✓	✓	✓	
nodeName	✓	✓			✓	✓	✓	✓	✓	✓	✓	✓		✓		✓	✓	✓	

Table 7.4 DOMDocument properties (continued)

nodeType	✓	✓			✓	✓	✓	✓	✓	✓	✓	✓		✓		✓	✓	✓	
nodeTypedValue	✓	✓			✓	✓	✓	✓	✓	✓	✓	✓		✓		✓	✓	✓	
nodeType-String	✓	✓			✓	✓	✓	✓	✓	✓	✓	✓		✓		✓	✓	✓	
nodeValue	✓	✓			✓	✓	✓	✓	✓	✓	✓	✓		✓		✓	✓	✓	
notations									✓										
notationName										✓									
ondata-available	✓																		
onreadystatechange	✓																		✓
ontransform-node	✓																		
owner-Document	✓	✓			✓	✓	✓	✓	✓	✓	✓	✓		✓		✓	✓	✓	
parentNode	✓	✓			✓	✓	✓	✓	✓	✓	✓	✓		✓		✓	✓	✓	
parsed	✓	✓			✓	✓	✓	✓	✓	✓	✓	✓		✓		✓	✓	✓	
parseError	✓																		
prefix	✓	✓			✓	✓	✓	✓	✓	✓		✓		✓			✓	✓	
preserve-WhiteSpace	✓																		
previous-Sibling	✓	✓			✓	✓	✓	✓	✓	✓	✓	✓		✓		✓	✓	✓	
publicId											✓			✓					
readyState	✓																		✓
reason															✓				
resolve-Externals	✓																		
responseBody																			✓
response-Stream																			✓
responseText																			✓
responseXML																			✓
specified	✓	✓			✓	✓	✓	✓	✓	✓	✓	✓		✓		✓	✓	✓	
srcText															✓				
status																			✓
statusText																			✓
systemId											✓			✓					
tagName									✓										

Table 7.4 DOMDocument properties (continued)

target														✓			
text	✓	✓		✓	✓	✓	✓	✓	✓	✓	✓		✓		✓	✓	✓
url	✓													✓			
validateOnParse	✓																
value				✓													
xml	✓	✓		✓	✓	✓	✓	✓	✓	✓	✓		✓		✓	✓	✓

Note: Boldface properties are explained in this chapter

We will use the People2.xml file example for the rest of this chapter. This file's source is:

```
<?xml version="1.0"?>
<!-- *********** Resumes for People *********** -->
<!DOCTYPE PEOPLE SYSTEM "http://mark/xmlcode/people.dtd">
<PEOPLE>
  <PERSON PERSONID="p1">
    <NAME>Mark Wilson</NAME>
    <ADDRESS>911 Somewhere Circle, Canberra, Australia</ADDRESS>
    <TEL>(++612) 12345</TEL>
    <FAX>(++612) 12345</FAX>
    <EMAIL>markwilson@somewhere.com</EMAIL>
  </PERSON>
  <PERSON PERSONID="p2">
    <NAME>Tracey Wilson</NAME>
    <ADDRESS>121 Zootle Road, Cape Town, South Africa</ADDRESS>
    <TEL>(++2721) 531 9090</TEL>
    <FAX>(++2721) 531 9090</FAX>
    <EMAIL>Tracey Wilson@somewhere.com</EMAIL>
  </PERSON>
  <PERSON PERSONID="p3">
    <NAME>Jodie Foster</NAME>
    <ADDRESS>30 Animal Road, New York, USA</ADDRESS>
    <TEL>(++1) 3000 12345</TEL>
    <FAX>(++1) 3000 12345</FAX>
    <EMAIL>Jodie Foster@somewhere.com</EMAIL>
  </PERSON>
  <PERSON PERSONID="p4">
    <NAME>Lorrin Maughan</NAME>
    <ADDRESS>1143 Winners Lane, London, &UK;</ADDRESS>
    <TEL>(++94) 17 12345</TEL>
    <FAX>++94) 17 12345</FAX>
    <EMAIL>Lorrin Maughan@somewhere.com</EMAIL>
  </PERSON>
  <PERSON PERSONID="p5">
```

```
        <NAME>Steve Rachel</NAME>
        <ADDRESS>90210 Beverly Hills, California, &USA;</ADDRESS>
        <TEL>(++1) 2000 12345</TEL>
        <FAX>(++1) 2000 12345</FAX>
        <EMAIL>Steve Rachel@somewhere.com</EMAIL>
    </PERSON>
</PEOPLE>
```

7.3.1 *async*

Is a member of:	DOMDocument

Syntax

```
blnValue = objDOMDocument.async
objDOMDocument.async = blnValue
```

Remark

The `async` property indicates or sets a boolean as to whether the XML document is downloaded asynchronously or synchronously. This should be set before loading the XML document, if you do not want to use the default.

The default for this property is set to `True`. This default is important to remember when dealing with the `load()` method of the DOMDocument, as it will load your information asynchronously. Therefore, as your DOMDocument is busy loading the XML, your VB code will continue to run without waiting for the documents to finish loading.

If you have set your DOMDocument to run asynchronously (or have forgotten to change it to *false*), it will then proceed to call another method afterwards, like:

```
Set objPeopleRoot = m_objDOMPeople.documentElement
```

This will cause an *object has not been set* error. This happens because the DOM-Document has not yet completed loading, and you are trying to access it. Therefore, before calling the `load()` method, don't forget to set the `async` property to `False`, if you want your XML document to be loaded synchronously.

Example

```
Dim objDOMDocument As DOMDocument
Dim objXMLDOMElement As IXMLDOMElement

Set objDOMDocument = New DOMDocument
objDOMDocument.async = False
objDOMDocument.Load "http://mark/xmlcode/people2.dtd"
```

The other approach is to use the `WithEvents` language statement in order to expose the event that come with the DOMDocument. Within these events, you can catch when the document has completed loading.

For a more detailed example of using `WithEvents` and the async method, see the section on *Loading a file asynchronously* in chapter 4, "Programming with XML."

7.3.2 Attributes

Is a member of:	DOMDocument XMLDOMNode XMLDOMAttribute XMLDOMCDATASection XMLDOMComment XMLDOMDocumentFragment XMLDOMDocumentType XMLDOMElement XMLDOMEntity XMLDOMEntityReference XMLDOMNotation XMLDOMProcessingInstruction XMLDOMText XTLRuntime

Syntax

```
set objXMLDOMNamedNodeMap = objDOMDocument.attributes
```

Remark

For more infor-
mation on
attributes, see
chapter 2, "XML
boot camp."

This property returns an `XMLDOMNamedNodeMap` object, which contains a collection of the attributes for this Node. The `XMLDOMNamedNodeMap` is an XML interface specifically designed for working with attributes.

Example

A common practice is to use attributes to store the ID (using the ID attribute type) from a database, which is declared in the DTD as:

```
<!ELEMENT PERSON ( NAME, ADDRESS, TEL, FAX, EMAIL ) >  ❶
<!ATTLIST PERSON PERSONID ID #REQUIRED>  ❷
```

❶ Declaring our Person element will contain the following elements (tags).
❷ The person element has an ID attribute called "PERSONID," which is always required.

In our XML example, this attribute is used as follows:

```
<PERSON PERSONID="p1">  ❶
  <NAME>Mark Wilson</NAME>
  <ADDRESS>911 Somewhere Circle, Canberra, Australia</ADDRESS>
  <TEL>(++612) 12345</TEL>
  <FAX>(++612) 12345</FAX>
  <EMAIL>markwilson@somewhere.com</EMAIL>
</PERSON>
```

❶ For this element, its ID attribute equals "p1."

In the following example in VB, we are busy populating the TreeView with data from a DOMDocument. We then want to store the PERSONID attribute in the tag property of the TreeView Node:

```
'the element Node is holding the id attribute that we want
'to store in the tag, as an identity reference.  We
'therefore need to get hold of this Node to get its value
Set objAttributes = objNode.Attributes  ❶

'check that there are attributes.
If objAttributes.length > 0 Then

    'we know that we've named our id reference as
    ''PERSONID', therefore tell the NameNodeListMap to get
    'this Node by using the getNamedItem method
    Set objAttributeNode = objAttributes.getNamedItem
       ("PERSONID")  ❷

    'store this value in the tag of the TreeView
    tvwElement.Tag = objAttributeNode.nodeValue
End If
```

❶ Get the attributes from the current Node (PERSON Node).
❷ getNamedItem only returns a single Node (IXMLDOMNode), because we have to specify that it must return the "PERSONID" attribute, of which there can only be one per element.

Read the sections on getNamedItem(), setNamedItem(), and nextNode() further in this chapter to learn more about working with attributes in the DOMDocument.

7.3.3 *childNodes*

Is a member of:	DOMDocument XMLDOMNode XMLDOMAttribute XMLDOMCDATASection XMLDOMComment XMLDOMDocumentFragment XMLDOMDocumentType XMLDOMElement XMLDOMEntity XMLDOMEntityReference XMLDOMNotation XMLDOMProcessingInstruction XMLDOMText XTLRuntime

Syntax

```
set objXMLDOMNodeList = objXMLDOMNode.childNodes
```

Remark

This property is read-only. The `childNodes` property returns the `IXMLDOMNodeList` collection object of the child Nodes for the parent object. Each Node that is returned from the child Node, may have `childNodes` themselves, which is consistent with the tree metaphor that the DOMDocument uses.

Example

```
Dim objDOMDocument As DOMDocument
Dim objXMLDOMNodeList As IXMLDOMNodeList
Set objDOMDocument = New DOMDocument
objDOMDocument.async = False
objDOMDocument.Load "http://mark/xmlcode/people2.dtd"

Set objXMLDOMNodeList = objDOMDocument.documentElement.childNodes
```

For the following explanations, we will use this XML example:

```
<?xml version="1.0" ?>
<!-- ********** Resumes for People ********** -->
<!DOCTYPE PEOPLE SYSTEM "http://mark/xmlcode/people.dtd">
<PEOPLE>
<PERSON id="1">
  <NAME>Mark Wilson</NAME>
  <ADDRESS>911 Somewhere Circle, Canberra, Australia</ADDRESS>
  <TEL>(++612) 12345</TEL>
  <FAX>(++612) 12345</FAX>
 <EMAIL>markwilson@somewhere.com</EMAIL>
```

```
</PERSON>
<PERSON id="2">
  <NAME>Tracey Wilson</NAME>
  <ADDRESS>121 Zootle Road, Cape Town, South Africa</ADDRESS>
  <TEL>(++2721) 531 9090</TEL>
  <FAX>(++2721) 531 9090</FAX>
  <EMAIL>Tracey Wilson@somewhere.com</EMAIL>
</PERSON>
</PEOPLE>
```

Common uses of the childNode property are:

- the child Node of the DOMDocument root consists of the processing instructions, DTDs, etc.
- the child Node of the root element consists of all the data in the DOMDocument
- the child Node of the `attributes` property of an element consists of the collection of attributes for the given element

What's so good about the childNodes property?

- Because the `childNodes` property is an `XMLDOMNodeList` collection, it is easy to iterate through, to collect the data.
- You can use the `XMLDOMNode` object to iterate through the `XMLDOMNodeList` collection, as it receives most of the other type of interfaces. See later in this section, *"Iterating through the childNodes."*

Getting the childNodes from the root of the DOMDocument

Here we look for the child Nodes of the actual root of the complete DOMDocument. To get these child Nodes from VB, our code would read:

```
set objXMLDOMNodeList = objDOMDocument.childNodes
```

This will return the four child Nodes shown in figure 7.2.

You might have noticed that we have specified the `Nodetypes` returned from each child Node. Please see the `nodeType` property for more details on these types of Nodes.

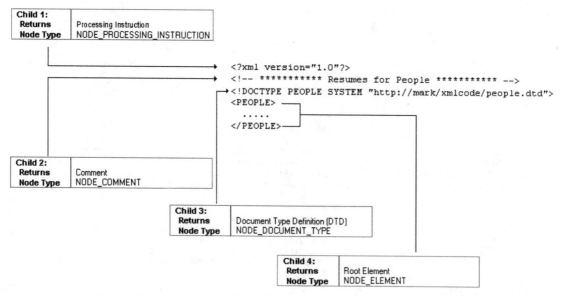

Figure 7.2 Returned childNodes from the DOMDocument root

Getting the childNodes from the documentElement element of the DOMDocument

This property returns all the Nodes associated with root Node, which is found in the documentElement property of the DOMDocument (i.e., all the PERSON's in the PEOPLE element). To get the childNodes from VB, our code would read:

```
set objXMLDOMNodeList = objDOMDocument.document-Element.childNodes
```

From our example, two child Nodes will be returned in this NodeList object, as shown in figure 7.3.

Getting all the childNodes from a single element

We now want to return all the elements between each section:

```
<PERSON PERSONID="p2">
   ...
</PERSON
```

This returns the NAME, ADDRESS, TEL, etc. This is the base of the child Nodes, but even these childNodes can once again iterate down to more childNodes, if they themselves have children.

In the following XML example, the child Node of Mark Wilson is Male:

```
<PERSON PERSONID="p2">
    <NAME>Mark Wilson</NAME>
        <GENDER>Male</GENDER>
    <ADDRESS>
    ...
</PERSON>
```

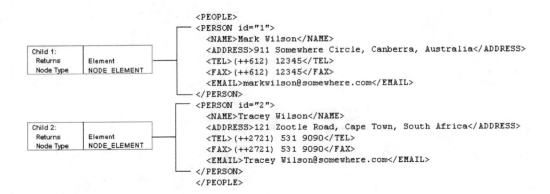

Figure 7.3   Returned childNodes from the DOMDocument root element

In our main example in table 7.5, there are five child Nodes found for each Person element, as shown in figure 7.4.

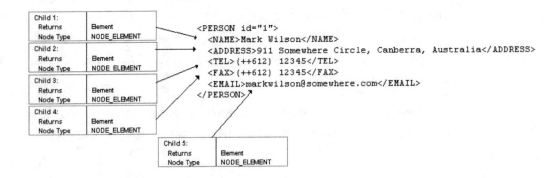

Figure 7.4   Returned childNodes from an element

Iterating through the childNodes

Because an `IXMLDOMNodeList` collection is returned from the `childNodes` property, you can iterate through each item using a `for each ... next` loop. Here we

demonstrate looping through the collection of child Nodes returned from the
documentElement property:

```
For Each objNode In objDOMDocument.document-Element.child-Nodes ❶
    populateTreeWithChildren objNode
Next
```

❶ The objNode has been declared as an IXMLDOMElement.

Note that an XMLDOMNodeList object is returned even if there are no children of
the Node. In such a case, the length of the list will be set to zero. To get the length
of the XMLDOMNodeList, use:

```
if objPeopleRoot.length > 0 then
  ...
end if
```

7.3.4   *data*

Is a member of:	XMLDOMCDATASection XMLDOMComment XMLDOMProcessingInstruction XMLDOMText

Syntax

```
strValue = objXMLDOMComment.data
objXMLDOMComment.data = strValue
```

Remark

This property is readable and writable. Depending on the type of Node, it returns
the same value as the nodeValue property. Please see the nodeValue property for
more details.

Example

```
Dim objDOMDocument As DOMDocument
Dim objXMLDOMNode As IXMLDOMNode
Dim objXMLDOMPI As IXMLDOMProcessingInstruction

Set objDOMDocument = New DOMDocument
objDOMDocument.async = False
objDOMDocument.Load "http://mark/xmlcode/people2.xml"
For Each objXMLDOMNode In objDOMDocument.childNodes
  If objXMLDOMNode.nodeType = NODE_PROCESSING_INSTRUCTION Then ❶
    Set objXMLDOMPI = objXMLDOMNode ❷
    MsgBox "The PI is : " & objXMLDOMPI.Data ❸
  End If
Next
```

❶ Check that the nodeType is a Processing Instruction.

❷ Cast the PI object from the Node object.

❸ Retrieve the PI's text using the data property, which from our XML example, returns version="1.0."

7.3.5 *docType*

Is a member of:	XMLDOMDocument

Syntax

```
set objXMLDOMNode = objXMLDOMNode.docType
set objXMLDOMDocumentType = objXMLDOMNode.docType
```

Remark

This property is read-only.

The docType is the DTD Node in the XML header. One problem that you may come across when using the DOMDocument is that you might like to add a DTD to your DOMDocument. However, because this property is read-only, you can't add a DTD and an error will occur.

So how does one get around adding a DTD to an XML file? You may think that you can just populate a string that will build up an XML file, which you can do. However, please read about the DOMDocument bug under the loadXML() method, which also explains a solution to this problem.

Example

The following XML code defines a DTD for the XML file:

```
<!DOCTYPE PEOPLE SYSTEM "http://mark/xmlcode/people.dtd">
```

This VB example shows that a DocumentType object or a Node object is returned from the docType property of the DOMDocument root:

```
Dim objDOMDocument As DOMDocument
Dim objXMLDOMDocumentType As IXMLDOMDocumentType

Set objDOMDocument = New DOMDocument
objDOMDocument.async = False
objDOMDocument.resolveExternals = True
objDOMDocument.Load "http://mark/xmlcode/people2.xml"

Set objXMLDOMDocumentType = objDOMDocument.doctype
```

Dual interfaces

What you may also have noticed in the properties syntax code example above is that the `doctype` property is being used to return values to two different objects. Take another look:

```
set objXMLDOMNode = objXMLDOMNode.docType
set objXMLDOMDocumentType = objXMLDOMNode.docType
```

The values are being *set*, which means an actual object is being passed.

If objectA and objectB are two totally different objects, how then can you `set objA = objC` and *also* `set objB = objC`? In other words, how can you place `objC` into the two *fundamentally different* objects of `objA` and `objB`?

This is one of our first examples of an object being able to return two interfaces. The `docType` property evidently implements two different interfaces. One of these is applicable to `objXMLDOMNode`, and the other to `objXMLDOMDocumentType`. This is because the `XMLDOMDocumentType` object inherits the `objXMLDOMNode` object. We can have a closer look at this.

Let's have a look at the *Local View* window in Visual Basic. This screen appears under the Tools/Local View menu and shows the local variable details. Under the Type section, you can see that this object returns the `IXMLDOMDocumentType` interface and the `IXMLDOMNode` interface. Therefore, you can use either interface to read this Node, depending on the type of interface you choose to use (whichever properties/methods you need to work with).

However, if you look in Visual Basic's Object Browser (press the F2 key to see the object browser), you will find that this object only returns the `IXMLDOMDocument-Type`. Figure 7.5 shows the `IXMLDOMDocumentType` interface in the Object Browser.

While we talk about the `docType` property, the `attributes` property of `IXMLDOMDocument` and `IXMLDOMNode` returns the actual URI of the DTD.

If you look closer at the `docTypes` child Node property, you will find a collection of the entities for the DTD.

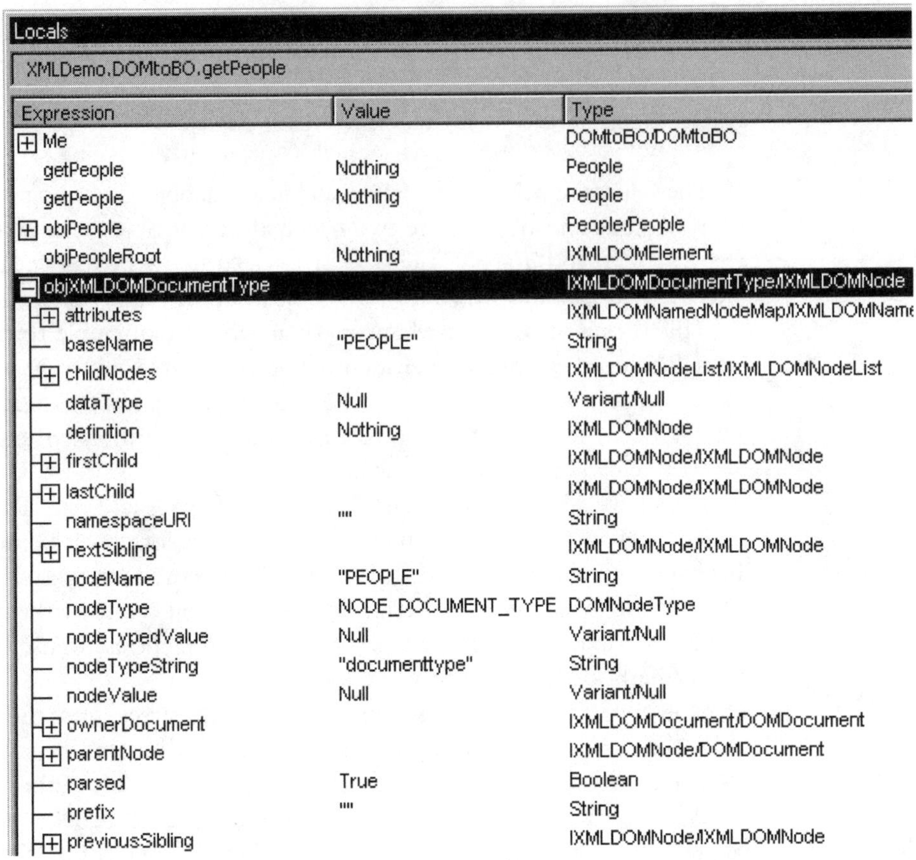

Locals		
XMLDemo.DOMtoBO.getPeople		
Expression	**Value**	**Type**
⊞ Me		DOMtoBO/DOMtoBO
getPeople	Nothing	People
getPeople	Nothing	People
⊞ objPeople		People/People
objPeopleRoot	Nothing	IXMLDOMElement
⊟ objXMLDOMDocumentType		IXMLDOMDocumentType/IXMLDOMNode
⊞ attributes		IXMLDOMNamedNodeMap/IXMLDOMName
— baseName	"PEOPLE"	String
⊞ childNodes		IXMLDOMNodeList/IXMLDOMNodeList
— dataType	Null	Variant/Null
— definition	Nothing	IXMLDOMNode
⊞ firstChild		IXMLDOMNode/IXMLDOMNode
⊞ lastChild		IXMLDOMNode/IXMLDOMNode
— namespaceURI	""	String
⊞ nextSibling		IXMLDOMNode/IXMLDOMNode
— nodeName	"PEOPLE"	String
— nodeType	NODE_DOCUMENT_TYPE	DOMNodeType
— nodeTypedValue	Null	Variant/Null
— nodeTypeString	"documenttype"	String
— nodeValue	Null	Variant/Null
⊞ ownerDocument		IXMLDOMDocument/DOMDocument
⊞ parentNode		IXMLDOMNode/DOMDocument
— parsed	True	Boolean
— prefix	""	String
⊞ previousSibling		IXMLDOMNode/IXMLDOMNode

Figure 7.5   Local View in VB of XMLDOMDocumentType

7.3.6   *documentElement*

Is a member of:	XMLDOMDocument

Syntax

```
set objXMLDOMElement = objDOMDocument.documentElement
set objXMLDOMNode = objDOMDocument.documentElement

set objDOMDocument.documentElement = objXMLDOMElement
set objDOMDocument.documentElement = objXMLDOMNode
```

Remark

This property is read-only.

Objects, objects, objects!! If you just want to get to the nitty-gritty and find the XML data in an XML document, this is the property for you! This is the *root element* of your XML (not the root).

Its child Node collection returns all the elements, which we have explained in detail for the `childNodes` property.

Once again, this property returns two interface types, namely `IXMLDOMElement` and `IXMLDOMNode`. As you read more about the other properties and methods later in this chapter, you can decide which interface you prefer to work with when viewing and manipulating your XML data.

If there is no root element, then Null is returned.

Example

```
Dim objDOMDocument As DOMDocument
Dim objXMLDOMElement As IXMLDOMElement

Set objDOMDocument = New DOMDocument
objDOMDocument.async = False
objDOMDocument.Load "http://mark/xmlcode/people2.dtd"
```

Set objXMLDOMElement = objDOMDocument.documentElement

7.3.7   firstChild, lastChild, nextSibling, and previousSibling

Is a member of:	DOMDocument
	XMLDOMNode
	XMLDOMAttribute
	XMLDOMCDATASection
	XMLDOMComment
	XMLDOMDocumentFragment
	XMLDOMDocumentType
	XMLDOMElement
	XMLDOMEntity
	XMLDOMEntityReference
	XMLDOMNotation
	XMLDOMProcessingInstruction
	XMLDOMText
	XTLRuntime

Syntax

```
set objXMLDOMNode = objDOMDocument.firstChild
set objXMLDOMNode = objDOMDocument.lastChild
set objXMLDOMNode = objDOMDocument.nextSibling
set objXMLDOMNode = objDOMDocument.previousSibling
```

Remark

These properties are read-only.

These properties allow us to read the values of the first Node, last Node, etc., from the current Node.

Example

Perhaps one only wants to get the first child of all the elements for an XML file. Therefore, in the following example, we know that we want to populate a text box with the Name and Address from our People2.xml example.

```
Dim objDOMDocument As DOMDocument
Dim objXMLDOMNodeList As IXMLDOMNodeList
Dim objXMLDOMNode As IXMLDOMNode
Dim strInfo As String

Set objDOMDocument = New DOMDocument
objDOMDocument.async = False
objDOMDocument.Load "http://mark/xmlcode/people2.dtd"

Set objXMLDOMNodeList = objDOMDocument.documentElement.childNodes

For Each objXMLDOMNode In objXMLDOMNodeList   ❶
   strInfo = strInfo & objXMLDOMNode.firstChild.text & vbCrLf   ❷
   strInfo = strInfo & objXMLDOMNode.nextSibling.text & vbCrLf & vbCrLf   ❸
Next

txtInfo.text = strInfo
```

❶ Iterate through the collection of elements in the NodeList object.

❷ The firstChild we know is going to return the Name element.

❸ The nextSibling returns the address element.

7.3.8 length

Is a member of:	XMLDOMNodeList
	XMLDOMNamedNodeMap
	XMLDOMComment
	XMLDOMText

Syntax

```
lngValue = objXMLDOMNodeList.length
```

Remark

This property is read-only.

Depending on the DOM object, the `length` property is used as follows:

For the XMLDOMNodeList and XMLDOMNamedNodeMap interfaces, the length property specifies the number of child Nodes in its collection. We use this property often to verify that an object has been loaded properly, by checking if the length property of the object is greater than zero.

For the XMLDOMComment and XMLDOMText interfaces, the length property returns the number of characters in the body of the Node.

Example

XMLDOMNodeList and XMLDOMNamedNodeMap Objects

In this example, we test the length to see if a DOMDocument has loaded properly. If the length is greater than zero, then we can proceed with the rest of the code for working with the DOMDocument object.

```
Dim objDOMDocument As DOMDocument
Dim objNode As IXMLDOMNode

Set objDOMDocument = New DOMDocument
objDOMDocument.async = False
objDOMDocument.Load "http://mark/xmlcode/people2.dtd"

If objDOMDocument.childNodes.length > 0 Then  ❶
   'run rest of code here
End If
```

❶ Our code has loaded the XML from our main example. The length returns 4, as there are 4 childNodes for this DOMDocument.

7.3.9 *namespaceURI*

Is a member of:	DOMDocument XMLDOMNode XMLDOMAttribute XMLDOMCDATASection XMLDOMComment XMLDOMDocumentFragment XMLDOMDocumentType XMLDOMElement XMLDOMEntity XMLDOMEntityReference XMLDOMNotation XMLDOMProcessingInstruction XMLDOMText XTLRuntime

Syntax

```
strValue = objDOMDocument.namespaceURI
```

Remark

This property is read-only. If a namespace has been specified in the XML document, this property returns a string of the location of the URI. As this property is read-only, you cannot add a namespaceURI to a DOMDocument.

Example

In the following example, we checking if the namespaceURI has been set for the DOMDocument.

```
Dim objDOMDocument As DOMDocument

Set objDOMDocument = New DOMDocument
objDOMDocument.async = False
objDOMDocument.Load http://mark/xmlcode/people2.dtd
If objDOMDocument.namespaceURI <> "" then  ❶
   'run some code here …
End If
```

❶   No namespaceURI has been set for this DOMDocument.

7.3.10   nodeName

Is a member of:	
	DOMDocument
	XMLDOMNode
	XMLDOMAttribute
	XMLDOMCDATASection
	XMLDOMComment
	XMLDOMDocumentFragment
	XMLDOMDocumentType
	XMLDOMElement
	XMLDOMEntity
	XMLDOMEntityReference
	XMLDOMNotation
	XMLDOMProcessingInstruction
	XMLDOMText
	XTLRuntime

Syntax

```
strValue = objDOMDocument.nodeName
```

Remark

This property is read-only. Depending on the type of Node, this property returns a string containing the Node's name. This is especially useful with elements and attributes. Table 7.5 details what is being represented by the `nodeName` property for the different interfaces of the DOMDocument.

Table 7.5   Return values for the different XMLDOM interfaces

Interface name	Return value
XMLDOMElement	The name of the element tag is returned, without the tag indicators (`</>`). XML Example: `<EMAIL>markwilson@somewhere.com</EMAIL>` Returns: EMAIL When dealing with namespaces, the full tag name is returned. XML Example: `<resume:EMAIL>markwilson@somewhere.com</resume:EMAIL>` Returns: resume:EMAIL
XMLDOMAttribute	The name of the element is returned. XML Example: `<PERSON PERSONID="p1">` Returns: PERSONID
XMLDOMProcessingInstruction	The target of the processing instruction is returned. This is the first word after the '`<?`' indicators. XML Example: `<?xml version="1.0" ?>` Returns: xml
XMLDOMEntityReference	The name of the entity that is being references is returned, stripping off the entity reference indicators, namely the "&;". XML Example: `<ADDRESS>`30 Animal Road, New York, **&USA;**`</ADDRESS>` Returns: USA
XMLDOMEntity	The name of the entity is returned. XML Example: `<!ENTITY USA "United States of America">` Returns: USA
XMLDOMDocumentType	The name of the document type (DTD) is returned. XML Example: `<!DOCTYPE PEOPLE SYSTEM "http://mark/xmlcode/people.dtd">` Returns: PEOPLE
XMLDOMNotation	The name of the notation is returned. XML Example: `<img src="http://mark/xmlcode/vbdev.gif">` Returns: img

The Node types listed in table 7.6 do not have nodeNames; therefore, they return the following string literals of what is being referenced.

Table 7.6   Return values for XMLDOM interfaces with no nodeNames

Interface name	Return value
XMLDOMText	#text
XMLDOMComment	#comment
XMLDOMCDATASection	#cdata-section
XMLDOMDocument	#document
XMLDOMDocumentFragment	#document-fragment

Example

When we want to populate the textboxes on a VB form, we use the `nodeName` property to work with a `Select Case` as the decider of which text box should be populated.

In the following example, we have already obtained a reference to an element, which in this case is the PERSON element from our main XML example. We are now looping through its child Nodes, differentiating which Node is current by its nodeName property.

```
For Each objChildElement In objPersonElement.childNodes
   If objChildElement.nodeType = NODE_ELEMENT Then
     Select Case UCase(objChildElement.nodeName)
     Case "NAME"
         txtName.Text = objChildElement.nodeTypedValue
     Case "ADDRESS"
         txtAddress.Text = objChildElement.nodeTypedValue
     Case "TEL"
         txtTel.Text = objChildElement.nodeTypedValue
     Case "FAX"
         txtFax.Text = objChildElement.nodeTypedValue
     Case "EMAIL"
         txtEmail.Text = objChildElement.nodeTypedValue
     End Select
   End If
Next objChildElement
```

7.3.11   nodeType

Is a member of:	DOMDocument XMLDOMNode XMLDOMAttribute XMLDOMCDATASection XMLDOMComment XMLDOMDocumentFragment XMLDOMDocumentType XMLDOMElement XMLDOMEntity XMLDOMEntityReference XMLDOMNotation XMLDOMProcessingInstruction XMLDOMText XTLRuntime

Syntax

```
objDOMNodeTypeEnum = objDOMDocument.nodeType
lngType = objDOMDocument.nodeType
```

Remark

This property is read-only.

Each Node will have a nodeType enumeration (enum) property to distinguish what type of Node we are currently working with. Knowing the Node type also determines whether the Node will have child Nodes.

Example

In each section, we mention what child Node types each Node type can have. Each Node type has its own interface; for example, NODE_ELEMENT uses the XML-DOMElement. However, as mentioned earlier, we will not discuss each one of these interfaces.

In the following example, we iterate through the child Nodes of the DOMDocument. Depending on what type of Node it its, using the nodeType property, we display a message box of what its type is.

```
Dim objDOMDocument As DOMDocument
Dim objNode as IXMLDOMNode

Set objDOMDocument = New DOMDocument
objDOMDocument.async = False
objDOMDocument.Load http://mark/xmlcode/people2.dtd

If objDOMDocument.length > 0 then

   For Each objNode In objDOMDocument.childNodes
      Select Case objNode.nodeType
         Case NODE_DOCUMENT_TYPE
            MsgBox "This is the dtd"
         Case NODE_ELEMENT
            MsgBox "This is an element"
```

```
        Case NODE_PROCESSING_INSTRUCTION
                MsgBox "This is a processing instruction"
        End Select
    Next objNode
End If
```

You may have noticed that we used an IXMLDOMNode object (objNode) for iterating through the collection of child Nodes in the DOMDocument. This is because most of the XML objects inherit the IXMLDOMNode interface. Due of this, you can cast the object into the preferred interface once you have assessed what type of Node you are dealing with.

For example, if your nodeType for your object is NODE_DOCUMENT_TYPE, then you can cast it like this:

```
set objXMLDOMDocumentType = objNode
```

Now you can work with a declared IXMLDOMDocumentType object and use its properties and methods. Let's look more closely at the different nodeTypes.

The 12 Node types

Table 7.7 lists the 12 Node types.

Table 7.7   The 12 Node types

Name	Enumeration number
NODE_ELEMENT	(1)
NODE_ATTRIBUTE	(2)
NODE_TEXT	(3)
NODE_CDATA_SECTION	(4)
NODE_ENTITY_REFERENCE	(5)
NODE_ENTITY	(6)
NODE_PROCESSING_INSTRUCTION	(7)
NODE_COMMENT	(8)
NODE_DOCUMENT	(9)
NODE_DOCUMENT_TYPE	(10)
NODE_DOCUMENT_FRAGMENT	(11)
NODE_NOTATION	(12)

Now let's look at each type in a bit more detail.

NODE_ELEMENT

Has an interface type of:	IXMLDOMElement
Can have the following children types:	Element Text Comment ProcessingInstruction CDATASection EntityReference

This `nodeType` specifies an element Node in the XML file.
Here is an example of an element in the XML code:

```
<PEOPLE> ... </PEOPLE>
```

This is also an example of an element in the XML code:

```
<TEL>(++) 61 2 12345</TEL>
```

The following XML code includes all the elements you can find in our DOMDocument:

```
<PEOPLE>  ❶
<PERSON id="p1">  ❷
  <NAME>Mark Wilson</NAME>  ❸
  <ADDRESS>911 Somewhere Circle, Canberra, Australia</ADDRESS>  ❹
  <TEL>(++612) 12345</TEL>  ❺


<FAX>(++612) 12345</FAX>  ❻
  <EMAIL>markwilson@somewhere.com</EMAIL>  ❼
</PERSON>
...
</PEOPLE>
```

❶ This element is returned by the documentElement property.

❷ This element is a childNode of PEOPLE.

❸ This element is the first childNode of PERSON.

❹ Second childNode of PERSON.

❺ Third childNode of PERSON.

❻ Fourth childNode of PERSON.

❼ Fifth childNode of PERSON.

NODE_ATTRIBUTE

Has an interface type of:	XMLDOMAttribute
Can have the following children types:	Text EntityReference

This `nodeType` specifies an attribute Node in the XML file. For more information on attributes, see the `attributes` property of this section, as well as chapter 4, "Programming with XML."

Our XML will read as follows:

```
<PERSON PERSONID="1"> ❶
```

❶ PERSONID="1" is the attribute.

In order to work with the XML file, these attributes need to be declared in the DTD file or a section of the XML file, which looks like:

```
<!ATTLIST PERSON PERSONID ID #REQUIRED> ❶
```

❶ In this example, an "id" type attribute declaration, which must exist for each Person element in the XML file as an id type attribute, is declared as "#REQUIRED."

NODE_TEXT

Has an interface type of:	XMLDOMText
Can have the following children types:	None

This `nodeType` specifies a text Node in the XML file. A text Node can appear as the child Node of Attribute, DocumentFragment, Element, and EntityReference Nodes. It never has any child Nodes.

In the following XML example, the highlighted text will be the value in a text Node:

```
<ADDRESS>911 Somewhere Circle, Canberra, Australia</ADDRESS> ❶
```

❶ The highlighted text is the Node text.

If you are working with an Element Node type, then you actually don't need to iterate down to its child Node to get the text of the element. You can just use the node-TypeValue property of the element Node. This will give you its text value, whether it contains a CDATA section, entities, or whatever.

However, there are a few tricks. The next Node type we will explain is the CDATA section. If your Node happens to be of this type, it will be represented as a CDATA section Node and not a text Node, even though it looks like a text Node. So, if you are looking for the text Node of an element Node, don't forget to look for the CDATA section Node as well.

NODE_CDATA_SECTION

Has an interface type of:	XMLDOMCDATASection
Can have the following children types:	None

Sometimes you will want to insert unusual characters in your XML Nodes. To do this, you need to use a CDATA section (also known as a Marked section).

Yes, we know that you can also use built-in entities instead of a CDATA section, but there are currently only five of these built-in entities that the DOMDocument will parse. (See the XMLDOMEntity object section earlier in this chapter.)

But built-in entities don't sort out all our problems. What do we do about a hash character (#)? An XML parser does not allow you to use a # character in your XML, but there is no DOMDocument built-in entity for a # character.

Note Built-in entities are like VB constants, but they are built into XML. Because XML has certain characters that are used specifically for XML (like a < character), you can use the entity to represent your character.

Here we talk specifically about what the DOMDocument can parse. Many browsers support numerous entities that they recognize, but the DOMDocument seems to support only these five built-in entities.

To use a CDATA section this in our XML code, instead of declaring an element in the DTD as CDATA element, we can use the following in our XML code:

```
![CDATA[]]
```

Here is an example of an element that uses a CDATA section with a # in it:

```
<ADDRESS><![CDATA[#911 Somewhere Circle, Canberra, Australia]]></ADDRESS>
```

Note If you do a Select Case in VB to find the enumeration of a Node, using the NODE_TEXT you will miss the text that is put into CDATA sections to protect reserved characters. Therefore, don't forget to look for NODE_CDATA_SECTION in your Select Case.

A CDATA section Node can be the child Node of Elements, EntityReferences, and DocumentFragments.

If you try to use an Entity in a CDATA section, the entity will not be parsed, and therefore not interpreted. For example the following XML code is embedded in a CDATA section:

```
<ADDRESS><![CDATA[#911 O&apos;Hara Circle, Canberra, Australia]]></ADDRESS>
```

Did you note the **'** entity? The ' entity represents an ' (apostrophe) and we would expect the output to display *O' Hara Circle,* wouldn't we? However, this will not be interpreted as O'Hara Circle, because the text is contained in CDATA section and won't be parsed. When we examine the above XML code from VB, using the `nodeTypedValue` property to get the value of the element, we observe the following:

```
strValue = objXMLElement.nodeTypedValue  ➊
```

➊ strValue returns: #911 O'Hara Circle, Canberra, Australia.

Note   When you allow users to add data to a DOMDocument, don't forget to check for any unparsable characters. Embed these unparsable characters in a CDATA section before saving the DOMDocument. If you do not this, when someone has typed in an apostrophe in one of the fields (e.g., O'Mally), the DOMDocument will save this and return no errors. However, when you try to load this saved XML file into the DOMDocument, you will receive an error because of this unparsable character.

NODE_ENTITY_REFERENCE

Has an interface type of:	XMLDOMEntityReference
Can have the following children types:	Element ProcessingInstruction Comment Text CDATASection EntityReference

This Node specifies a reference to an entity (see the next section on the Entity Node).

In the DTD file, we specify the entity as:

```
<!ENTITY USA   "United States of America">
```

In the XML file, the following code in an element Node will have two child Nodes, one a text Node and the other an EntityReference:

```
<ADDRESS>30 Animal Road, New York, &USA;</ADDRESS>
```

In the DOMDocument, the XML example above can be extracted, for the element, as follows:

First child Node

```
strValue = objXMLElement.childNodes(1).nodeTypedValue  ❶
enumType = objXMLElement.childNodes(1).nodeType  ❷
```

❶ Returns: strValue = "30 Animal Road, New York."

❷ Returns: enumType = NODE_TEXT.

Second child Node

```
strValue = objXMLElement.childNodes(2).Text  ❶
enumType = objXMLElement.childNodes(2).nodeType  ❷
```

❶ Returns: strValue = "United States of America."

❷ Returns: enumType = NODE_ENTITY_REFERENCE.

However, why have we changed from using the `nodeTypedValue` property in the first child to using the text value in the second child? It's because we are dealing with two different Node types. Therefore, depending on your Node type, you get the data you need to access different properties. See the `nodeTypedValue` and `nodeValue` in this section for more information on this.

Note If you only want to get the value of the element Node, you don't have to go through this long procedure to get the value. You only have to do this if you specifically want to analyze the EntityReference Node, for example.

The following XML code specifies an entity "&USA;":

```
<ADDRESS>30 Animal Road, New York, &USA;</ADDRESS>
```

In the DOMDocument, you can get straight to finding its parsed value from the element Node:

```
strValue = objXMLElement.nodeTypedValue  ❶
```

❶ Returns: strValue = "30 Animal Road, New York, United States of America."

NODE_ENTITY

Has an interface type of:	XMLDOMEntity
Can have the following children types:	Text EntityReference

As mentioned earlier, an entity can only be *specified* in the DTD section or file, and not in the XML file. Therefore, entities will always be child Nodes of the DocumentType Node (see the docType property in this section).

An example of entities in the DTD is:

```
<!ENTITY USA    "United States of America">
<!ENTITY UK     "United Kingdom">
```

As you can see in figure 7.6, there are two child Nodes (Item 1 and Item 2) for the docType property of this object.

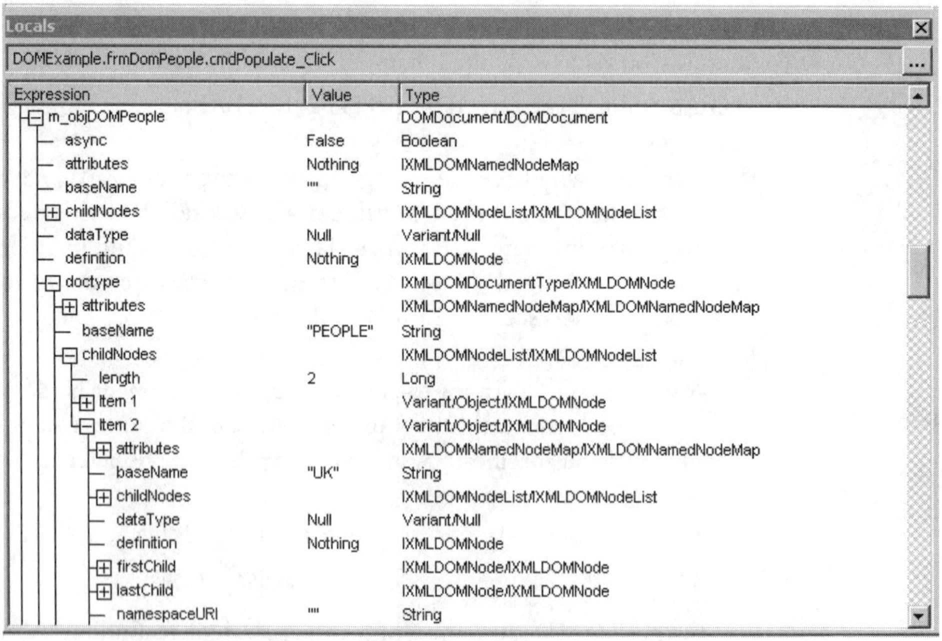

Figure 7.6   ChildNodes property of the docType in the VB Local Views window

From our DTD sample code above, the DOMDocument's `docType` child-Nodes property has two child Nodes. Our `nodeName` property for the first child Node of `nodeType` `NODE_ENTITY` is *USA*. This Node consists of one child Node, which is of the type `NODE_TEXT`. However, as you might have noticed, you can reference the text property—this will give you the same value as the child Node, without having to iterate to the child Nodes.

Although they are referenced (`NODE_ENTITY_REFERENCE` Node types) later in the XML file, among the elements, the parser will automatically handle expanding these entities—unless it's in a CDATA section, which we have explained in the `NODE_CDATA_SECTION` in this section.

NODE_PROCESSING_INSTRUCTION

Has an interface of:	XMLDOMProcessingInstructor
Can have the following children types:	None

This type of Node specifies a PI in the XML document. Processing Instructions are declared in the XML file as:

```
<?xml version="1.0" ?>
```

PIs can be found as part of the `childNodes` property in Document, DocumentFragment, Element, and EntityReference Nodes. Therefore, don't be deceived—they are not only found as the PI at the header of a document.

We could easily put the following XML code, "`<?realaudio version="4.0"?>`", among our elements, which would cause no harm to the DOMDocument. This will return six child Nodes for the PERSON element. The realaudio PI is returned as a PI Node (and in case you were wondering, the parser will ignore it completely).

```
<PERSON id="p1">
  <?realaudio version="4.0"?>
  <NAME>Mark Wilson</NAME>
  <ADDRESS>911 Somewhere Circle, Canberra, Australia</ADDRESS>
  <TEL>(++612) 12345</TEL>
  <FAX>(++612) 12345</FAX>
  <EMAIL>markwilson@somewhere.com</EMAIL>
</PERSON>
```

NODE_COMMENT

Has an interface type of:	XMLDOMComment
Can have the following children types:	None

This Node is a comment. Comments can be inserted anywhere, so this is another Node to be aware of when iterating through a Node collection. It's good practice to check the type of Node that you are working with, in case PIs or comments pop up. The following XML example includes a comment about this person's address that someone inserted.

```
<PERSON id="p1">
   <!-- Person not available for another contract until September -->
   <NAME>Mark Wilson</NAME>
   <ADDRESS>911 Somewhere Circle, Canberra, Australia</ADDRESS>
   <TEL>(++612) 12345</TEL>
   <FAX>(++612) 12345</FAX>
   <EMAIL>markwilson@somewhere.com</EMAIL>
</PERSON>
```

In the following VB example, we iterate through our child Nodes for an element. For this example, we only want to check for Element, Comments, or PI Nodes. The nodeType property enables us to do this check.

```
For Each objNode In objElement.childNodes
    Select Case objNode.nodeType
       Case NODE_COMMENT
            'Do something to handle comments
       Case NODE_ELEMENT
            'Do something to handle elements
       Case NODE_PROCESSING_INSTRUCTION
            'Do something to handle PI's
    End Select
    Next objNode
```

NODE_DOCUMENT

Has an interface type of:	XMLDOMDocument
Can have the following children types:	Element ProcessingInstruction Comment DocumentType

This Node type specifies that this Node is the document object, which is the root of the whole document. There can only be one document Node per XML file. In the following example, we load a DOMDocument from an XML file:

```
Dim objDOMDocument As DOMDocument

Set objDOMDocument = New DOMDocument
objDOMDocument.async = False
objDOMDocument.Load http://mark/xmlcode/people2.dtd  ❶
```

❶ If all is fine with our XML code, we now have a loaded DOMDocument.

In this example, if you look at the objDOMDocument's nodeType property, you will see that it's a NODE_DOCUMENT type Node.

Of its childNodes, the Element Node type can only consist of one element (who in itself has child Nodes), as there is only one root element (see the documentElement property for a detailed explanation and example of this Node).

NODE_DOCUMENT_TYPE

Has an interface type of:	XMLDOMDocumentType
Can have the following children types:	Notation Entity

This Node type specifies that this is the DTD Node, which is represented in the XML code as:

```
<!DOCTYPE PEOPLE SYSTEM "http://mark/xmlcode/people.dtd">
```

For a more detailed explanation of the DocumentType Node, see the docType property in this section.

NODE_NOTATION

Has an interface type of:	XMLDOMNotation
Can have the following children types:	None

This is a notation Node. These notations can only be declared in the document type declaration, just like the Entity type Node. Therefore, it will only be found as a child of the Document type Node.

An example of a notation is when we want to tell the browser how to include an image or realaudio or whichever type of file; we can then specify the following:

```
<img src="http://mark/xmlcode/vbdev.gif">
```

7.3.12 nodeTypedValue

Is a member of:	DOMDocument XMLDOMNode XMLDOMAttribute XMLDOMCDATASection XMLDOMComment XMLDOMDocumentFragment XMLDOMDocumentType XMLDOMElement XMLDOMEntity XMLDOMEntityReference XMLDOMNotation XMLDOMProcessingInstruction XMLDOMText XTLRuntime

Syntax

```
vntValue = objXMLDOMElement.nodeTypedValue
```

Remark

In VB's object browser, its description of this propery is: property *get the strongly typed value of the node*. For an element Node, it returns a variant datatype of the contents of the Node. If you're working with an attribute Node, you will only get the value of *attribute*, which does not return much value. (See `nodeValue` for working with attribute Nodes.)

If you have used a Schema in your XML, which does not have a datatype specified for the element in the Schema, a string value datatype is the default datatype returned. Otherwise, it returns the data in the specified datatype value. This is the main strength of this property.

When working with an element Node, you could also use the `Text` property to get the value of a Node. It's a matter of preference.

Example

You cannot use the nodeTyped-Value *property to set the value of a Node, as it will return a runtime error. You need to use the text property to do this.*

In the following example, after loading our DOMDocument, we want to get the value of the first child's value of the first element (firstChild) of the root element (documentElement), using the nodeTypedValue property:

```
Dim objDOMDocument As DOMDocument
Dim objXMLDOMElement As IXMLDOMElement
Dim strFirstValue As String

Set objDOMDocument = New DOMDocument
objDOMDocument.async = False
objDOMDocument.Load "http://mark/xmlcode/people2.dtd"

Set objXMLDOMElement = objDOMDocument.documentElement.first-Child  ❶
strFirstValue = objXMLDOMElement.firstChild.nodeTypedValue  ❷
```

❶ Get the root Node's first child element.

❷ From the first child of the root Node, get the first child of that element. This returns "Mark Wilson" from our main XML example.

7.3.13 nodeTypeString

Is a member of:	DOMDocument
	XMLDOMNode
	XMLDOMAttribute
	XMLDOMCDATASection
	XMLDOMComment
	XMLDOMDocumentFragment
	XMLDOMDocumentType
	XMLDOMElement
	XMLDOMEntity
	XMLDOMEntityReference
	XMLDOMNotation
	XMLDOMProcessingInstruction
	XMLDOMText
	XTLRuntime

Syntax

```
strValue = objXMLDOMNode.nodeTypeString
```

Remark

The nodeTypeString returns the nodeType of the current Node in a string. This can be used instead of the nodeType property, if you want to work with a string instead of an enumeration datatype. You can use the same examples from the `nodeType` property in this section, except use this property to make it return a string. Table 7.8 lists the `nodeTypeString` return values.

Table 7.8   nodeTypeString return values

Type of Node	nodeTypeString value
Element	"element"
Attribute	"attribute"
Text	"text"
CDATA section	"cdatasection"
Entity Reference	"entityreference"
Processing Instruction	"processinginstruction"
Comment	"comment"
Document Fragment	"documentfragment"

7.3.14   *nodeValue*

Is a member of:	DOMDocument XMLDOMNode XMLDOMAttribute XMLDOMCDATASection XMLDOMComment XMLDOMDocumentFragment XMLDOMDocumentType XMLDOMElement XMLDOMEntity XMLDOMEntityReference XMLDOMNotation XMLDOMProcessingInstruction XMLDOMText XTLRuntime

Syntax

```
vntValue = objXMLDOMAttribute.nodeValue
```

Remark

This property is readable and writable. The VB object browser specifies that this is the *value stored in the node*. For each nodeType these values can differ as shown in table 7.9.

Table 7.9   nodeValue returned for nodeTypes

XMLDOMAttribute	The nodeValue returns a string containing the value of the attribute. If the current attribute has child Nodes, then the string will be a concatenation of all its child Nodes. XML Example: `<PERSON PERSONID="p1">` Returns: p1
XMLDOMText	The nodeValue returns a string of the contents of a text Node. XML Example: `<EMAIL>markwilson@somewhere.com</EMAIL>` Returns: markwilson@somewhere.com
XMLDOMComment	The nodeValue returns a string of the contents of a comment, stripping off the comment indicators and white space. XML Example: `<!-- ******** Resumes for People ******** -->` Returns: ********* Resumes for People *********
XMLDOMCDATASection	The nodeValue returns a string of the contents of a CDATASection. As mentioned under the nodeTypes properties, beware of including an entity in a CDATASection, as it does not expand. In the following example, the hash (#) key is not permitted in XML; therefore, it needs to be embedded in a CDATA section. XML Example: `<ADDRESS><![CDATA[#911 Somewhere Circle, Canberra, Australia]]></ADDRESS>` Returns: #911 Somewhere Circle, Canberra, Australia
XMLDOMProcessingInstruction	The nodeValue returns a string of the contents of a processing instruction, stripping off the processing instruction indicators and white space. XML Example: `<?xml version="1.0" ?>` Returns: xml version="1.0"

Table 7.9   nodeValue returned for nodeTypes (continued)

XMLDOMElement **XMLDOMDocument** **XMLDOMDocumentType** **XMLDOMDocumentFragment** **XMLDOMNotation** **XMLDOMEntityReference**	The nodeValue returns Null.

Example

In the following example, we load a DOMDocument. Then we want to insert the Processing Instruction Node's `nodeValue` property into a text box (`txtPI`), after iterating through each Node of the DOMDocument Node collection, until we find the Processing Instruction Node.

```
Dim objDOMDocument As DOMDocument

Dim objNode As IXMLDOMNode

Set objDOMDocument = New DOMDocument
objDOMDocument.async = False
objDOMDocument.Load "http://mark/xmlcode/people2.dtd"

If objDOMDocument.childNodes.length > 0 Then   ❶

For Each objNode In objDOMDocument.childNodes
  Select Case objNode.nodeType
    Case NODE_PROCESSING_INSTRUCTION   ❷
        txtPI.Text = objNode.nodeValue   ❸
    End Select
  Next objNode
End If
```

❶ Make sure that there are childNodes after loading the document.

❷ Check the Node's nodeType enumeration for a PI Node.

❸ Display the nodeValue of the PI in a text box.

7.3.15 *ondataavailable*

Is a member of:	DOMDocument

Syntax

```
strValue = objDOMDocument.ondataavailable
```

Remark

This property is write-only. When an XMLDOMDocument is large, waiting for the XML to load can take quite a while. The DOMDocument provides this property to let you know when the data has started to become available. You can then start working with this data as it arrives.

This property works in conjunction with the `ontransformnode()` event. For more information on this property, see the *"Loading a file asynchronously"* section in chapter 4, "Programming with XML."

7.3.16 ownerDocument

Is a member of:	DOMDocument XMLDOMNode XMLDOMAttribute XMLDOMCDATASection XMLDOMComment XMLDOMDocumentFragment XMLDOMDocumentType XMLDOMElement XMLDOMEntity XMLDOMEntityReference XMLDOMNotation XMLDOMProcessingInstruction XMLDOMText XTLRuntime

Syntax

```
set objDOMDocument = objXMLDOMNode.ownerDocument
```

Remark

This property is read-only. It returns the parent document to which this Node object belongs. This is always going to be the root of the document (DOMDocument).

7.3.17　parentNode

Is a member of:	DOMDocument XMLDOMNode XMLDOMAttribute XMLDOMCDATASection XMLDOMComment XMLDOMDocumentFragment XMLDOMDocumentType XMLDOMElement XMLDOMEntity XMLDOMEntityReference XMLDOMNotation XMLDOMProcessingInstruction XMLDOMText XTLRuntime

Syntax

```
set objXMLDOMNode = objXMLDOMNode.parentNode
```

Remark

This property is read-only. Whereas the `ownerDocument` object returns the root of the document, the `parentNode` returns the `parentNode` for the current Node. All Nodes except Document, DocumentFragment, and Attribute Nodes can have a `parentNode`.

When we create a Node and it has not yet been added to the tree—or if it has been removed from the tree—the parent is NULL. (See the `createNode()` or `createElement()` methods later in this section for more information on how to do this.)

7.3.18　parsed

Is a member of:	DOMDocument XMLDOMNode XMLDOMAttribute XMLDOMCDATASection XMLDOMComment XMLDOMDocumentFragment XMLDOMDocumentType XMLDOMElement XMLDOMEntity XMLDOMEntityReference XMLDOMNotation XMLDOMProcessingInstruction XMLDOMText XTLRuntime

Syntax

```
blnParsed = objDOMDocument.parsed
```

Remark

This property returns `True/False`, regarding whether the document is parsed, after it is loaded (i.e., indicates whether it is a well-formed document). It will only parse a document if you have set the `resolveExternals` property of DOMDocument to `True`. (See the `resolveExternals` property for more details.)

Example

The following example is the same as found in the `length` property example, except we use this property to check whether the XML file is parsed.

```
Dim objDOMDocument As DOMDocument
Dim objNode As IXMLDOMNode

Set objDOMDocument = New DOMDocument
objDOMDocument.async = False
objDOMDocument.Load "http://mark/xmlcode/people2.dtd"

If objDOMDocument.parsed = True Then
'run rest of code here
End If
```

7.3.19   *parseError*

Is a member of:	XMLDOMDocument

Syntax

```
set objXMLDOMParseError = objDOMDocument.parseError
```

Remark

This property is read-only. This property returns an `XMLDOMParseError` object. The returned object is always a valid object. When you are dealing with the DOMDocument interface, it inherits the `XMLDOMParseError` interface; therefore all the properties of the `XMLDOMParseError` object are exposed in the DOMDocument object (for example, the `parseError` property). This means you can interrogate any errors immediately after you have loaded your DOMDocument, without having to set an `XMLDOMParseError` object.

Example

In the following example, we demonstrate using the reason property of the XML-DOMParseError object from the DOMDocument object.

```
If objDOMDocument.parseError.reason <> "" Then
  'there has been an error with the loaded XML - show the reason
  MsgBox objDOMDocument.parseError.reason
End If
```

However, if you want to interrogate any errors in any of the other types of Nodes, you have to get the XMLDOMParseError object to find any of the error properties:

```
Set objXMLDOMParseError = objXMLDOMElement.parseError
If objXMLDOMParseError.reason <> "" then
  Msgbox objXMLDOMParseError.reason
end if
```

7.3.20 prefix

Is a member of:	DOMDocument XMLDOMNode XMLDOMAttribute XMLDOMCDATASection XMLDOMComment XMLDOMDocumentFragment XMLDOMDocumentType XMLDOMElement XMLDOMEntity XMLDOMEntityReference XMLDOMNotation XMLDOMProcessingInstruction XMLDOMText XTLRuntime

Syntax

```
strVAlue = objXMLDOMNode.prefix
```

Remark

This property is read-only. When working with a namespace in your document, this property returns the prefix for that namespace.

Example

In your XML file:

```
<resume:EMAIL>markwilson@somewhere.com</resume:EMAIL>
```

VB returns:

```
strValue = objNode.prefix ❶
```

❶ strValue returns: resume.

7.3.21 *preserveWhiteSpace*

Is a member of:	XMLDOMDocument

Syntax

```
blnValue = objDOMDocument.preserveWhiteSpace
objDOMDocument.preserveWhiteSpace = blnValue
```

Remark

This property is a readable and writable property that returns True/False. The default is False. White space is a space, tab, or carriage return (new line) character in your XML file.

This property is useful when you need to preserve the layout (white space) of the data in your XML document. For example, you have as one of your elements a comment that consists of sentences. You would need to preserve the two spaces after a full stop, the carriage return between paragraphs. Well, if you did not specify to preserve the white space for this element, you would lose all this formatting.

In the XML specifications, all white space is meant to be preserved; however, the default behavior of this property in the DOMDocument is False, and as such, the XML and TEXT properties do not preserve the white space.

The text and XML properties will preserve white space when the user has set the preserveWhiteSpace property to True and/or when the xml:space attribute on the XML element has the value *preserve*. Depending on which you choose from the previous line; the DOMDocument object handles the white space differently.

There are different types of white space:

- **Preserved**: the content of the DOMDocument will be exactly as it's found in the XML file
- **Trimmed**: the leading and trailing spaced in your XML file are removed
- **Half-preserved**: the white space inside your text is preserved, but the white space between tags is *normalized*

To find more information about how setting your white space affects the output of your text in the DOMDocument, go to the Microsoft website, which explains this quite well.

Example

The following XML example specifies that the white space needs to be preserved:

```
<ADDRESS>xml:space="preserve">
    911 Somewhere Circle,
    Canberra,
    Australia
</ADDRESS>
```

Now this data will keep its form when it is displayed.

7.3.22 resolveExternals

Is a member of:	XMLDOMDocument

Syntax

```
blnVal = objDOMDocument.resolveExternals
objDOMDocument.resolveExternals = blnVal
```

Remark

This property is readable and writable. `True/False` is returned/set, defaulting to `True`. Remember that there is a difference between valid and well-formed. A *merely* well-formed XML document has matching tags and is syntactically correct. Valid means that the entire XML document is correct, including the use of a Schema, DTD, or other externals.

Externals are items that are referenced from within the XML document, such as namespaces, DTDs, and other included files or objects.

When the DOMDocument is parsed, validation can occur or not. We can turn validation off—as is the default for IE5 when it displays XML files—by setting `validateOnParse` property to `False`.

During parsing, if validation occurs, validation will fail unless `resolveExternals` is set to `True`.

Example

To resolve a namespace, the Microsoft DOM objects require that the URI prefix begins with "x-schema."

In the following example, the DOM document loaded has a DTD. Before the load takes place, the DOMDocument needs to resolve the DTD. Therefore, the `resolveExternals` property needs to be set before loading the document. But if we want the XML file validated against the DTD file request, we must set the `validateOnParse` property to `True`:

```
Dim objDOMDocument As DOMDocument

Set objDOMDocument = New DOMDocument
objDOMDocument.async = False
```

```
objDOMDocument.resolveExternals = True
objDOMDocument.validateOnParse = True
objDOMDocument.Load "http://mark/xmlcode/people2.xml"
```

7.3.23   tagName

Is a member of:	XMLDOMElement

Syntax

```
strValue objXMLDOMElement.tagName
```

Remark

This property is read-only. For an element, this property returns the tagName of the element. It therefore is the same as the `nodeName` property, except that it is only found in the `XMLDOMElement` interface. Please see the `nodeName` property for a detailed explanation and example.

7.3.24   text

Is a member of:	DOMDocument
	XMLDOMNode
	XMLDOMAttribute
	XMLDOMCDATASection
	XMLDOMComment
	XMLDOMDocumentFragment
	XMLDOMDocumentType
	XMLDOMElement
	XMLDOMEntity
	XMLDOMEntityReference
	XMLDOMNotation
	XMLDOMProcessingInstruction
	XMLDOMText
	XTLRuntime

Syntax

```
strValue = objXMLDOMNode.text
```

Remark

For writing the values to a Node, the `text` property is used. The `text` property normalizes white space, unless the DOMDocument has been specified to preserve the white space (see the `preserveWhiteSpace` property).

When reading the value of a Node, using the text property can lead to some strange behavior if your current Node has children.

Example

The following XML example explains what we meant by the previous comment.

```
<PEOPLE>
<PERSON id="1">
  <NAME>Mark Wilson</NAME>
  <ADDRESS>911 Somewhere Circle, Canberra, Australia</ADDRESS>
  <TEL>(++612) 12345</TEL>
  <FAX>(++612) 12345</FAX>
  <EMAIL>markwilson@somewhere.com</EMAIL>
</PERSON>
….
</PEOPLE>
```

For the other properties, like the nodeType property, we explained how to get references to CDATA sections, etc. However, if you are looking for the text of a Node and are not too concerned about interrogating whether the sub-children consist of CDATA sections or entities, then just getting the text property will return the parsed data of your element.

In our example we have loaded our DOMDocument, which consists of our People2.xml file. We then get a reference to the `firstChild` property (`objNode = '<PERSON id="1">'`) of the `documentElement` property:

```
Dim objDOMDocument As DOMDocument
Dim objNode As IXMLDOMNode
Dim strText as String

Set objDOMDocument = New DOMDocument
objDOMDocument.async = False
objDOMDocument.resolveExternals = True
objDOMDocument.validateOnParse = True
objDOMDocument.Load "http://mark/xmlcode/people2.xml"

Set objNode = objDOMDocument.documentElement.firstChild
strText = objNode.text
```

Our `objNode` has child Nodes; therefore, its text property returns the values of all its child Nodes. The string `strText` returns the following:

```
Mark Wilson 911 Somewhere Circle, Canberra, Australia (++612) 12345 (++612)
  12345 markwilson@somewhere.com"
```

The value return has all the tags, and the less than (<) and greater than (>) signs have been removed, with a space inserted between each child for the current Node.

7.3.25 *url*

Is a member of:	XMLDOMDocument

Syntax

```
strValue = objDOMDocument.url
```

Remark
This property is read-only. This property returns the URL for the loaded XML document.

7.3.26 *validateOnParse*

Is a member of:	XMLDOMDocument

Remark
See the `resolveExternals` property for more information, as these two properties are interlinked.

7.3.27 *value*

Is a member of:	XMLDOMAttribute

Syntax
```
vntValue = objXMLDOMAttribute.value
```

Remark
This property returns the value (content) of an attribute. For the `XMLDOMAttribute` object, this is the same as the `nodeValue` property.

Example
In the following example, we first get a reference to the `firstChild` of the `documentElement`. We then get a reference to the attribute for the `firstChild`, and then find the value of that attribute.
```
Dim objDOMDocument As DOMDocument
Dim objNode As IXMLDOMNode
Dim objAttritube As IXMLDOMAttribute
Dim strValue as String

Set objDOMDocument = New DOMDocument
objDOMDocument.async = False
objDOMDocument.resolveExternals = True
objDOMDocument.validateOnParse = True
objDOMDocument.Load "http://mark/xmlcode/people2.xml"

Set objNode = objDOMDocument.documentElement.firstChild
Set objAttritube = objNode.Attributes(0)
strValue = objAttribute.value
```

From our People2.xml file example, `strValue` returns `p1`.

7.4 DOM object methods

Here are some of the methods we think would be useful in the context of this book. More complete descriptions can be read from the documentation or on the Microsoft website.

The listing below is a list of all the methods for all of the XMLDom objects. Use this chart when you need to find a method in one of the interfaces that could be useful for something that you are trying accomplish. We have found this list very useful for when we want to do something, like finding the value of an attribute, but don't know what methods are available because there are so many DOM objects. We discover that in the XMLDOMElement interface, there is a method called getAttribute(). If you didn't know it existed there, you might try to do the same thing using the XMLDOMNode interface.

As with the properties before them, the methods that are bolded in table 7.10 are the ones that we will explain.

Table 7.10 DOMDocument methods

Methods	DOMDocument	XMLDOMNode	XMLDOMNodeList	XMLDOMNamedNodeMap	XMLDOMAttribute	XMLDOMCDATASection	XMLDOMComment	XMLDOMDocumentFragment	XMLDOMDocumentType	XMLDOMElement	XMLDOMEntity	XMLDOMEntityReference	XMLDOMImplementation	XMLDOMNotation	XMLDOMParseError	XMLDOMProcessingInstruction	XMLDOMText	XTLRuntime	XMLHTTPRequest
abort	✓																		✓
absoluteChildNumber																		✓	
ancestorChildNumber																		✓	
appendChild	✓	✓			✓	✓	✓	✓	✓	✓	✓	✓		✓		✓	✓	✓	
appendData						✓	✓										✓		
childNumber																		✓	
cloneNode	✓	✓			✓	✓	✓	✓	✓	✓	✓	✓		✓		✓	✓	✓	
createAttribute	✓																		
createCDATA-Section	✓																		
createComment	✓																		

Table 7.10 DOMDocument methods (continued)

Method																		
createDocument-Fragment	✓																	
createElement	✓																	
createEntity-Reference	✓																	
createNode	✓																	
createProcessing-Instruction	✓																	
createTextNode	✓																	
deleteData					✓	✓									✓			
depth																	✓	
formatDate																	✓	
formatIndex																	✓	
formatNumber																	✓	
formatTime																	✓	
getAllResponseHeaders																		✓
getResponseHeader																		✓
getAttribute									✓									
getAttributeNode									✓									
getElementsByTagName	✓								✓									
getNamedItem			✓															
getQualifiedItem			✓															
hasChildNodes	✓	✓		✓	✓	✓	✓	✓	✓	✓	✓		✓		✓	✓	✓	
hasFeature												✓						
insertBefore	✓	✓		✓	✓	✓	✓	✓	✓	✓	✓		✓		✓	✓	✓	
insertData					✓	✓									✓			
load	✓																	
loadXML	✓																	
nextNode		✓	✓															
nodeFromID	✓																	
open																		✓
normalize									✓									
removeAttribute									✓									

Table 7.10 DOMDocument methods (continued)

	1	2	3	4	5	6	7	8	9	10	11	12	13	14	15	16	17	18	19
removeAttribute-Node												✓							
removeChild	✓	✓			✓	✓	✓	✓	✓	✓	✓	✓		✓		✓	✓	✓	
removeNamedItem				✓															
removeQualifiedItem				✓															
replaceChild	✓	✓			✓	✓	✓	✓	✓	✓	✓	✓		✓		✓	✓	✓	
replaceData					✓	✓										✓			
reset			✓	✓															
save	✓																		
selectNodes	✓	✓			✓	✓	✓	✓	✓	✓	✓	✓		✓		✓	✓	✓	
selectSingleNode	✓	✓			✓	✓	✓	✓	✓	✓	✓	✓		✓		✓	✓	✓	
send																			✓
setRequestHeader																			✓
setAttribute												✓							
setAttributeNode												✓							
setNamedItem				✓															
splitText					✓											✓			
substringData					✓	✓										✓			
transformNode	✓	✓			✓	✓	✓	✓	✓	✓	✓	✓		✓		✓	✓	✓	
transformNodeTo-Object	✓	✓			✓	✓	✓	✓	✓	✓	✓	✓		✓		✓	✓	✓	
uniqueID																		✓	

Note: Boldface methods are explained in this chapter.

7.4.1 *abort()*

Is a member of:	XMLDOMDocument

Syntax

```
objDOMDocument.abort()
```

Remark

This method stops the parsing and discards any portion of the XML tree already built. The XMLDOMParseError object then shows that the download was stopped. If the parsing is complete, the current document is not changed.

This could be useful if the processing of a DOMDocument was taking too long or the user hit a cancel button. If you change it to `False`, you could use this property to stop the document loading.

7.4.2 appendChild()

Is a member of:	DOMDocument XMLDOMNode XMLDOMAttribute XMLDOMCDATASection XMLDOMComment XMLDOMDocumentFragment XMLDOMDocumentType XMLDOMElement XMLDOMEntity XMLDOMEntityReference XMLDOMNotation XMLDOMProcessingInstruction XMLDOMText XTLRuntime

Syntax

```
set objXMLDOMNode = objDOMDocument.appendChild(objNewChildNode)
```

Remark

This method's function is to append (add) a new child Node to the end of a Node.

Before we can append a new Node (element, attribute, etc.), we need to first create this Node. Then once we have a reference to this Node, we can append it to the current `parentNode` by passing the parameter (`objNewChildNode`), which is the newly created Node. This new child will be added to the end of the list of children on this `parentNode`.

The child (`objXMLDOMNode`) will be returned if it is successfully added. It will be set to nothing if it fails.

Appending to the root (DOMDocument)

If you recall, we mentioned that the DOMDocument root could only have the following child Nodes:

- element—only one, because the DOMDocument can only have one root element Node (createElement)
- processing instruction (createProcessingInstruction)
- comment (createComment)
- document type (DocumentType)

Of these child Nodes, the only one that you cannot currently add to the DOM-Document is a DocumentType (DTD).

Example

Before we can append a child Node, we need to fist create a Node of whichever type you want (attribute, element, etc.) and set a few properties to it if needed. This example creates a new DOMDocument, and then the `documentElement` gets added to it:

```
Dim objDOMDocument As DOMDocument
Dim objPeople As IXMLDOMNode
Dim objNode As IXMLDOMNode

Set objDOMDocument = new DOMDocument
Set objPeople = objDOMDocument.createElement("People")  ❶  ❷
Set objNode = objDOMDocument.appendChild (objPeople)    ❶  ❸
```

❶ Add the root Node to the XML document.

❷ Create the element first.

❸ Append this childNode to the end of the DOMDocument.

Consider the following code:

```
Set objNode = objDOMDocument.appendChild (objPeople)
```

You only need to say `Set objNode = ....` if you want to check that this Node was created properly. You could just say:

```
objDOMDocument.appendChild objPeople
```

Appending to the root element (documentElement)

If you try to add a second element-type Node to the DOMDocument, you'll get a run-time error—because the DOMDocument only allows one root element.

How do you go about adding more data to your DOMDocument?

No matter how many levels deep your tree goes, you need to add your first branch, which is your `documentElement`. Thereafter you need to append (add) the rest of the XML data.

The following steps show the sequence for adding data to your XML code, starting with adding the root Node.

Step 1:

```
<PEOPLE>
....
</PEOPLE>
```

Then you need to add your next level branch, which will be the your first sub-element of the root Node.

Step 2:

```
<PEOPLE>
  <PERSON>
  ...
  </PERSON>
</PEOPLE>
```

To this subelement we can then add the elements (data).

Step 3:

```
<PEOPLE>
  <PERSON>
    <NAME>Mark Wilson</NAME>
    <ADDRESS>911 Somewhere Circle, Canberra, Australia</ADDRESS>
    <TEL>(++612) 12345</TEL>
    <FAX>(++612) 12345</FAX>
    <EMAIL>markwilson@somewhere.com</EMAIL>
  </PERSON>
</PEOPLE>
```

You now need to append the root element. The following code shows Step 2 and Step 3 added to the XML code in VB. (See createElement() to create the element.)

```
Dim objPerson As IXMLDOMNode
Dim objChild As IXMLDOMNode

Set objPerson = objDOMDocument.createElement("PERSON")   ❶
objDOMDocument.documentElement.appendChild objPerson   ❷

Set objChild = objDOMDocument.createElement("NAME")   ❸
objChild.Text = "Monty Python"   ❹

objPerson.appendChild objChild   ❺
objDOMDocument.save
```

❶ Create a new element DOMDocument.

❷ We have already inserted our documentElement. Now we need to append a new Person element to the documentElement.

❸ Create a new childNode for the Person element and give it a few properties.

❹ Append this new child to the Person element.

❺ To actually add any new change to the DOMDocument, you need to save the DOMDocument.

Note   The Node may be added to the instantiated DOMDocument, but it is not added to the actual XML file until you have called the *save()* method.

In Line 2 above we could also say:

```
objPeople.appendChild objPerson
```

Either method is fine. Both `objPeople` and `objDOMDocument.documentEle-`
`ment` refer to the Document Element.

7.4.3 *cloneNode()*

Is a member of:	DOMDocument XMLDOMNode XMLDOMAttribute XMLDOMCDATASection XMLDOMComment XMLDOMDocumentFragment XMLDOMDocumentType XMLDOMElement XMLDOMEntity XMLDOMEntityReference XMLDOMNotation XMLDOMProcessingInstruction XMLDOMText XTLRuntime

Syntax

```
set objXMLDOMNode = objXMLDOMNode.cloneNode(deep)
```

Remark

Pass one parameter (`deep`) that is either `True` or `False`. It indicates if the Node
should be cloned (copied) with its children included or not. Any changes made to
this Node will not be reflected in the DOMDocument.

Note that the new Node returned will be of the `XMLDOMNode` interface.

7.4.4 *createAttribute(), createCDATASection(), createComment(), createElement(), createEntityReference(), createProcessingInstruction(), createTextNode()*

Is a member of:	DOMDocument

Syntax

```
objXMLDOMAttributr = objDOMDocument.createAttribute(name)
```

Remark

Adding Nodes to the DOMDocument is done in two phases:

1 You first need to create a Node of the type you want (Element, Comment, etc.)

2 Then you append the created Node to the DOMDocument

Creating an element

```
objXMLDOMElement = objDOMDocument.createElement(tagName)
```

These methods are only applicable to the DOM-Document interface.

When creating an element, we need to pass the `createElement()` method the tag name of the element to be created. This tag name is case-sensitive. Once we've established a new element, then we need to give it its values. See the example below.

In the code for the `appendChild()` method, we see how an element is created and added to a `parentNode`. Therefore, we have already created a DOMDocument and its `documentElement` property (root element). Now we want to add children to the `documentElement`:

```
Dim objPerson As IXMLDOMNode
Dim objChild As IXMLDOMNode

Set objPerson = objDOMDocument.createElement("PERSON")  ❶
objDOMDocument.documentElement.appendChild objPerson  ❷

Set objChild = objDOMDocument.createElement("NAME")  ❸
objChild.Text = "Monty Python"
objPerson.appendChild objChild  ❹
```

❶ The tag name (element name) is passed as a string to say which element to create. We get a reference to objPerson, because we will add childNodes (Name, Address etc.) to this parentNode.

❷ Add objPerson Node to the documentElement Node.

❸ Create another element—note that we are using the DOMDocument object here.

❹ Add this childNode to the Person element.

Before appending the element to its `parentNode`, don't forget to give it its properties, like the text, etc.

Here again we see the append method being used to actually add this element to the `parentNode`. If this is not done, then the new element's parent will be NULL and not part of the DOMDocument.

This create-Element() *method does not add the new child-Node to the document tree. To actually add it to the document, you need to call the* append-Child() *method.*

You now need to use a method such as `insertBefore()`, `replaceChild()`, or `appendChild()` to add the new child to the DOMDocument. Then you need to use the `save()` method on the DOMDocument to actually write the change to the XML file. This applies to the methods that follow as well.

Namespaces

If you have specified a namespace in your document (namespaceURI = ...), the element will be added in the context of this namespace. If no prefix is used before a `tagName`, then element is added to the default namespace. If you say:

```
Set objChild = objDOMDocument.createElement("resume:NAME")
```

the colon will be ignored.

Creating an attribute

The VB code line:

```
objXMLDOMAttribute = objDOMDocument.createAttribute(name)
```

creates an attribute with a specific name, where name is the name of the attribute. You then need to give the attribute its details. See the example below.

Attributes can only be added to created or current elements. Therefore, you need to first get access to an element object to which you are about to add an attribute.

There are several methods used to add an attribute to an element (which you will see as you go through the methods). If you use the createAttribute() method, this is how to go about it:

```
Dim objNode As IXMLDOMNode
Dim objAttrib As IXMLDOMAttribute

Set objNode = m_objDOMPeople.createElement("PERSON")          ❶
Set objAttrib = m_objDOMPeople.createAttribute("PERSONID")    ❷
objAttrib.Text = "p7"   ❸
objNode.Attributes.setNamedItem objAttrib   ❹
m_objDOMPeople.documentElement.appendChild objNode   ❺
```

❶ Create the element Node if it's a new element.

❷ Create the attribute type, passing it a string of its name.

❸ Give the attribute properties.

❹ To the created Node (element), add the attribute object.

❺ Append the created Node to the documentElement.

See the setAttribute() method in this chapter.

Creating a CDATA section

The following VB code creates a CDATA section in an element Node in the DOMDocument:

```
objXMLDOMCDATASection = objElement.createCDATASection(data)
```

This method can be really handy if you need to find an easy way to put those crazy brackets (<![CDATA[#]]>) around a CDATA section, without having to put the brackets around yourself when you are busy modifying a DOMDocument.

In the following example, we need to have the following in our address Node:

```
#123 Narrabundah Avenue
```

We accomplish this by wrapping the hash (#) in a CDATA section:

```
Dim objCDATA As IXMLDOMCDATASection

Set objCDATA = objDOMDocument.createCDATASection("#")
Set objChild = objDOMDocument.createElement("ADDRESS")
objChild.Text = objCDATA.XML & "123 Narrabundah Avenue"
Set objNode = objDOMDocument.documentElement.appendChild(objChild)
```

If you query the text property for this Node (objNode), it returns:

```
<![CDATA [#]]>123 Narrabundah Avenue
```

Creating a comment

The following VB code creates a comment in the DOMDocument:

```
objXMLDOMComment = objDOMDocument.createComment(data)
```

If you need to add a comment to your XML, then you need to use the following method. It automatically adds the correct characters (<!-- -->) around the comment; you only need to add the data.

In the following example, we add a comment to the DOMDocument:

```
Dim objDOMDocument As DOMDocument
Dim objComment As IXMLDOMComment

Set objDOMDocument = New DOMDocument        ❶
Set objComment = objDOMDocument.createComment("This is a comment.")   ❷
objDOMDocument.appendChild objComment        ❸
objDOMDocument.save http://mark/xmlcode/people2.xml
```

❶ Create your DOMDocument.

❷ Create a Comment object, passing just your comment, no XML tags. Note that this object can also be an XMLDOMNode object.

❸ Add this new comment object to the DOMDocument.

If you run this example and look at the xml property for the objComment object, you will see that the comment tags (<!-- -->) have been automatically added, but the text property does not have these tags.

Creating an entity reference

The following VB code creates a CDATA section in an element Node in the DOMDocument:

```
objXMLDOMEntityReference = objElement.createEntityReference(name)
```

This creates an entity reference with a specified case-sensitive name. This method is important when you want to create a Node that needs to have the entity reference in the XML. The entity is defined in the DTD. In our DTD example (people2.dtd), we have specified the following entity:

```
<!ENTITY UK    "United Kingdom">
```

In the following example, we need to create an address element for a person. However, our example is a bit more complicated, because the entity UK needs to come at the end of the address. Therefore, we need to create an element for the address, plus we need to create an entity reference Node for the address element. This is how we need to combine the two:

```
Dim objDOMDocument As DOMDocument
Dim objPerson As IXMLDOMNode
Dim objChild As IXMLDOMNode
Dim objEntityRef As IXMLDOMEntityReference

Set objDOMDocument = New DOMDocument        ❶
objDOMDocument.async = False
objDOMDocument.resolveExternals = True
objDOMDocument.validateOnParse = True
objDOMDocument.Load http://mark/xmlcode/people2.xml

Set objPerson = objDOMDocument.createElement("PERSON")    ❷
objDOMDocument.documentElement.appendChild objPerson

Set objChild = objDOMDocument.createElement("ADDRESS")    ❸
Set objEntityRef = objDOMDocument.createEntityReference("UK")    ❹
objChild.Text = "34 Erica Street, Isle of Dogs,"    ❺
objChild.appendChild objEntityRef    ❻
objPerson.appendChild objChild
```

❶ Load a DOMDocument from file.

❷ Create a person element and add it to the documentElement NodeList.

❸ Create the child Node for the Address element.

❹ Create an entity reference Node, which we know is the "UK" entity from our DTD.

❺ To our address element (objChild), add the address text, excluding the entity reference.

❻ Append the entity reference object to the address element as a child Node. This creates the correct syntax for an element that has normal text, plus an entity reference in it.

When running this example, after the line

```
objChild.appendChild objEntityRef
```

```
 the objChild xml and text properties are as follows:
objChild.xml: <ADDRESS>34 Erica Street, Isle of Dogs, &UK;</ADDRESS>
objChild.text: 34 Erica Street, Isle of Dogs, United Kingdom
```

7.4.5   *createNode()*

Is a member of:	DOMDocument

Syntax

As an alternative to the `createElement()`, `createAttribute()`, etc. methods, you can also use the `createNode()` method, which creates any type of Node, using the following syntax:

```
set objXMLDOMNode = objDOMDocument.createNode(Type, name, namespaceURI)
```

Table 7.11 describes the syntax of `createNode()`.

Table 7.11   Signature of the createNode method

Type	Specify the type of Node, which can be the numeric value of the nodeType or a string of the nodeTypeString.
name	Specify the name of the Node or, if there is no name, then an empty string (""). Remember that if you're dealing with an element or an entity reference, the name is case-sensitive.
namespaceURI	Specify the namespace or, if there is no namespaceURI, then an empty string ("").

Remark

Before we continue, please refer to the `nodeType` *property section, which explains in detail the different Node types, their enumeration values, and descriptions.*

You cannot create a Node of the following types:

- Document—it is the root of the XML; it cannot be a childNode. The `create-Node()` method only creates child Nodes. To create the root of your XML, you initialize a DOMDocument object as we have seen in most examples so far.

- Document type—DTDs cannot be added to the DOMDocument. See the `docType` property in this section.

- Entity—entities are declared in the DTD; therefore, being external to the XML file restricts their creation

- Notation—this is the same as entities

If you attempt to create any of the above, an error will occur.

Table 7.12 lists what to insert in the `Type` and `Name` parts of the `create-Node()` signature. We have not added the namespace property in the signature, as this only applies to element and attribute Nodes, where you can specify the namespace. If there is not a namespace, you need to add an empty string (""), as this signature has no `optional` addresses.

In the `Type` part of the `createNode()` signature, you can insert either the `nodeType` value or the `nodeTypeString` value. You can insert the `Name` section in the `name` part of the signature.

Table 7.12 Specifications of values to insert in createNode signature

Type of Node	node Type value	nodeTypeString value	name
Element	1	"element"	tagName/nodeName (e.g., "PERSON")
Attribute	2	"attribute"	name of the attribute/nodeName (e.g., "PERSONID")
Text	3	"text"	empty string ("")
CDATA section	4	"cdatasection"	empty string ("")
Entity Reference	5	"entityreference"	name of the referenced entity/nodeName (e.g., "USA")
Processing Instruction	7	"processinginstruction"	target/nodeName ("realaudio')
Comment	8	"comment"	empty string ("")
Document Fragment	11	"documentfragment"	empty string ("")

Example

In the following examples, we create the different `nodeTypes` and append them to the `documentElement` property of the DOMDocument.

To create an element Node, pass the `nodeTypeString` as the type:

```
Set objNode = m_objXMLDOM.createNode("element", "PERSON", "")
m_objXMLDOM.documentElement.appendChild objNode
```

It is such a pity that the DOM-NodeType enum for the Node type in the signature was not used as the passed variable. (Instead, an integer or string was inserted.) It would have made the Intellisense auto-complete in VB so much easier to read.

Alternatively, you can pass the `nodeType` enumeration as the type:

```
Set objNode = m_objXMLDOM.createNode(NODE_ELEMENT, "PERSON", "")
m_objXMLDOM.documentElement.appendChild objNode
```

Otherwise, you can pass the `nodeType` enumeration value as the type:

```
Set objNode = m_objXMLDOM.createNode(1, "PERSON", "")
m_objXMLDOM.documentElement.appendChild objNode
```

The example from the `createComment()` method example would change as follows for the `createNode()` method:

```
Dim objDOMDocument As DOMDocument
Dim objComment As IXMLDOMComment

Set objDOMDocument = New DOMDocument
Set objComment = objDOMDocument.createNode(NODE_COMMENT, "", "")   ❶
objComment.Text = "This is a comment."   ❷
objDOMDocument.appendChild objComment   ❸
```

❶ We've used the nodeType enumuration for the nodeType. Don't forget to pass empty strings for the other two parameters, as they are not optional.

❷ Add the comment text.

❸ Append the comment Node to its parent, which in this case is the DOMDocument.

7.4.6 getAttribute()

Is a member of:	XMLDOMElement

Syntax

```
vntValue = objXMLDOMElement.getAttribute(strAttributeName)
```

Remark

If your element has an associated attribute, you can look up the string value of that attribute its name. It then returns the attributes value (nodeValue) in a variant datatype.

Example

In the following example, we have already loaded our people2.xml file into a DOMDocument (objDOMDocument). We add a new Person element and its attribute. Once we have added this element, we get the value of the attribute for this element.

```
Dim objPerson As IXMLDOMElement
Dim objAttrib As IXMLDOMAttribute
Dim vntValue As Variant

Set objPerson = objDOMDocument.createElement("PERSON")
Set objAttrib = objDOMDocument.createAttribute("PERSONID")
objAttrib.Text = "p7"
objPerson.Attributes.setNamedItem objAttrib
objDOMDocument.documentElement.appendChild objPerson
vntValue = objPerson.getAttribute("PERSONID")  ❶
```

❶ vntValue returns "p7," the value of the attribute.

As an alternative to this method, see the nodeFromID() method for getting an attribute when you know the id value but you want to find its associated Node.

7.4.7   *getAttributeNode()*

Is a member of:	XMLDOMElement

Syntax

```
objXMLDOMAttribute = objXMLDOMElement.getAttributeNode(strAttributeName)
```

Remark

This method is the same as the `getAttribute()` method, except that it returns an attribute object instead of the attribute's value. If your element has an associated attribute, you look up the attribute Node object using the name of the attribute (`nodeName`). If `NULL` is returned, then there is no attribute for the Node.

Example

Using the same example as in `getAttribute()` method, we change the last line so that it returns an attribute object.

```
Dim objPerson As IXMLDOMElement
Dim objAttrib As IXMLDOMAttribute
Dim strValue As String

Set objPerson = objDOMDocument.createElement("PERSON")
Set objAttrib = objDOMDocument.createAttribute("PERSONID")
objAttrib.Text = "p7"
objPerson.Attributes.setNamedItem objAttrib
objDOMDocument.documentElement.appendChild objPerson
Set objAttrib = obj-Person.getAttribute("PERSONID")   ❶
```

❶ `objAttrib` returns the attribute in the `objPerson` element.

7.4.8   *getElementsByTagName()*

Is a member of:	DOMDocument XMLDOMElement

Syntax

```
set objXMLDOMNodeList = objDOMDocument.getElementsByTagName(tagname)
```

Remark

The parameter `Tagname` in the `getElementsByTagName()` signature is a string, specifying the element name to find. If you specify that the tagname is an asterisk ("*"), then all the elements are returned in the DOMDocument.

The returned `NodeList` of this method is different from the `nodeLists` that we have dealt with so far. You normally work with a `NodeList` that returns a collection from the `documentElement`, such as:

```
set objXMLDOMNodeList = objDOMDocument.documentElement
```

This will return a `NodeList` collection that returns its child Nodes as shown in figure 7.7.

```
PERSON: Child 1
      L             Child 1: NAME
      L             Child 2: ADDRESS
      L             Child 3: TEL
      L             Child 4: FAX
      L             Child 5: EMAIL
PERSON: Child 2
      L             Child 1: NAME
      L             Child 2: ADDRESS
      L             Child 3: TEL
      L             Child 4: FAX
      L             Child 5: EMAIL
```

Figure 7.7   NodeList returned from the documentElement property

You can call `getElementsByTagName()` from the DOMDocument root, specifying that you want everything (*****):

```
set objXMLDOMNodeList = objDOMDocument.getElementsByTagName("*")
```

In the above example, `getElementsByTagName()` returns a `NodeList` collection that has `child Nodes` as follows in figure 7.8:

This method returns a `NodeList` object in which each child Node is grouped by their element names, instead of being grouped by the normal TreeView effect.

Example

To get a clearer view of what we are trying to explain, look in your Local Views in VB for the following examples. See the difference in the collections of the `NodeList` object by calling:

```
Dim objDOMDocument As DOMDocument
Dim objNodeList As IXMLDOMNodeList

Set objDOMDocument = New DOMDocument
objDOMDocument.async = False
objDOMDocument.Load "http://mark/xmlcode/people2.dtd"
Set objNodeList = objDOMDocument.documentElement
```

NAME: Child 1	
L	Child 1: NAME
L	Child 2: NAME
ADDRESS: Child 2	
L	Child 1: ADDRESS
L	Child 2: ADDRESS
TEL: Child 3	
L	Child 1: TEL
L	Child 2: TEL
FAX: Child 4	
L	Child 1: FAX
L	Child 2: FAX
EMAIL: Child 5	
L	Child 1: EMAIL
L	Child 2: EMAIL

Figure 7.8   NodeList returned from the getElementsByTagName() method

Now look at the returned NodeList object in the Local Views in VB. Try the following:

```
Dim objDOMDocument As DOMDocument
Dim objNodeList As IXMLDOMNodeList

Set objDOMDocument = New DOMDocument
objDOMDocument.async = False
objDOMDocument.Load "http://mark/xmlcode/people2.dtd"
Set objNodeList = objDOMDocument.getElementsByTagName("*")
```

You can use this method when you want to get a specific Node, like NAME. However, take note that it returns a NodeList object; therefore, you need to iterate through the returned Nodes.

An example of this is when we want to put the NAME values of our element into a text box.

```
Set objNodeItems = objNode.getElementsByTagName("NAME")  ❶
txtName.Text = objNodeItems.Item(0).nodeTypedValue  ❷
```

❶ We indicate that we want the "NAME" element returned from the current Node.

❷ We want to get the value from the first Node in our collection.

For an easier method, look at the selectSingleNode() method later in this section.

7.4.9   getNamedItem()

Is a member of:	XMLDOMNamedNodeMap

Syntax

```
Set objXMLDOMNode = objXMLDOMNamedNodeMap.getNamedItem(strAttributeName)
```

Remark

The `XMLDOMNamedNodeMap` object is used to find and manipulate attributes for a Node, although the `XMLDOMElement` interface gives you many methods as well to do this.

This method takes the name of an attribute to find the Node associated with that attribute. However, to be able to do this, we first need to get a hold of the `XMLDOMNamedNodeMap` object, which is the `attributes` property of a Node. If there are attributes in the current Node, then we can query the `XMLDOMNamedNodeMap` collection.

Example

In the following example, we want to store the value of the elements ID attribute in the tag of a TreeView. We have already loaded a DOMDocument from our people2.xml. We have passed a `person` element in the following example.

```
Dim objNode As IXMLDOMNode
Dim objAttributes As IXMLDOMNamedNodeMap
Dim objAttributeNode As IXMLDOMNode

Set objAttributes = objNode.Attributes     ❶

If objAttributes.length > 0 Then
    Set objAttributeNode = objAttributes.getNamedItem("PERSONID")  ❷
    tvwElement.Tag = objAttribute-Node.nodeValue  ❸
End If
```

❶ Get the XMLDOMNamedNodeMap from the Nodes attribute property.

❷ Check that there are available attributes.

❸ Our id reference is "PERSONID"; therefore, tell the NameNodeListMap to get this Node by using the getNamedItem method.

7.4.10   *hasChildNodes()*

Is a member of:	DOMDocument XMLDOMNode XMLDOMAttribute XMLDOMCDATASection XMLDOMComment XMLDOMDocumentFragment XMLDOMDocumentType XMLDOMElement XMLDOMEntity XMLDOMEntityReference XMLDOMNotation XMLDOMProcessingInstruction XMLDOMText XTLRuntime

Syntax

```
blnValue = objXMLDOMNode.hasChildNodes()
```

Remark

This method is read-only. This method returns a boolean indicating whether the current Node has any children. It can be used instead of the `length` property, as explained earlier in this chapter.

Example

We have snatched the following example from the `length` property and changed it to show how to use the `hasChildNodes()` method.

In this example, we test the `hasChildNodes()` method to see if a DOMDocument has loaded properly. If the `hasChildNodes()` returned `True`, then we can proceed with the rest of the code working with the DOMDocument object.

```
Dim objDOMDocument As DOMDocument
Dim objNode As IXMLDOMNode

Set objDOMDocument = New DOMDocument
objDOMDocument.async = False
objDOMDocument.Load "http://mark/xmlcode/people2.dtd"

If objDOMDocument.hasChildNodes Then  ❶
  'run rest of code here
End If
```

❶ Our code has loaded the XML from our main XML example. The hasChildNodes() method returns True; therefore, we can proceed with our DOMDocument.

7.4.11 *insertBefore()*

Is a member of:	DOMDocument
	XMLDOMNode
	XMLDOMAttribute
	XMLDOMCDATASection
	XMLDOMComment
	XMLDOMDocumentFragment
	XMLDOMDocumentType
	XMLDOMElement
	XMLDOMEntity
	XMLDOMEntityReference
	XMLDOMNotation
	XMLDOMProcessingInstruction
	XMLDOMText
	XTLRuntime

Syntax

```
set objXMLDOMNode = objXMLDOMNode.insertBefore(newChild, refChild)
```

Remark

This method inserts a new child Node before the current Node (objXMLDOMNode).

From the methods signature, if you do not include a parameter, refChild, then this function acts the same as the appendChild() method. Here the refChild must be a child Node of the current Node (objXMLDOMNode). This indicates that the new child must be inserted before this refChild Node (which is the left sibling).

The DOMDocument checks that the refChild is a child Node of the current Node (objXMLDOMNode). If it is not, then an error will occur.

This method returns the child that has been successfully inserted. The method will return an error if you have tried to do an impossible operation, such as adding a Node of type NODE_DOCUMENT_TYPE (which cannot be a child Node), or the refChild is not a child Node of the current Node. See the nodeType property and the createNode() method for more information on types of Nodes.

7.4.12 *load()*

Is a member of:	DOMDocument

Syntax

```
blnValue = objDOMDocument.load(url)
```

Remark

When you load a DOMDocument, any existing contents in the DOMDocument are discarded.

This is one of the two common ways to load XML into a DOMDocument. In the methods signature, the URL is a string that is the location of an XML file. True or False is returned to indicate success or failure of the load.

See the `async` property for related information on using this method and an example.

7.4.13   *loadXML()*

Is a member of:	DOMDocument

Syntax

```
blnValue = objDOMDocument.loadXML(xmlString)
```

Remark

When you call the loadXML() method for a DOM-Document, any existing contents in the DOM-Document are discarded.

This is one of the two common ways to load XML into a DOMDocument (see the `load()` method). In the loadXML signature, `xmlString` is either a string that is an entire XML document or a well-formed fragment.

`True` or `False` is returned to indicate success or failure of the load.

loadXML bug in XML 2.0

In the Microsoft XML 2.0 object, there is a bug in the `loadXML()` method. Unfortunately, when used from VB or VBScript, your code may return an error that says that there is a parse error. The error usually complains that you are using an element in your XML that is not declared in the DTD you have referenced.

The error looks something like this:

The element "PEOPLE" is used but not declared in the DTD/Schema.

The reason is that the `loadXML()` method, when called from VB or VBA, will always act as if the `resolveExternals` property of the document was `false`. There is no work-around, but it will be fixed for the next release of the Microsoft XML objects.

7.4.14   *nextNode()*

Is a member of:	XMLDOMNodeList XMLDOMNamedNodeMap

Syntax

```
set objXMLDOMNode = objXMLDOMNodeList.nextNode()
```

Remark

This method is used to iterate through either the collection returned from child Node of an element (XMLDOMNodeList collection) or the collection returned from the attributes property of an element (XMLDOMNamedNodeMap collection).

The pointer after returning either of these collections is set to before the first Node in the list. Therefore, when you call the nextNode() method for the first time, it returns the first Node in the list.

As you iterate through this collection, NULL will be returned when the current Node is the last Node or there are no items in the list.

Example

In previous examples, we showed you a similar example of iterating through the Nodes in an XMLDOMNodeList collection:

```
Dim objDOMDocument As DOMDocument
Dim objXMLDOMNode As IXMLDOMNode

Set objDOMDocument = New DOMDocument
objDOMDocument.async = False
objDOMDocument.Load "http://mark/xmlcode/people2.xml"

For Each objXMLDOMNode In objDOMDocument.childNodes
   'do something with this
Next
```

Let's change this example to demonstrate using the nextNode property:

```
Dim objDOMDocument As DOMDocument
Dim objNodeList As IXMLDOMNodeList
Dim objXMLDOMNode As IXMLDOMNode

Set objDOMDocument = New DOMDocument
objDOMDocument.async = False
objDOMDocument.Load "http://mark/xmlcode/people2.xml"

Set objNodeList = objDOMDocument.childNodes       ❶
Set objXMLDOMNode = objNodeList.nextNode          ❷
Do Until objXMLDOMNode Is Nothing                 ❸
   ' do something with this node
   Set objXMLDOMNode = objNodeList.nextNode4       ❹
Loop
```

❶ Get a reference to the XMLDOMNodeList collection.

❷ Fetch the first Node.

③ Prepare your loop, exiting once the last Node has been fetched.

④ Fetch the next Node.

7.4.15 *nodeFromID()*

Is a member of:	XMLDOMDocument

Syntax

```
set objXMLDOMNode = objDOMDocument.nodeFromID(strId)
```

Remark

The `nodeFromID()` method was designed to work specifically with ID and IDREF type attributes. (See the `attributes` property in this section.) Because this method is only available for the `XMLDOMDocument` interface, it will find any child Node that has the ID value that you have specified. If no child Node is found, it returns NULL.

Example

In the following example, we have stored the PERSONID attribute in the TreeView tag. When the user clicks on the TreeView, we fetch the Node in the DOMDocument using this method.

```
Dim objPersonElement As IXMLDOMElement

If Trim(objSelNode.Tag) <> "" Then  ①
    Set objPersonElement = m_objDOMPeople.nodeFromID(objSelNode.Tag)  ②
    lblElement.Caption = objPersonElement.nodeName & ": " & _
                        objPersonElment.Attributes(0).nodeValue  ③
End If
```

① Check that this is not a TreeView Node that has an empty tag.

② Find the Node in the DOMDocument that has the tag value.

③ Set a label's caption with details from the found Node.

open()

Is a member of:	XMLHTTPRequest

Syntax

```
objHTTPRequest.open
```

Remark

The `open()` method is used extensively in the examples in this book. It is used to open a connection to a web server so that you can use the `send()` method to use a `GET()`, `PUT()`, or similar HTTP command.

Example

```
Dim objXMLHttp As New XMLHTTPRequest
Dim objDOMDocument As DOMDocument

objXMLHttp.Open "POST", "http://mark/xmlcode/demo.asp", False ❶
objXMLHttp.Send ❷
Set objDOMDocument= objXMLHttp.responseXML ❸
```

❶ Open the POST (or GET) connection to the web server.

❷ Establish the connection.

❸ Receive the response—note there are different types of responses; binary and text are also supported.

7.4.16 removeAttribute()

Is a member of:	XMLDOMElement

Syntax

```
objXMLDOMElement.removeAttribute strAttributeName
```

Remark

If your element has an associated attribute, you can remove it from the Node by specifying the attribute's name. This method does not return anything. If you try to remove an attribute that does not exist, nothing happens and there is no warning.

Example

In the following example, we remove the PERSONID attribute from the first child Node of the `documentElement` child Node collection.

```
Dim objDOMDocument As DOMDocument
Dim objXMLDOMElement As IXMLDOMElement
Dim strFirstValue As String

Set objDOMDocument = New DOMDocument
objDOMDocument.async = False
objDOMDocument.Load "http://mark/xmlcode/people2.dtd"

Set objXMLDOMElement = objDOMDocument.documentElement.firstChild
objXMLDOMElement.removeAttribute "PERSONID"
```

7.4.17 *removeAttributeNode()*

Is a member of:	XMLDOMElement

Syntax

```
set objXMLDOMAttribute = objXMLDOMElement.removeAttribute-
  Node(objXMLDOMAttribute)
```

Remark

You can remove an attribute from a Node if you have an associated XMLDOMAttribute Node type for the element Node. If the attribute was successfully removed, it will return the removed attribute Node. If not, it will return NULL.

Example

Using the example from the removeAttribute() method, we will show how to do the same function using the removeAttributeNode() method. Here we need to first get a reference to the attribute before we can remove it. The difference with this method is that we can test if the removal of the attribute was successful.

```
Dim objDOMDocument As DOMDocument
Dim objXMLDOMElement As IXMLDOMElement
Dim objAttrib As IXMLDOMAttribute

Set objDOMDocument = New DOMDocument
objDOMDocument.async = False
objDOMDocument.Load "http://mark/xmlcode/people2.dtd"

Set objXMLDOMElement = objDOMDocument.documentElement.firstChild
Set objAttrib = objXMLDOMElement.removeAttributeNode _  ❶
                (objXMLDOMElement.getAttributeNode("PERSONID"))
If objAttrib Is Nothing Then  ❷
  ' this removal was unsuccessful, show warning
End If
```

❶ We have chosen to use the getAttributeNode() method to get a reference to the attribute that we want to remove. The returned attribute (objAttribute) from the method is the removed attribute.

❷ If the attribute removal was successful, then show a warning.

7.4.18 removeChild()

Is a member of:	DOMDocument XMLDOMNode XMLDOMAttribute XMLDOMCDATASection XMLDOMComment XMLDOMDocumentFragment XMLDOMDocumentType XMLDOMElement XMLDOMEntity XMLDOMEntityReference XMLDOMNotation XMLDOMProcessingInstruction XMLDOMText XTLRuntime

Syntax

```
Set objXMLDOMNode = objXMLDOMNode.removeChild(oldChild)
```

Remark

The parameter `oldChild` is the Node to be removed from the list of children for this Node. If the removal is successful, this method returns the removed child Node (`objXMLDOMNode`).

Although this method has been added to most of the DOMDocument interfaces, it cannot actually be used with all of them, as they may not have child Nodes to remove.

This method returns the Node that has just been removed (see the `nodeType` property for more information on Node types). It works successfully with the following Node types:

- Document
- Element
- Attribute
- Document Fragment
- Node (if its type is one of the above)

The following types of Nodes cannot have childNodes; therefore, this method cannot be used successfully for the following nodeTypes:

- Comment
- Text
- Processing Instruction

- CDATA section
- Notation

Although the following can have children, they are childNodes that cannot be removed, as they may be part of a DTD:

- Document type
- Entity
- Entity reference

Example

The following example removes the firstChild of the child Node collection of the documentElement **property.**

```
Dim objDOMDocument As DOMDocument
Dim objXMLDOMElement As IXMLDOMElement
Dim objRemovedElement As IXMLDOMElement

Set objDOMDocument = New DOMDocument
objDOMDocument.async = False
objDOMDocument.Load "http://mark/xmlcode/people2.dtd"

Set objXMLDOMElement = objDOMDocument.documentElement.firstChild
Set objRemovedElement = objDOMDocument.documentElement.removeChild(objXML-
  DOMElement) ❶
If objRemovedElement Is Nothing Then   ❷
  ' this removal was unsuccessful, show warning
End If
```

❶ The object objRemovedElement returns the removed Node if the removeChild execution was successful.

❷ If the removal was unsuccessful, then it returns a warning.

7.4.19 *removeNamedItem()*

Is a member of:	XMLDOMNamedNodeMap

Syntax

```
set objXMLDOMNode = objXMLDOMNamedNodeMap.removeNamedItem(strAttribute)
```

Remark

Here we repeat our introduction to getNamedItem(). The XMLDOMNamedNodeMap object is used to find and manipulate attributes for a Node, although the XML-DOMElement interface gives you many methods as well to do this.

For all the remove type methods, the Node may be removed from the instantiated DOMDocument —but it is not yet removed from the actual XML file —until you have called the save() method

This method takes the name of an attribute to remove the attribute from an element Node. It is the similar to the removeAttribute() method, except that it returns the removed attribute, and it's a method for a different object.

Example

In the following example, we get a reference to an XMLDOMNamedNodeMap object, in order to use the removeNamedItem() method.

```
Dim objDOMDocument As DOMDocument
Dim objNamedNodeMap As IXMLDOMNamedNodeMap
Dim objAttrib As IXMLDOMAttribute

Set objDOMDocument = New DOMDocument
objDOMDocument.async = False
objDOMDocument.Load "http://mark/xmlcode/people2.dtd"

Set objNamedNodeMap = objDOMDocument.documentElement.first-
  Child.Attributes ❶
Set objAttrib = objNamedNodeMap.removeNamedItem("PERSONID")  ❷

If objAttrib Is Nothing Then
  ' this removal was unsuccessful, show warning
End If

 This method can also be done in one line of code:
Set objAttrib = objDOMDocument.documentElement.firstChild. _
               Attributes.removeNamedItem("PERSONID")
```

❶ Get a reference to the XMLDOMNamedNodeMap object, which is returned from the attributes property.

❷ Remove the attribute using the attributes name.

7.4.20 replaceChild()

Is a member of:	DOMDocument
	XMLDOMNode
	XMLDOMAttribute
	XMLDOMCDATASection
	XMLDOMComment
	XMLDOMDocumentFragment
	XMLDOMDocumentType
	XMLDOMElement
	XMLDOMEntity
	XMLDOMEntityReference
	XMLDOMNotation
	XMLDOMProcessingInstruction
	XMLDOMText
	XTLRuntime

Syntax

```
set objXMLDOMNode = objXMLDOMNode.replaceChild(newChild, oldChild)
```

Remark

This method replaces one child Node with another child Node, instead of removing the old child and then appending the new child.

The parameter `newChild` is the Node that will replace the `oldChild` Node. If `newChild` is NULL, `oldChild` is removed without a replacement. The `oldChild` that had been replaced is returned in the `objXMLDOMNode` object, if the execution of this method is successful.

Again, take note of the types of Nodes you are dealing with. Some types of Nodes cannot be children, and therefore cannot be used with this method.

7.4.21 reset()

Is a member of:	XMLDOMNodeList
	XMLDOMNamedNodeMap

Syntax

```
objXMLDOMNodeList.reset()
```

Remark

This method resets the iterator to point before the first Node in the XMLDOMNodeList object, so that the next call to `nextNode()` returns the first item in the list.

7.4.22 save()

Is a member of:	XMLDOMDocument

Syntax

```
objDOMDocument.save(objTarget)
```

Remark

The parameter `objTarget` can be a file name, an ASP response object, an XML document object, or a custom object that supports persistence and specific interfaces.

If you have manipulated the DOMDocument in any way by appending, removing, or whatever, remember that it is not saved to the XML file until you have called the `save()` method.

The `save()` method does not return anything; however, if an error is reported, the error can expose one of the return values listed in table 7.13.

Table 7.13   save() method return values

Returned	Description
S_OK	Success
XML_BAD_ENCODING	The document contains a character that does not belong in the specified encoding
E_INVALIDARG	A string was provided but it is not a valid file name. or an object was provided that does not support any of the above interfaces
E_ACCESSDENIED	save() operation is not permitted
E_OUTOFMEMORY	save() cannot allocate buffers
Other values	Any other file system error

Saving in ADO 2.5

You may have noticed in previous examples that we tend to save our XML to a file and then load the file into a DOMDocument. In Microsoft ADO 2.5 that ships with Windows 2000, you will be able to save directly to a DOMDocument.

This is how you will be able to do it:

```
Dim strSQL As String
Dim adoCon As ADODB.Connection
Dim adoRst As ADODB.Recordset
Dim objDOMDocument As DOMDocument

strSQL = "SELECT * FROM categories"

Set adoCon = New ADODB.Connection     ❶
Set adoRst = New ADODB.Recordset

  adoCon.ConnectionString = "northwind"     ❷
  adoCon.CursorLocation = adUseClient
  adoCon.Open
  Set adoRst.ActiveConnection = adoCon

  adoRst.Open strSQL, , adOpenForwardOnly, _     ❸
  adLockReadOnly, adCmdText

Set objDOMDocument = New DOMDocument     ❹
objDOMDocument.async = False
adoRst.Save objDOMDocument, 1  ' save this to DOM     ❺
adoRst.Close
adoCon.Close
Set adoCon = Nothing
```

① Prepare ADO objects.

② Open database connection.

③ Get resultset.

④ Prepare the DOMDocument.

⑤ Save the recordset to the DOMDocument.

7.4.23 *selectNodes()*

Is a member of:	DOMDocument XMLDOMNode XMLDOMAttribute XMLDOMCDATASection XMLDOMComment XMLDOMDocumentFragment XMLDOMDocumentType XMLDOMElement XMLDOMEntity XMLDOMEntityReference XMLDOMNotation XMLDOMProcessingInstruction XMLDOMText XTLRuntime

Syntax

```
Set objXMLDOMNode  = objDOMDocument.selectNodes(strXQLQuery)
```

Remark

For more information on XSL pattern matching, see chapter 5, "XSL—adding style to XML."

This method returns an XMLDOMNodeList collection of all the Nodes for a specified XQL query.

Example

In the following example, we retrieve an XMLDOMNodeList collection of all the NAME elements from our DOMDocument that are in the PERSON element.

```
Dim objDOMDocument As DOMDocument
Dim objNodeList As IXMLDOMNodeList

Set objDOMDocument = New DOMDocument
objDOMDocument.async = False
objDOMDocument.Load "http://mark/xmlcode/people2.dtd"
Set objNodeList = objDOMDocument.selectNodes("//PERSON//NAME")
```

7.4.24   *selectSingleNode()*

Is a member of:	DOMDocument XMLDOMNode XMLDOMAttribute XMLDOMCDATASection XMLDOMComment XMLDOMDocumentFragment XMLDOMDocumentType XMLDOMElement XMLDOMEntity XMLDOMEntityReference XMLDOMNotation XMLDOMProcessingInstruction XMLDOMText XTLRuntime

Syntax

```
Set objXMLDOMNode = objXMLDOMElement.selectSingleNode(strXQLQuery)
```

Remark

Once again, as in the `selectNodes()` method, `selectSingleNode()` uses XQL to find the required Node. However, it only returns a single Node, `XMLDOMNode` object, which is the first Node that matches the pattern if it's found. If no match is found, it returns `NULL`.

Example

The select-Nodes() and selectSingle-Node() methods can also be used to search for Nodes that have certain attribute values. As we mentioned, you will need to do a bit of research to work out how to work with XQL, which we do not cover in detail here.

In the following example, we iterate through all the `childNodes` in the `documentElement` collection. We only want to find the `NAME` element in each `PERSON` element.

```
Dim objDOMDocument As DOMDocument
Dim objXMLDOMNode As IXMLDOMNode
Dim objElement As IXMLDOMElement

Set objDOMDocument = New DOMDocument
objDOMDocument.async = False
objDOMDocument.Load "http://mark/xmlcode/people2.xml"

For Each objXMLDOMNode In objDOMDocument.documentElement.childNodes
  Set objElement = objXMLDOMNode.selectSingleNode("NAME")
  ' do something with this name element
Next
```

Look at `getElementsByTagName()`, which does almost the same thing as this method. The beauty of this method, however, is that it returns a single Node instead of an `XMLDOMNodeList`. Therefore, this method is easier to work with, as you don't need to iterate through a `NodeList` collection to just get the one value out of it.

7.4.25   send()

Is a member of:	XMLHTTPRequest

Syntax

```
objHTTPRequest.send([varBody])
```

Remark

The `send()` method is used extensively in the examples in this book. Once you have opened a connection to a web server with the open method, you can use the send method to communicate with the webserver and then use `PUT()`, `GET()`, or similar HTTP commands against the webserver.

Example

```
Dim objXMLHttp As new XMLHTTPRequest
Dim objDOMDocument As DOMDocument

objXMLHttp.Open "POST", "http://mark/xmlcode/demo.asp", False  ❶
objXMLHttp.Send  ❷
Set objDOMDocument= objXMLHttp.responseXML  ❸
```

❶ Open the POST (or GET) connection to the web server.

❷ Establish the connection.

❸ Receive the response—note there are different types of responses; binary and text are also supported.

7.4.26   setAttribute()

Is a member of:	XMLDOMElement

Syntax

```
objXMLDOMElement.setAttribute strAttributeName, vntValue
```

Remark

There are so many ways to add an attribute to a DOMDocument. Here are a few:

- setAttribute
- setAttributeNode

- setNamedItem
- appendChild

We find this method, setAttribute(), the easiest way to add an attribute. However, you need to have a reference to the element interface before you can add the attribute. You can directly give the attribute its most important values, the name of the attribute (strAttributeName) and its value (vntValue), in one call through this method.

Example

In the following example, we add another PERSON element to our document-Element in a DOMDocument, which needs to have an attribute.

```
Dim objPerson As IXMLDOMElement

Set objPerson = m_objDOMPeople.createElement("PERSON")  ❶
objPerson.setAttribute "PERSONID", "p7"  ❷
m_objDOMPeople.documentElement.appendChild objPerson  ❸
```

❶ Create the PERSON element.

❷ Add the attribute to this element.

❸ Add this new element with its attribute to the DOMDocument.

7.4.27 setAttributeNode()

Is a member of:	XMLDOMElement

Syntax

```
set objXMLDOMAttribute = objXMLDOMElement.setAttribute-
  Node(objXMLDOMAttribute)
```

Remark

As we mentioned, this is one of the methods used to add or manipulate an attribute. As with the setAttribute() method, you can only use this method with the XMLDOMElement interface. However, instead of passing a string, you need to pass an XMLDOMAttribute object when adding the attribute to the element. This attribute Node is added to the element after using the createAttribute() method to create the attribute.

Example

By modifying the example for the setAttribute() method, we will show how the setAttributeNode() method differs from the setAttribute() method:

```
Dim objPerson As IXMLDOMElement
Dim objAttrib As IXMLDOMAttribute
Set objPerson = m_objDOMPeople.createElement("PERSON")      ❶
Set objAttrib = m_objDOMPeople.createAttribute("PERSONID")  ❷
objAttrib.text = "p7"  ❸
objPerson.setAttributeNode objAttrib  ❹
m_objDOMPeople.documentElement.appendChild objPerson  ❺
```

❶ Create the PERSON element.

❷ Create the PERSONID element.

❸ Give the attribute Node its value.

❹ Add the attribute to the PERSON element.

❺ Add this new element with its attribute to the DOMDocument.

7.4.28 *setNamedItem()*

Is a member of:	XMLDOMNamedNodeMap

Syntax

```
set objXMLDOMNode = objXMLDOMNamedNodeMap.setNamedItem(objXMLDOMNode)
```

Remark

This is true for all the methods used to add/manipulate an attribute: if you add an attribute with the same name as an existing attribute, it will replace the existing attribute.

Surprise, this is yet another method to add/manipulate an attribute to the DOM-Document. This time it is done using the XMLDOMNamedNodeMap interface.

You don't need to create an XMLDOMNamedNodeMap object to use this method, because the attributes property of a Node is a XMLDOMNamedNodeMap object.

Example

In the following example, we show how to add an attribute using this method.

```
Set objPerson = m_objDOMPeople.createElement("PERSON")
Set objAttrib = m_objDOMPeople.createAttribute("PERSONID")  ❶
objAttrib.text = "p7"  ❷
objPerson.attributes.setNamedItem objAttrib  ❸
m_objDOMPeople.documentElement.appendChild objPerson  ❹
```

❶ Create an attribute Node.

❷ Add the attribute's key details.

❸ The attributes property returns a NodeList object; therefore you can use the setNamedItem() method.

❹ Add this new "PERSON" element to the DOMDocument.

7.4.29 *transformNode()*

Is a member of:	DOMDocument XMLDOMNode XMLDOMAttribute XMLDOMCDATASection XMLDOMComment XMLDOMDocumentFragment XMLDOMDocumentType XMLDOMElement XMLDOMEntity XMLDOMEntityReference XMLDOMNotation XMLDOMProcessingInstruction XMLDOMText XTLRuntime

Syntax

```
strVAlue = objDOMDocument.transformNode(strStylesheet)
```

Remark

The `transformNode()` method applies a stylesheet to the current Node and its child Nodes. It returns this data in a string, which is very useful for when you want to pass your data back as HTML (which means that your XSL file needs to convert your XML data to HTML):

```
strValue = objDOMDocument.transformNode(strStylesheet)
```

The string `strValue` will contain the contents to transform the Node into the required string. For more information, see chapter 5, "XSL—adding style to XML."

Example

The following example shows the string from the transformed Node being passed back using the `transformNode()` method. We use people2.xml to demonstrate the `transformNode()` method.

Our XSL example looks as follows:

```
<?xml version="1.0"?>
<xsl:stylesheet xmlns:xsl="http://www.w3.org/TR/WD-xsl">
<xsl:template match="/">
<HTML>
<BODY>
  <TABLE BORDER="2">
  <TR>
    <TD>Name</TD>
    <TD>Address</TD>
```

```
    <TD>Tel</TD>
    <TD>Fax</TD>
    <TD>Email</TD>
  </TR>
  <xsl:for-each select="PEOPLE/PERSON">
  <TR>
    <TD><xsl:value-of select="NAME"/></TD>
    <TD><xsl:value-of select="ADDRESS"/></TD>
    <TD><xsl:value-of select="TEL"/></TD>
    <TD><xsl:value-of select="FAX"/></TD>
    <TD><xsl:value-of select="EMAIL"/></TD>
  </TR>
  </xsl:for-each>
  </TABLE>
</BODY>
</HTML>
</xsl:template>
</xsl:stylesheet>

Dim objXMLStyle As New DOMDocument
Dim objDOMDocument As New DOMDocument
Dim strXMLFromXSL As String

Call objDOMDocument.Load("http://mark/xmlcode/people2.xml")
Call objXMLStyle.Load("http://mark/xmlcode/people.xsl")
strXMLFromXSL = objDOMDocument.transformNode(objXML-
  Style.documentElement)
```

The `strXMLFromXSL` string returns the following HTML:

```
<HTML>
<BODY>
<TABLE BORDER="2">
<TR>
<TD>Name</TD>
<TD>Address</TD>
<TD>Tel</TD>
<TD>Fax</TD>
<TD>Email</TD>
</TR>
<TR>
<TD>Mark Wilson</TD>
<TD>911 Somewhere Circle, Canberra, Australia</TD>
<TD>(++612) 12345</TD>
<TD>(++612) 12345</TD>
<TD>markwilson@somewhere.com</TD>
</TR>
<TR>
<TD>Tracey Wilson</TD>
<TD>121 Zootle Road, Cape Town, South Africa</TD>
<TD>(++2721) 531 9090</TD>
<TD>(++2721) 531 9090</TD>
```

```
<TD>Tracey Wilson@somewhere.com</TD>
</TR>
<TR>
<TD>Jodie Foster</TD>
<TD>30 Animal Road, New York, USA</TD>
<TD>(++1) 3000 12345</TD>
<TD>(++1) 3000 12345</TD>
<TD>Jodie Foster@somewhere.com</TD>
</TR>
<TR>
<TD>Lorrin Maughan</TD>
<TD>1143 Winners Lane, London, United Kingdom</TD>
<TD>(++94) 17 12345</TD>
<TD>++94) 17 12345</TD>
<TD>Lorrin Maughan@somewhere.com</TD>
</TR>
<TR>
<TD>Steve Rachel</TD>
<TD>90210 Beverly Hills, California, United States of America</TD>
<TD>(++1) 2000 12345</TD>
<TD>(++1) 2000 12345</TD>
<TD>Steve Rachel@somewhere.com</TD>
</TR>
</TABLE>
</BODY>
</HTML>
```

7.4.30 *transformNodeToObject()*

Is a member of:	DOMDocument
	XMLDOMNode
	XMLDOMAttribute
	XMLDOMCDATASection
	XMLDOMComment
	XMLDOMDocumentFragment
	XMLDOMDocumentType
	XMLDOMElement
	XMLDOMEntity
	XMLDOMEntityReference
	XMLDOMNotation
	XMLDOMProcessingInstruction
	XMLDOMText
	XTLRuntime

Syntax

```
objDOMDocument.transformNode(objXMLStyle.documentElement, vntNewDOMDocument)
```

Remark

This is similar to the `transformNode()` method; however, it doesn't actually change the underlying DOMDocument. Instead it returns a variant (`vntNewDOM-Document`) with a new transformed DOMDocument that has the stylesheet applied to it.

Schemas, BizTalk, and eCommerce

8

What this chapter covers:

- eCommerce is here to stay and it affects everything!
- Where does Biztalk fit in?
- BizTalk Server and BizTalk Framework
- Why are Schemas so important?
- Getting to know the BizTalk Framework Schemas

8.1 *An introduction to eCommerce*

Looking back on the (sometimes turbulent) history of computing, it is clear that the Internet and specifically the World Wide Web have been an incredible success. They have already had a huge impact on many businesses and markets. In some cases, completely new industries and markets have popped up. That is the power of this new interconnected economy, which has only just begun.

Let's travel back in time and take a look at the growth of the Internet and pick out some key trends, which will demonstrate the imminent impact of eCommerce and the Internet on your business and your relationships with your partners, customers, and competitors.

Table 8.1 shows the total number of registered Internet DNS host names (such as http://www.news.com) at different times in the past.

Table 8.1   The growth of DNS hosts on the Internet

Date:	Number of DNS hosts:
1988	30,000
January 1993	1,313,000
July 1993	1,776,000
January 1994	2,217,000
July 1994	3,212,000
January 1995	5,846,000
July 1995	8,200,000
January 1996	14,352,000
July 1996	16,729,000
January 1997	21,819,000
July 1997	26,053,000
January 1998	29,670,000
July 1998	36,739,000
January 1999	43,230,000
July 1999	56,218,000

The first trend that we can assume was instrumental in the massive growth of the Internet was the combination of HTML (which is easy to learn and use) with the inexpensive and wide availability of Internet access. The statistics also show the demand for information and for connectivity between businesses.

With all this activity, the second trend we now see is that more companies are turning to the Internet to buy goods and services from their suppliers and trading partners, placing orders on everything from office supplies to safety equipment to temporary personnel. IDC research estimates that the Internet commerce procurement market, worth 147 million U.S. dollars in 1998, will be worth five billion U.S. dollars by 2003, with 46% of this activity taking place outside the U.S. Overall, Internet commerce will top one trillion U.S. dollars in the same year.

The third trend we already see is that HTML is becoming simply a part of XML. This flexibility and extensibility has resulted in Schemas, which are themselves XML-based.

8.2 Why do our systems need a Schema?

When people talk about eCommerce, they don't mean put a button on the website that says "call 1-800...." No, what they are talking about are computer systems that describe themselves to other machines and computing devices. These systems are able to sustain automated relationships with each other—moving information around, fulfilling just-in-time orders, providing receipts, and more.

Schemas are the key link in that chain, because they provide the reliable structure for data, which is so desperately needed on the Internet. Schemas are therefore, without doubt, the key to providing automated eCommerce between companies.

There are many more reasons to use XML and Schemas.

8.2.1 Development of flexible web applications

Because a Schema is basically a vocabulary you have defined to describe your data, you can use the same vocabularies in different programs. You can also query other systems to discover their Schemas and learn to exchange data with that system. If the Schema is stored within a document repository such as BizTalk (see http://www.biztalk.org), then entire vertical industries could rely on a select number of Schemas, and the benefits of interoperability would be huge.

Your software development teams will begin programming in a more flexible way, using Schemas and DOM objects to understand data, rather than accessing table structures directly. The benefit of this is substantial. Provided the Schema is maintained and is correct, table designs can change, data can be moved, and new data can be added without breaking your programs.

8.2.2 So, how does it work then?

XML is meant to be readable to humans and not overly complex. Here is a very simple XML file for a resumé:

```
<?xml version="1.0" ?>
<PEOPLE xmlns="x-schema:PEOPLE.DTD">
<PERSON>
 <NAME>Mark Wilson</NAME>
```

```
<ADDRESS>911 Somewhere Circle, Canberra, Australia</ADDRESS>
<TEL>(++612) 12345</TEL>
<FAX>(++612) 12345</FAX>
<EMAIL>Mark.Wilson@somewhere.com</EMAIL>
</PERSON>
</PEOPLE>

<PEOPLE xmlns="x-schema:PEOPLE.DTD">
```

The text xmlns="x-schema:PEOPLE.DTD" is the pointer to the Schema document against which this XML document will be validated.

XML has already been described in the earlier chapters in this book, so let's now focus on the values and relationships in and between the elements, which is the strength of Schemas. In the example above, there is a group called <PEOPLE>, which contains one <PERSON>.

You automatically understand that this design or structure is correct by relying on your own experience and how documents like this should be structured. You also know it's OK to have several <PERSON> tags within a single <PEOPLE> tag, but there should only ever be one <NAME> value per position.

A computer (or in a more broad sense, we should say machines) cannot make those judgments, as they have no previous experience to draw on—unless we had already defined which values are acceptable and what the relationships are between the elements. Therefore, when creating a Schema, we define what the acceptable values of each of the tags are and how they relate to each other.

So, what would a Schema for the above PEOPLE XML look like? The following XML Schema would be the minimum Schema needed to enforce that the XML document has the required tags and structure:

```
<?xml version ="1.0"?>
<Schema name = "people.dtd"
 xmlns = "urn:schemas-microsoft-com:xml-data"
 xmlns:dt = "urn:schemas-microsoft-com:datatypes">
<ElementType name = "PEOPLE" content = "eltOnly" order = "seq">
 <element type = "PERSON" minOccurs = "1" maxOccurs = "*"/>
</ElementType>
<ElementType name = "PERSON" content = "eltOnly" order = "seq">
 <element type = "NAME"/>
 <element type = "ADDRESS"/>
 <element type = "TEL"/>
 <element type = "FAX"/>
 <element type = "EMAIL"/>
</ElementType>
<ElementType name = "ADDRESS" content = "textOnly"/>
<ElementType name = "EMAIL" content = "textOnly"/>
<ElementType name = "FAX" content = "textOnly"/>
<ElementType name = "NAME" content = "textOnly"/>
```

```
<ElementType name = "TEL" content = "textOnly"/>
</Schema>
```

Let's pick the Schema above apart a bit so that you can get a sense of some of the exciting features that are available to Schema designers.

```
<Schema name="myschema" xmlns="urn:schema-microsoft-com:xml-data"
      xmlns:dt="urn:schema-microsoft-com:datatypes">
<!-- ... -->
</Schema>
```

This is called the *Schema document element,* and it contains the *namespace declarations* that indicate to the parser that the Microsoft built-in data types are being used. Once you have included the Microsoft datatype namespaces, you can prefix your tags with dt:type, which allows you to reference the Microsoft data types in the Internet Explorer 5 XML objects.

This Schema document element is called a *top-level declaration.*

```
<ElementType name = "PEOPLE" content = "eltOnly" order = "seq">
<element type = "PERSON" minOccurs = "1" maxOccurs = "*"/>
</ElementType>
```

Inside this top-level declaration (called an ElementType), we declare the element types that are being used. There is only one, and it has a name of PERSON. The PERSON element is permitted to have contents of a type called eltOnly. Type eltOnly means that the element cannot contain any free text, only the specified elements. (These are listed later in this chapter as Address, Email, Fax, Name, and Tel.)

You can provide more attributes for this element to ensure your data is correctly defined and structured. For example, you can set the number of instances of PERSON. This is defined in the minOccurs and maxOccurs attributes.

```
<element type = "PERSON" minOccurs = "1" maxOccurs = "*"/>
```

The order of the elements within PERSON (Address, Email, Fax, Name, and Tel) is set as seq, which means the specified elements must appear in the required order.

Already you may be getting the feeling that Schemas can define your data and even outline appropriate user interactions to a certain extent. This is clearly a very useful feature of XML, and properly used, it can lead to massive productivity gains as data and systems begin to describe themselves accurately.

Attributes are very similar to elements, and you would use one over the other because of their different characteristics. The following XML snippet has two elements, NAME and FULL_NAME:

```
<NAME>
<FULL_NAME>Mark Wilson</FULL_NAME>
</NAME>
```

The element below, NAME, has an attribute called FULL_NAME and is functionally the same as the preceding snippet:

```
<NAME FULL_NAME="Mark Wilson" />
```

The Microsoft XML-Data Reduced Schemas also provide for a lot of control and definition if we use attributes in our XML. If you used an attribute called colors, which is a selection of one of 3 colors, in your XML, an example of the Schema could be:

```
<AttributeType name="colors" dt:type="enumeration" dt:values="red green blue" required="yes">
```

The attribute above has a name of colors, it has a type of enumeration, and the values are red, green, and blue. Lastly, this attribute must have a supplied value.

Although Schemas are very useful and will be used in most instances, they are optional, not required. If your XML application doesn't require validation, you do not need to specify a Schema file. A Schema is an excellent alternative to DTDs, the document that provides similar structure details for SGML and which existed for decades before XML blossomed.

As we discussed before, Schemas have several advantages over DTDs, one of which is the massively improved data typing that is available to you as a developer.

8.3 *Using the data types that are available*

To make use of the data type support included with Internet Explorer 5, your XML Schema must include the datatype namespace. The top-level Schema element declaration looks like this:

```
<Schema name="myschema"
        xmlns="urn:schemas-microsoft-com:xml-data"
        xmlns:dt="urn:schemas-microsoft-com:datatypes">
 <!-- ... -->
</Schema>
```

Within that Schema element, we already know that data can be structured as an <ElementType> or <AttributeType>. Also, in the Schema element declaration, we used the namespace declarations to indicate that we intend to use the Microsoft data types. We can now use a data type in one of two forms:

```
dt:type attribute
<datatype> element
```

Both forms are demonstrated below as two equivalent and valid samples. This declaration of an ElementType called pages has a data type of an integer:

```
<ElementType name="pages" dt:type="int"/>
```

This declaration of an `ElementType` is also called "pages" and also has a data type of an integer:

```
<ElementType name="pages">
  <datatype dt:type="int" />
</ElementType
```

The same applies to attributes. The `<datatype>` or `dt:type` attribute can be used directly on the `<AttributeType>` declaration.

Although XML Schema support in Internet Explorer 5 allows data types to be specified within attributes, only the following data types are supported within attributes by the parser and DOM: `string`, `id`, `idref`, `idrefs`, `nmtoken`, `nmtokens`, `entity`, `entities`, `enumeration`, and `notation`. Support for the other data types will be added in a future release.

Table 8.2 provides a complete list of data types supported by the Microsoft DOM Objects. This list can be found at http://msdn.microsoft.com/xml/reference/schema/datatypes.asp

8.3.1 *Full list of Microsoft data types supported*

Table 8.2 Datatypes that are supported

Datatype	Description
bin.base64	MIME-style Base64 encoded binary BLOB
bin.hex	Hexadecimal digits representing octets
boolean	0 or 1, where 0 == "false" and 1 =="true"
char	String, one character long
date	Date in a subset ISO 8601 format, without the time data. For example: "1994-11-05".
dateTime	Date in a subset of ISO 8601 format, with optional time and no optional zone. Fractional seconds can be as precise as nanoseconds. For example, "1988-04-07T18:39:09".
dateTime.tz	Date in a subset ISO 8601 format, with optional time and optional zone. Fractional seconds can be as precise as nanoseconds. For example: "1988-04-07T18:39:09-08:00".
fixed.14.4	Same as "number" but no more than 14 digits to the left of the decimal point, and no more than 4 to the right
float	Real number, with no limit on digits; can potentially have a leading sign, fractional digits, and optionally an exponent. Punctuation as in U.S. English. Values range from 1.7976931348623157E+308 to 2.2250738585072014E-308.
int	Number, with optional sign, no fractions, and no exponent

Table 8.2 Datatypes that are supported (continued)

number	Number, with no limit on digits; can potentially have a leading sign, fractional digits, and optionally an exponent. Punctuation as in U.S. English. (Values have same range as most significant number, R8, 1.7976931348623157E+308 to 2.2250738585072014E-308.)
time	Time in a subset ISO 8601 format, with no date and no time zone. For example: "08:15:27".
time.tz	Time in a subset ISO 8601 format, with no date but optional time zone. For example: "08:1527-05:00".
i1	Integer represented in one byte. A number, with optional sign, no fractions, no exponent. For example: "1, 127, -128".
i2	Integer represented in one word. A number, with optional sign, no fractions, no exponent. For example: "1, 703, -32768".
i4	Integer represented in four bytes. A number, with optional sign, no fractions, no exponent. For example: "1, 703, -32768, 148343, -1000000000".
r4	Real number, with no limit on digits; can potentially have a leading sign, fractional digits, and optionally an exponent. Punctuation as in U.S. English. Values range from 3.40282347E+38F to 1.17549435E-38F.
r8	Same as "float". Real number, with no limit on digits; can potentially have a leading sign, fractional digits, and optionally an exponent. Punctuation as in U.S. English. Values range from 1.7976931348623157E+308 to 2.2250738585072014E-308.
ui1	Unsigned integer. A number, unsigned, no fractions, no exponent. For example: "1, 255".
ui2	Unsigned integer, two bytes. A number, unsigned, no fractions, no exponent. For example: "1, 255, 65535".
ui4	Unsigned integer, four bytes. A number, unsigned, no fractions, no exponent. For example: "1, 703, 3000000000".
uri	Universal Resource Identifier (URI). For example, "urn:schemas-microsoft-com:Office9".
uuid	Hexadecimal digits representing octets, optional embedded hyphens that are ignored. For example: "333C7BC4-460F-11D0-BC04-0080C7055A83".

8.3.2 *Primitive types*

The W3C XML 1.0 recommendation also defines enumerated types (notations and enumerations) and a set of tokenized types. These types, defined in the W3C XML 1.0 recommendation, are referred to as *primitive types* within this Microsoft XML documentation.

Table 8.3 lists some of the primitive types defined in Section 3.3.1 of the W3C XML 1.0 Recommendation.

Table 8.3 Supported W3C primitive types

Primitive datatype	Description
entity	Represents the XML ENTITY type
entities	Represents the XML ENTITIES type
enumeration	Represents an enumerated type (supported on attributes only)
id	Represents the XML ID type
idref	Represents the XML IDREF type
idrefs	Represents the XML IDREFS type
nmtoken	Represents the XML NMTOKEN type
nmtokens	Represents the XML NMTOKENS type
notation	Represents a NOTATION type
string	Represents a string type

8.3.3 *Supported data type conversions*

Table 8.4 lists the data type conversions supported by the Microsoft XML processor in Microsoft Internet Explorer 5.

Table 8.4 Datatype conversions supported by Microsoft XML processors

Datatype	Variant type
string	VT_BSTR, VT_BOOL, VT_CY, VT_DATE, VT_VARIANT, VT_DECIMAL, VT_UI1, VT_I2, VT_I4, VT_R4, VT_R8, VT_EMPTY, VT_NULL, VT_ARRAY
number	VT_BSTR, VT_BOOL, VT_CY, VT_VARIANT, VT_DECIMAL, VT_UI1, VT_I2, VT_I4, VT_R4, VT_R8, VT_EMPTY, VT_NULL
int	VT_BSTR, VT_BOOL, VT_VARIANT, VT_UI1, VT_I2, VT_I4, VT_EMPTY, VT_NULL
float	VT_BSTR, VT_CY, VT_VARIANT, VT_DECIMAL, VT_UI1, VT_I2, VT_I4, VT_R4, VT_R8, VT_EMPTY, VT_NULL
fixed.14.4 (currency)	VT_BSTR, VT_CY, VT_VARIANT, VT_DECIMAL, VT_UI1, VT_I2, VT_I4, VT_R4, VT_EMPTY, VT_NULL
boolean	VT_BSTR, VT_BOOL, VT_VARIANT, VT_DECIMAL, VT_UI1, VT_I2, VT_I4, VT_EMPTY, VT_NULL
dateTime	VT_BSTR, VT_DATE, VT_VARIANT
i1	VT_BSTR, VT_BOOL, VT_VARIANT, VT_DECIMAL, VT_EMPTY, VT_NULL
i2	VT_BSTR, VT_BOOL, VT_VARIANT, VT_DECIMAL, VT_I2, VT_EMPTY, VT_NULL
i4	VT_BSTR, VT_BOOL, VT_VARIANT, VT_DECIMAL, VT_I2, VT_I4, VT_EMPTY, VT_NULL
i8	VT_BSTR, VT_BOOL, VT_CY, VT_VARIANT, VT_DECIMAL, VT_I2, VT_I4

Table 8.4 Datatype conversions supported by Microsoft XML processors (continued)

ui1	VT_BSTR, VT_BOOL, VT_VARIANT, VT_DECIMAL, VT_UI1, VT_EMPTY, VT_NULL
ui2	VT_BSTR, VT_BOOL, VT_VARIANT, VT_UI1, VT_I2, VT_EMPTY, VT_NULL
ui4	VT_BSTR, VT_BOOL, VT_VARIANT, VT_UI1, VT_I2, VT_I4, VT_EMPTY, VT_NULL
ui8	VT_BSTR, VT_BOOL, VT_CY, VT_VARIANT, VT_DECIMAL, VT_UI1, VT_I2, VT_I4, VT_EMPTY, VT_NULL
r4	VT_BSTR, VT_CY, VT_VARIANT, VT_DECIMAL, VT_I2, VT_I4, VT_R4, VT_EMPTY, VT_NULL
r8	VT_BSTR, VT_CY, VT_VARIANT, VT_DECIMAL, VT_I2, VT_I4, VT_R4, VT_R8, VT_EMPTY, VT_NULL
uuid	VT_BSTR, VT_VARIANT
uri	VT_BSTR, VT_VARIANT
bin.hex	VT_BSTR, VT_VARIANT, VT_ARRAY
char	VT_BSTR, VT_VARIANT, VT_I2, VT_EMPTY, VT_NULL

8.4   *BizTalk, where it's all happening!*

With BizTalk you will be able to submit your XML-described messages (such as a subscription request or a just-in-time purchase order) in many different ways and from any platform. You can use Microsoft Message Queue Server, the SMTP email protocol, the Internet's HTTP protocol, various COM interfaces, and even FTP, to name just a few ways to get your information into and receive it out of BizTalk.

BizTalk is also aware of existing data storage systems and ERP systems such as SAP and can exchange messages and routing documents with them automatically.

You have to use some predefined XML tags and the associated BizTalk namespace within your XML. Let's take a look at how you do that.

8.4.1   *A BizTalk XML example*

So, what does a BizTalk Framework XML document look like? Below is a simple example of a generic BizTalk Framework data document.

```
<?xml version="1.0"?>
<BizTalk xmlns:="urn:schemas-biztalk.org:BizTalk/biztalk-0.8.xml">
<Body xmlns:= "urn:your-namespace-goes-here">
<Route>
<From Location ID="value" LocationType="value" Process="value"
Path="value" Handle="value"/>
<To Location ID="value" LocationType="value" Address="value" Path="value"
Handle="value"/>
</Route>
<MessageType>
```

-- Your XML document data goes here --

```
</MessageType>
</Body>
</BizTalk>
```

Also, you can see that all the BizTalk tags relate to message exchange and do not include industry-specific tags. This makes the BizTalk Framework industry-neutral and suitable for widespread use.

Let's take a closer look at the tags your BizTalk XML document must use.

The root of the matter

A BizTalk Framework document must begin and end with the BizTalk XML "root" tag:

```
<BizTalk xmlns="urn:schemas-biztalk-org:BizTalk/biztalk-0.8.xml">
</BizTalk>
```

If you take a close look, you will see that a BizTalk namespace is used.

Body and identity tags

The `<MessageType>` tag shown is a placeholder for the actual document type name tag. It could actually hold a tag for a Purchase Order, Flight, or other entity. The XML document would be marked up with XML tags consistent with the XML-Data proposal.

```
<Body>
<MessageType xmlns="urn:your-namespace-here">
</MessageType>
</Body>
```

Note that this is where your Schema is inserted.

Routing tags

Two types of routing tags are defined in the BizTalk Framework. These are the `To` and `From` tags that are required to support point-to-point message exchanges. These `To` and `From` tags take the general form described below:

```
<Route>
<From locationID="111111111" locationType="DUNS"
   process="" path="" handle="3"/>
<To locationID="222222222" locationType="DUNS"
   process="" path="" handle="23CF15"/>
</Route>
```

So, now that you have had a taste of Schemas, and you may have a good grasp of BizTalk and the impact it will have on automated messaging between systems, you may wonder *what's next?*

8.4.2 *Get your schemas here!*

Ah, yes, the million dollar question is: does anyone in your industry already have a Schema for certain areas or concerns in your industry? At the BizTalk website, http://www.biztalk.org/, the Microsoft website builders are building a library. It is a catalog with accompanying features that will help you locate Schemas that others have registered and cataloged. Members will be given the opportunity to register their organizations and establish publishing rights.

8.4.3 *Cool tools and websites*

Go to http://www.biztalk.org, http://www.xml.com, and http://www.xmltree.com for more information on your particular industry. You can also take a look at these business-to-business websites that are taking the lead in XML documents and communication, http://www.marketsite.net and http://www.commerceone.com, which is marketing itself as "Industry's First Comprehensive XML Document Library." For more information, sample code, or to find other developers who program with XML or the BizTalk Framework Toolkit, visit http://www.vbxml.com

For your own interest, there are also at least five more Schema formats, which are also trying to take over DTDs:

- DCD (Document Content Description), http://www.w3.org/TR/NOTE-dcd

- XML-Data Reduced (XDR), http://www.w3.org/TR/1998/NOTE-XML-data/ and http://msdn.microsoft.com/xml/XMLGuide/schema-overview.asp

- DDML (also known as XSchema) http://www.w3.org/TR/NOTE-ddml

- W3C XML Schema Definition Language (XSDL), http://www.w3.org/TR/xmlSchema-1/, http://www.w3.org/TR/xmlSchema-1/, http://www.w3.org/TR/xmlSchema-2/, and http://www.w3.org/TR/xmlschema-2/

- Schema for Object-oriented XML (SOX), http://www.w3.org/TR/NOTE-SOX/

Of course, building Schemas would be easier if there were a visual tool that could help you, right? A company called Extensibility, http://www.extensibility.com/, has just that kind of tool. XML Authority is their product, and it presents Schemas in a visual way so you can set your constraints visually without getting stuck in the syntax. Even better, it handles all the different Schema proposals essentially the same.

XML Authority is aware of all the different types of Schemas. It does not force you to use any particular one because it is a visual design tool that allows you to "save as" the different types of Schemas.

8.4.4 *How different are all the Schemas?*

Well, to answer that, let's look at some examples. In this book, we have been using the following XML code snippet:

```
<?xml version="1.0" ?>
<PEOPLE>
<PERSON>
<NAME>Mark Wilson</NAME>
<ADDRESS>911 Somewhere Circle, Canberra, Australia</ADDRESS>
<TEL>(++612) 12345</TEL>
<FAX>(++612) 12345</FAX>
<EMAIL>Mark.Wilson@somewhere.com</EMAIL>
</PERSON>
</PEOPLE>
```

DTD example

For that XML code, this is the correct DTD structure:

```
<!ELEMENT PEOPLE ( PERSON+ ) >
<!ELEMENT PERSON ( NAME, ADDRESS, TEL, FAX, EMAIL ) >
<!ELEMENT ADDRESS ( #PCDATA ) >
<!ELEMENT EMAIL ( #PCDATA ) >
<!ELEMENT FAX ( #PCDATA ) >
<!ELEMENT NAME ( #PCDATA ) >
<!ELEMENT TEL ( #PCDATA ) >
```

Here we investigate the five Schemas that XML Authority generates:

- W3C Schema
- Microsoft XML-data reduced
- Commerce One
- DCD
- DDML

W3C Schema (XSDL) example

You can down-load your own free trial copy of XML Authority at http://www. extensibility.com/

For the W3C Schema definition, you will use:

```
<?xml version ="1.0"?>
<!DOCTYPE schema PUBLIC "-//W3C//DTD XMLSCHEMA 19990506//EN
    "http://www.w3.org/1999/05/06-xmlschema-1/structures.dtd">
<!--Generated by XML Authority. Conforms to w3c http://www.w3.org/
    TR/xmlschema-1/-->
<schema name = "people.dtd"
```

```
    xmlns = "http://www.w3.org/1999/05/06-xmlschema-1/structures.xsd">
<elementType name = "PEOPLE">
 <sequence>
  <elementTypeRef name = "PERSON" minOccur = "1" maxOccur = "*"/>
 </sequence>
</elementType>
<elementType name = "PERSON">
 <sequence>
  <elementTypeRef name = "NAME"/>
  <elementTypeRef name = "ADDRESS"/>
  <elementTypeRef name = "TEL"/>
  <elementTypeRef name = "FAX"/>
  <elementTypeRef name = "EMAIL"/>
 </sequence>
</elementType>
<elementType name = "ADDRESS">
 <datatypeRef name = "string"/>
</elementType>
<elementType name = "EMAIL">
 <datatypeRef name = "string"/>
</elementType>
<elementType name = "FAX">
 <datatypeRef name = "string"/>
</elementType>
<elementType name = "NAME">
 <datatypeRef name = "string"/>
</elementType>
<elementType name = "TEL">
 <datatypeRef name = "string"/>
</elementType>
</schema>
```

Microsoft XML-data reduced (XDR) Schema example

For this Schema definition, you will use:

```
<?xml version ="1.0"?>
<!--Generated by XML Authority. Conforms to XML Data subset for IE 5-->
<Schema name = "people.dtd"
 xmlns = "urn:schemas-microsoft-com:xml-data"
 xmlns:dt = "urn:schemas-microsoft-com:datatypes">
<ElementType name = "PEOPLE" content = "eltOnly" order = "seq">
 <element type = "PERSON" minOccurs = "1" maxOccurs = "*"/>
</ElementType>
<ElementType name = "PERSON" content = "eltOnly" order = "seq">
 <element type = "NAME"/>
 <element type = "ADDRESS"/>
 <element type = "TEL"/>
 <element type = "FAX"/>
 <element type = "EMAIL"/>
</ElementType>
```

```
<ElementType name = "ADDRESS" content = "textOnly"/>
<ElementType name = "EMAIL" content = "textOnly"/>
<ElementType name = "FAX" content = "textOnly"/>
<ElementType name = "NAME" content = "textOnly"/>
<ElementType name = "TEL" content = "textOnly"/>
</Schema>
```

Commerce One SOX Schema example

For this Schema definition, you will use:

```
<?xml version ="1.0"?>
<!DOCTYPE schema SYSTEM "schema.dtd">
<!--Generated by XML Authority. Conforms to w3c NOTE-SOX-19980930-->
<schema name = "people.dtd">
<h1>people.dtd</h1>
<elementtype name = "PEOPLE">
 <model>
   <sequence>
     <element name = "PERSON" occurs = "+"/>
   </sequence>
 </model>
</elementtype>
<elementtype name = "PERSON">
 <model>
   <sequence>
     <element name = "NAME"/>
     <element name = "ADDRESS"/>
     <element name = "TEL"/>
     <element name = "FAX"/>
     <element name = "EMAIL"/>
   </sequence>
 </model>
</elementtype>
<elementtype name = "ADDRESS">
 <string/>
</elementtype>
<elementtype name = "EMAIL">
 <string/>
</elementtype>
<elementtype name = "FAX">
 <string/>
</elementtype>
<elementtype name = "NAME">
 <string/>
</elementtype>
<elementtype name = "TEL">
 <string/>
</elementtype>
</schema>
```

DCD Schema example

For this Schema definition, you will use:

```
<?xml version ="1.0"?>
<!DOCTYPE DCD SYSTEM "tbd">
<!--Generated by XML Authority. Conforms to DCD 1.0-->
<DCD xmlns:RDF = "http://www.w3.org/1999/02/22-rdf-syntax-ns#">
<ElementDef type = "PEOPLE" Content = "Closed" Model = "Elements">
 <Group RDF:Order = "Seq">
   <Group Occurs = "OneOrMore">
     <Element>PERSON</Element>
   </Group>
 </Group>
</ElementDef>

<ElementDef type = "PERSON" Content = "Closed" Model = "Elements">
 <Group RDF:Order = "Seq">
   <Element>NAME</Element>
   <Element>ADDRESS</Element>
   <Element>TEL</Element>
   <Element>FAX</Element>
   <Element>EMAIL</Element>
 </Group>
</ElementDef>

<ElementDef type = "ADDRESS" Content = "Closed" Model = "Data"/>
<ElementDef type = "EMAIL" Content = "Closed" Model = "Data"/>
<ElementDef type = "FAX" Content = "Closed" Model = "Data"/>
<ElementDef type = "NAME" Content = "Closed" Model = "Data"/>
<ElementDef type = "TEL" Content = "Closed" Model = "Data"/>
</DCD>
```

DDML Schema example

For this Schema definition, you will use:

```
<?xml version ="1.0"?>
<!DOCTYPE DocumentDef [
]>
<!--Generated by XML Authority. DDML version 1.0-->
<DocumentDef name = "people.dtd"
 xmlns = "http://www.purl.org/NET/ddml/v1"
 xmlns:DDML = "http://www.purl.org/NET/ddml/v1" Version = "1.0">
<ElementDecl Name = "PEOPLE">
 <Model>
   <Ref Element = "PERSON" Frequency = "OneOrMore"/>
 </Model>
</ElementDecl>
<ElementDecl Name = "PERSON">
 <Model>
   <Seq>
```

```
        <Ref Element = "NAME"/>
        <Ref Element = "ADDRESS"/>
        <Ref Element = "TEL"/>
        <Ref Element = "FAX"/>
        <Ref Element = "EMAIL"/>
      </Seq>
    </Model>
  </ElementDecl>
  <ElementDecl Name = "ADDRESS">
   <Model>
    <PCData/>
   </Model>
  </ElementDecl>
  <ElementDecl Name = "EMAIL">
   <Model>
    <PCData/>
   </Model>
  </ElementDecl>
  <ElementDecl Name = "FAX">
   <Model>
    <PCData/>
   </Model>
  </ElementDecl>
  <ElementDecl Name = "NAME">
   <Model>
    <PCData/>
   </Model>
  </ElementDecl>
  <ElementDecl Name = "TEL">
   <Model>
    <PCData/>
   </Model>
  </ElementDecl>
</DocumentDef>
```

8.5 Summary

With potentially as many as 56 million places to visit on the Internet, you may be thinking the words *information overload*. Frequently we wonder how we will be able to find information we need in all that unstructured information out there. But with the growing use of XML, DTDs, RDF, RDF Schemas, and the various versions of XML Schemas, we can look forward to better software and a more accurate understanding of that information.

But that's not all. We can also look forward to businesses sharing their Schemas and (hopefully) using the same ones, or at least mapping their Schemas to each other. When this happens, transparent data transfer, automatic billing and reconciliation, and loads of other things will begin to make our lives easier.

The XML/Schema/BizTalk combination is undoubtedly a knockout punch and will help usher in widespread, inexpensive, and worldwide use of eCommerce. Its potential to provide a platform for business-to-business exchange is enormous.

However, as XML travels across this sea of information, it may become more like a modern-day Gulliver than a Christopher Columbus. While Columbus discovered the New World, Gulliver became tied down by thousands of bit-part players. The same thing could happen to XML if poorly defined Schemas become prevalent and are used in document repositories such as BizTalk.

Since the jury is still out on where all of this is going, and since the Schema specification is not finalized, we have not focused on using Schemas in this book. We have been using DTDs, as they are a mature, easy-to-use, and stable standard. Going from DTDs to Schemas is not a complex step, and you will be able to make your own decision on which route to take.

Where to go from here 9

What this chapter covers:

- Community websites
- Meet the authors
- Links and suggestions

9.1 *The End*

Go to this book's website at http://www.thespot4.com or http://www.vbxml.com and download the source code, share opinions, and join in the discussions. You can also go to http://www.manning.com

Welcome to the end of this book! Thank you for reading this far. We hope you found it enjoyable. You can contact Tracey and Mark via email at tracewilson@my-deja.com and mark@vbxml.com.

Give us a shout. We would love to hear from you.

There are many more resources on the Internet where you can go to continue your learning. There are tens of thousands of people feverishly learning and exchanging information in discussion groups, newsgroups, and on websites.

Here are a few useful URLs that we have found. Please note that at the time of writing, these URLs were OK to be used.

9.2 *Check out the online glossary*

Confused by a word or two? Go to http://www.thespot4.com and check out the huge glossary of technical words, phrases, relationships, and meanings.

9.3 *Investigate future technologies*

BIZTALK—the framework for interbusiness XML data exchange. It's going to be huge!

http://www.biztalk.org

Check out this W3C submission list—it includes links and descriptions:

http://www.xml.com/xml/pub/submlist

9.4 *Join the http://www.vbxml.com VB, ASP, and XML discussions*

Go to http://www.thespot4.com and http://www.vbxml.com and join in the discussion! We have a vibrant and exciting community of readers and passers-by who are discussing XML, XSL, CSS, VB, ASP, Cold Fusion, and more.

Regular articles and open source code projects are available. Download the source code for this book and more!

9.5 *Author Online at http://www.manning.com*

Go to Manning Publisher's Author Online forum, where you can ask the authors questions about this book and interact with other readers.

http://www.manning.com/wilson

9.6 Newsgroups

For XML, try:
    Microsoft.public.xml
    Comp.text.xml

If any of these links are broken, please go to http://www. thespot4.com and get some fresh ones!

For RDF, try:
    Netscape.public.mozilla.rdf
    (NOTE: The news server must be set to news.mozilla.org.)

For SGML, try:
    Comp.text.sgml

9.7 W3C discussion groups

For a (huge) collection of discussion lists at the W3C, go to:
    http://www.w3.org/Mail/Lists.html

9.8 Links, links, and more links

The W3C, the new center of the standards universe... well, almost!
    http://www.w3c.com

Complete list of W3C activity for XML:
    http://www.w3.org/XML/Activity

Excellent overview of the W3C standards situation:
    http://www.wdvl.com/Authoring/Languages/XML/
    Specifications.html

Microsoft's XML website is excellent:
    http://msdn.microsoft.com/xml

Microsoft conformance to XSL W3C standards can be found here:
    http://msdn.microsoft.com/xml/XSLGuide/conformance.asp

Alternative DOM objects can be found at:
    http://www.vivid-creations.com
    http://www.cuesoft.com

XML:
    http://www.xml.com
    http://wdvl.com/Authoring/Languages/XML/
    http://www.ibm.com/developer/xml/
    http://www.w3.org/XML/Overview.HTML
    http://developer.netscape.com/tech/metadata/index.HTML?cp=dev01mtec

CSS:
    http://wdvl.com/Authoring/Style/Sheets/
    http://builder.com/Authoring/CSS/?st.bl.HTML..dvlp

If any of these links are broken, please go to http://www. thespot4.com and get some fresh ones!

SGML:
    http://wdvl.com/Authoring/Languages/SGML.HTML
    http://www.oasis-open.org/HTML/getstart.htm
    http://www.sgml.u-net.com/

RDF:
    http://www.irt.org/articles/js086/index.htm
    http://www.w3.org/RDF/Overview.HTML

Schemas:
    http://www.Schema.net/
    http://www.stars.com/Seminars/Languages/XMLSpecifications.HTML
    http://www.oasis-open.org/cover/
    http://www.xml.com/xml/pub/Guide/DTDs
    http://xdev.datachannel.com/directory/industry_resources.HTML

Want to get an interpretation of the entire XML Specification? Look no further:
    http://www.xml.com/axml/axml.HTML

Want to know which websites are using XML and how? Check out XMLTree—it's cutting edge stuff:
    http://www.xmltree.com/

DTD-to-Schema converter—OK, it is out of date...but it's interesting!
    http://www.informatik.tu-darmstadt.de/DVS1/staff/bourret/
      xSchema/convert.HTML

Want research on who is doing what on the web?
    http://www.commerce.net/research/

Dublin Core Metadata Initiative:
   http://purl.oclc.org/dc/

And last but not least... how about submitting an XML file and getting a DTD back?
   http://www.pault.com/Xmltube/dtdgen.HTML

index

Symbols

#PCDATA 21
&gt 22, 51, 52

A

abort( ) 224
ADO 75, 120, 121, 251
   ADO 1.5 xxi
   ADO 2.0 xxi, 75, 76
   ADO 2.1 xxi, xxii, 31, 32, 76, 77, 132, 145
   ADO 2.5 xxi
adPersistADTG 75, 76
adPersistXML 76, 77, 124, 135, 145
appendChild 229
appendChild( ) 225
Asynchronously 180
   Loading an XML file 56
attribute 14
   adding an attribute 254, 255, 256
   creating 230
   getting an attribute 235, 236, 239
   getting an element from the ID 244
   removing 245, 246, 249
AttributeType 266, 267
Author Online xxii

B

B2B xix
B2C xix
BizTalk 17, 261, 263, 270, 271, 272, 278
Bound Property 46

browser 5, 6, 17, 18, 19, 25
business objects 117
business-to-business xix

C

CallByName 117
Cascading Stylesheet 19
case-sensitive
   XML is... 20
CDATA 21
CDATA section 173, 201, 205, 230
CDF
   Channel Definition Framework 6
CGI 78, 110
character data 22
Chemical Markup Language (CML) 5
childNodes 183
class 116
comment
   creating 231
Commerce One 275
ContentType 78, 145
createAttribute( ) 228
createCDATASection( ) 228
createComment( ) 228
createElement( ) 228
createEntityReference( ) 228
createNode( ) 233
CreateObject 120
createProcessingInstruction( ) 228
createTextNode( ) 228
CSS 19, 25, 82, 280, 282
   CSS Object Model 82
   CSS-OM 82

D

data 187
data brokering 109
Data Island xxi, 40, 42, 43, 46–54, 71, 90, 92–97
datatype 208, 209, 235, 265, 266, 267, 269
DCD 276
   Document Content Description 272
DCOM 110
DDML 272, 276
Distributed Component Object Model 110
DOCTYPE 19, 173, 188
Document Object Model xx, xxi, 15, 16, 26, 36, 37, 38, 39, 40, 57, 58, 61, 62, 66, 82, 108, 148, 153, 167, 168, 281
Document Type Definition 15, 19
documentElement 190
DOM
   Document Object Model 36
   DOM object methods 222
   DOM object properties 176
   DOMDocument 170
DSO
   Data Source Object 40
   Data Source Objects xxi, 42, 45, 46, 47, 49, 92
dual interfaces 189

E

ECMAscript 83
eCommerce xix, 2, 6, 17, 109, 261, 262, 263, 278
Electronic Data Interchange (EDI) xx, 6, 27
element 13, 14, 15, 16, 24, 73, 83
   creating 229
   getting an element 236
encoding 18
entities 14, 174, 201, 204
entity reference
   creating 231
EntityReference 203
extensibility 272

F

firstChild 191
frameworks 111
FrontPage xxii, 143

G

getAttribute() 235
getAttributeNode() 236
getElementsByTagName() 236, 253
getNamedItem() 238

H

hasChildNodes() 240
hierarchical 12
HTML elements 46
HTTP 3, 78, 118, 119, 140
HTTPRequest 119

I

IE5 xx, xxi, xxii, 17, 19, 25, 26, 39, 40, 42, 46, 49, 55, 74, 75, 78, 82, 83, 84, 93, 94, 99, 108, 110, 141, 146, 153, 154, 168
   Internet Explorer 5 19
implements 115
innerHTML 46
innerText 46
insertBefore 229
insertBefore() 241
interface 116, 117
interfaces 116, 117, 251
IPersistStream 117
IpersistStreamInit 117
IStream 117
IXMLDOMDocument 116

J

Java Servlets 78

L

lastChild 191
length 192
load 241
loadXML() 242

M

mainframes 3
markup
  Marking up your Website 6
MathML 5
MessageType 271
metadata 2, 5, 111, 282
Microsoft XML 2.0 55, 116
middleware 78
MusicML 5

N

Namespaces 16, 17, 22–25, 83, 89, 169, 172, 194, 195, 216, 229, 233, 265, 266, 270, 271
namespaceURI 193
newsgroups
  A list of... 281
nextNode() 242
nextSibling 191
Node type enumeration 198
nodeFromID() 244
nodeName 194
nodeType 197
  creating a Node 234
  NODE_ATTRIBUTE 200
  NODE_CDATA_SECTION 201
  NODE_COMMENT 206
  NODE_DOCUMENT 206
  NODE_DOCUMENT_TYPE 207
  NODE_ELEMENT 199
  NODE_ENTITY 204
  NODE_ENTITY_REFERENCE 202
  NODE_NOTATION 207
  NODE_PROCESSING_INSTRUCTION 205
  NODE_TEXT 200
nodeTypedValue 208
nodeTypeString 209
nodeValue 210
notation 233

O

object browser 116
object orientation 115

Office 2000 xix
OLEDB 2
ondataavailable 212
ontransformnode 213
open 244
ownerDocument 213

P

PARAM 46
parentNode 214
parsed 214
parsed character data 22
parseError 215
Parsing 19
persisted 118
PersistFormat 75, 76
Personal Web Server xxi, xxii, 78
prefix 216
preserveWhiteSpace 217
previousSibling 191
processing instruction 205
push
  Push technology 6
PWS xxi, xxii, 75

R

RDF 5, 26, 27, 111, 276, 277, 281, 282
reference
  Adding to your VB project 55
removeAttribute() 245
removeAttributeNode() 246
removeChild() 247
removeNamedItem() 248
replaceChild 229
replaceChild() 249
res://msxml.dll/DEFAULTSS.XSL 83
reset() 250
resolveExternals 218
Resource Description Framework 5
resources
  XML Resources 281
root element 20

S

save() 250
saving an XML object to a file 70
schema for object-oriented XML 272
schemas 11, 15, 17, 169, 208, 218, 263–268, 270–276, 278, 282
    difference between schema and DTD 261
search Engines
    optimizing 2
selectNodes 253
selectNodes() 252
selectSingleNode 253
selectSingleNode() 253
send() 254
sequence diagram 112, 113, 119, 120, 121, 125, 126, 127, 139
setAttribute() 254
setAttributeNode() 255
setNamedItem() 256
SGML 2, 10
sorting
    using XSL 99
SOX 272, 275
src 46
standalone 48
synchronously
    loading an XML file 55
SYSTEM 19, 20

T

tagName 219
tags
    HTML tags 5
text 219
three tier 112, 113, 115, 125, 146
transforming XML to HTML 86
transformNode() 94, 257
transformNodeToObject() 259

U

UML 112, 113
UNIX 3
Updateable 46
Universal Resource Indicator (URI) 23

url 220
UTF 18

V

valid 20
validateOnParse 221
validation 19
value 221
VBScript 55
VBXML
    Visual Basic and ASP XML group 280
Vector Markup Language 6
Visual Basic 6.0 xx
Visual Interdev xx, 116, 143
VML 6
vocabulary
    DTD or schemas 5, 12
VRML
    Virtual Reality Modeling Language 6

W

W3C 7, 8, 10, 25, 26, 36, 39, 82, 99, 101, 102, 273, 280, 281
    discussion groups to follow 281
    Worldwide Web Consortium 3, 7, 8, 10, 19, 22, 24, 25, 27, 36, 281
W3C XML Schema Definition Language 272
webclass 108, 121, 143
well-formed 20
whitespace 217
Windows 2000 xxi
Word 2000 xix

X

XDR 274
xGUI 2
XML
    Description 2
XML Authority 272–276
XML header 18
XML syntax
    learning more about... 11
XML version 18
XML-Data Reduced 274

XML-Data Reduced Schema 266
XMLDOMAttribute 169, 173, 200, 246, 255
XMLDOMCDATASection 169, 173, 196, 201
XMLDOMDocument
  cloneNode() 228
XMLDOMDocumentType 169, 173, 190, 207
XMLDOMElement 169, 170, 219, 239, 248, 255
XMLDOMEntity 169, 174, 201, 204
XMLDOMNamedNodeMap 169, 172, 173, 181,
  239, 243, 248, 249, 256
XMLDOMNode 169, 171, 184, 228, 231
XMLDOMNodeList 169, 172, 184, 243, 250,
  252, 253
XMLDOMNodeListMap 170

XMLDOMParseError 169, 175, 215
XMLDOMProcessingInstruction 169, 175
XMLHTTPRequest 169, 176, 244
XMLstylesheet 18
XQL 83, 101, 102
XSchema 272
XSDL 272, 273
XSL 19, 81
  transforming XML to HTTP 257

Y

Y2K xxi